# Microsoft System Center 2012 R2 Operations Manager Cookbook

Learn how to deploy, configure, and maintain System Center Operations Manager with 50 recipes designed to help you meet the challenges of managing a complex IT system

**Steve Beaumont (MVP)**

**Jonathan Horner**

**Chiyo Odika**

**Robert Ryan**

[PACKT] PUBLISHING enterprise
professional expertise distilled

BIRMINGHAM - MUMBAI

# Microsoft System Center 2012 R2 Operations Manager Cookbook

First published: April 2015

Production reference: 1080415

Published by Packt Publishing Ltd.
Livery Place
35 Livery Street
Birmingham B3 2PB, UK.

ISBN 978-1-78217-624-4

www.packtpub.com

# Credits

# About the Authors

**Steve Beaumont** has worked for more years than he cares to admit within IT, starting with desktop support. He is now the technical director of PowerONPlatforms and an MVP within the System Center Cloud and Datacenter Management group, where he helps organizations realize the benefits of the hybrid cloud. He is the coauthor of *Microsoft System Center 2012 Service Manager Cookbook* and *System Center 2012 Orchestrator Cookbook*. He maintains his own blog at `http://systemcenter.ninja`. It covers all System Center components and areas related to desktop design, deployment, and optimization.

His passion for everything about System Center and IT systems management reflects through all areas of his work, presentation, and day-to-day life in the form of new and innovative solutions brought to the market by PowerONPlatforms.

> This book is dedicated to my wife and family, who are patient enough to put up with me when I get lost for hours, immersed in challenges.

**Jonathan Horner** has worked in the IT industry for over 25 years. Starting his career at a small consultancy company, he took up many diverse roles, from implementing PC rollouts to running the infrastructure for a major online supermarket.

For the last 14 years, Jonathan has been using multiple versions of System Center to help with his tasks. Over many of these years, he specialized in Operations Manager and gained expertise in writing custom management packs for specialized solutions, using many authoring tools along the way.

He was one of the earliest people to gain an MCSE in private cloud by passing the exams before they were publically released. He is also a qualified MCT and provides training in many areas of System Center.

Jonathan now works at Inframon, a specialist in cloud transformation, where he is the head of the support services team. His team provides telephone support on System Center issues as well as remote-managed and remote-hosted System Center solutions for multiple clients.

I would like to thank my wife for her love and support in giving me the time to write my chapters of this book. I want to express my gratitude to Gordon McKenna and Sean Roberts for helping me take my career to the next level. Indeed, the entire team at Inframon deserves thanks for pushing and inspiring me to continually develop and progress, especially Steve Veitch, with his management pack authoring skills and general approach to technology. Finally, thanks to the many other people, too numerous to mention individually, who have helped me during my career and made me the person I am today.

**Chiyo Odika** is a senior consultant with Concurrency Inc., a US-based IT solutions provider. While at Concurrency, and also prior to joining it, he architected and configured a wide range of System Center deployments, from small single-site deployments to deployments spanning global infrastructures. He has over 8 years of experience in IT, managing systems, and architecting solutions using a broad range of technologies and platforms. Chiyo holds bachelor's and master's degrees in business and information systems, respectively, and holds an ever-growing list of technology certifications. He has a keen interest in strategies to optimize the service delivery of IT to businesses, and he shares his technology experiences with the community through his blogs at http://mrchiyo.com and http://www.concurrency.com/blog/.

Chiyo balances a life of passion for business and technology with his passion for entrepreneurship and service leadership. He has cofounded various business endeavors and is involved in nonprofit and other causes that are of interest to him. When he is not working on the latest cloud technologies, you can find him learning about economic theory, analyzing the markets, and following the latest news and strategies about chess.

I would like to acknowledge and thank my coauthors, Steve Beaumont, Robert Ryan, and Jonathan Horner, for their tenacity and contributions to making this project a reality. I would also like to thank my family for their prayers and well wishes, and I thank Anna for her friendship.

**Robert Ryan** is an IT professional with over 15 years of industry experience. He works in both public and private sectors to provide third-line infrastructure support across the globe. He is responsible for major technology projects, including server rationalization, virtualization, and messaging. Currently, he is focusing on private cloud deployments using the Microsoft System Centre suite.

In his free time, Robert enjoys technology and films. He likes to spend time with his wife, Natalie, and their five children. He is a frequent blogger at http://scnuggets.blogspot.com.

# About the Reviewers

**Steve Buchanan** is a regional solution lead at Concurrency Inc., a three-time Microsoft System Center MVP, and author of several technical books about the System Center platform. He has been an IT professional for over 15 years. He has held various positions ranging from infrastructure architect to IT manager.

Steve focuses on transforming IT departments through DevOps, service management, systems management, and cloud technologies. He has authored these books: *System Center 2012 Service Manager Unleashed*, SAMS Publishing (2014); *Microsoft System Center Data Protection Manager 2012 SP1*, Packt Publishing (2013); and *Microsoft Data Protection Manager 2010*, Packt Publishing (2011).

Steve holds certifications in A+, Linux+, MCSA, MCITP (server administrator), and MCSE (private cloud). He is active in the System Center community and enjoys blogging about his adventures in the world of IT at www.buchatech.com. You can also follow him on Twitter at @buchatech for his latest blog posts.

**M. Sencer DEMIR** his BSc in computer engineering and soon after, he started work as a systems engineer for different consulting firms. He is an MCT and holds many Microsoft certifications (MCP, MCSE, MCSA, and so on). He also has a certificate from the ITIL foundation. He focuses on Microsoft technologies, especially the System Center suite, Active Directory, RDS, and Citrix.

Sencer is new to Azure, but he is considered a deployment, PowerShell, SBC, and VDI expert. He works on different projects as a subject matter expert but mostly in financial institutions. He also participates in different events and user group meetings as a speaker or the organizer.

**Richard Skinner** has over 10 years of experience in the field of IT. Starting as a software developer, he has had a varied career covering many aspects of IT, including Windows desktop deployment, SQL Server administration, SAN implementation, document management, SharePoint, and Hyper-V. He is a blogger at http://richardstk.com. His Twitter handle is @_richardstk.

# www.PacktPub.com

## Support files, eBooks, discount offers, and more

For support files and downloads related to your book, please visit www.PacktPub.com.

Did you know that Packt offers eBook versions of every book published, with PDF and ePub files available? You can upgrade to the eBook version at www.PacktPub.com and as a print book customer, you are entitled to a discount on the eBook copy. Get in touch with us at service@packtpub.com for more details.

At www.PacktPub.com, you can also read a collection of free technical articles, sign up for a range of free newsletters and receive exclusive discounts and offers on Packt books and eBooks.

https://www2.packtpub.com/books/subscription/packtlib

Do you need instant solutions to your IT questions? PacktLib is Packt's online digital book library. Here, you can search, access, and read Packt's entire library of books.

## Why subscribe?

- ▶ Fully searchable across every book published by Packt
- ▶ Copy and paste, print, and bookmark content
- ▶ On demand and accessible via a web browser

## Free access for Packt account holders

If you have an account with Packt at www.PacktPub.com, you can use this to access PacktLib today and view 9 entirely free books. Simply use your login credentials for immediate access.

## Instant updates on new Packt books

Get notified! Find out when new books are published by following @PacktEnterprise on Twitter or the *Packt Enterprise* Facebook page.

# Table of Contents

# Preface

Microsoft System Center 2012 R2 Operations Manager is the longstanding monitoring solution from Microsoft and a component of the larger System Center 2012 R2 product.

System Center 2012 R2 Operations Manager (SCOM) has many capabilities and doesn't focus purely on Windows Server monitoring. It has cross-platform monitoring capabilities, from the Unix and Linux operating systems to network and bare-metal (hardware) monitoring.

SCOM's focus on event monitoring of servers and infrastructure has also changed with recent releases. The idea of monitoring services and applications at a much deeper level is now a core focus area, giving businesses a very granular view of their environment, even all the way down to code-level problem discovery.

This cookbook aims to deliver recipes across the various areas of SCOM and unlock it's potential, while making complex solutions easier to learn and utilize to a greater extent.

## What this book covers

*Chapter 1, Architecting System Center 2012 R2 Operations Manager*, helps you design the deployment of System Center 2012 R2 Operations Manager based on your business requirements.

*Chapter 2, Deploying System Center 2012 R2 Operations Manager*, shows you how to deploy System Center 2012 R2 Operations Manager, and includes methods used to automate the deployment.

*Chapter 3, Configuring System Center 2012 R2 Operations Manager*, has recipes for post-deployment configuration of System Center 2012 R2 Operations Manager, and shows you how to deploy monitoring agents and the admin console.

*Chapter 4, Operating System Center 2012 R2 Operations Manager*, describes the best recipes for practice overrides and tuning. This chapter also has recipes for the steps usually performed via manual efforts in the GUI, and shows you how these tasks can be performed using PowerShell or set up with automatic actions.

*Chapter 5, Maintaining System Center 2012 R2 Operations Manager,* covers how to maintain System Center 2012 R2 Operations Manager after installation, the common tasks that should be performed, and how to optimize for scale and performance.

*Chapter 6, Monitoring Applications and IT Services with System Center 2012 R2 Operations Manager,* has recipes for monitoring applications across different platforms within your environment using System Center 2012 R2 Operations Manager.

*Chapter 7, Authoring Custom Monitoring Solutions with System Center 2012 R2 Operations Manager,* teaches you how to create your own advanced customizations with System Center 2012 R2 Operations Manager, and explains which tools and design methodologies may be best suited to your needs.

*Chapter 8, Authoring Management Packs in Visual Studio,* delves deeper into using Visual Studio to author custom monitoring solutions. Visual Studio can be a complex tool if you have not used it before, and it is often used for relatively complex custom monitoring solutions. This chapter covers its use in an easy-to-understand way.

*Chapter 9, Integrating System Center 2012 R2 with Other Components,* has recipes for integrating Operations Manager with the other components within the System Center 2012 R2 solution, and shows you how to utilize these integration points to gain a greater degree of flexibility and a more advanced solution.

*Chapter 10, Reporting in System Center 2012 R2 Operations Manager,* teaches you how to provide an in-depth view of the data collected by System Center 2012 R2 Operations Manager with reporting, and how to present it in a meaningful and relevant manner across different areas of your business.

*Appendix, Resourceful Links,* covers useful links to community content and third-party System Center 2012 R2 Operations Manager extensions.

# What you need for this book

To deploy a test environment of SCOM, you will need at least three virtual servers and access to the System Center 2012 and SQL 2012 media.

If you're performing the recipes for SQL AlwaysON, you will need an additional server, that is, four virtual servers. Similarly, another virtual server will be required to deploy Linux to for the cross-platform recipe.

More virtual servers may be required if you are creating custom applications and services to monitor.

The book is based on the Windows Server 2012 R2 version of the operating system, and previous versions may not have the same steps as those used in the recipes here.

# Who this book is for

This book is designed to take new, aspiring SCOM administrators through the process of designing their new deployment and deploying SCOM in a more automated manner to support private cloud methodologies of implementation. It will also help refine the skills and knowledge of existing SCOM administrators in the areas of maintenance, authoring, integration, and reporting.

# Sections

In this book, you will find several headings that appear frequently (Getting ready, How to do it, How it works, There's more, and See also).

To give clear instructions on how to complete a recipe, we use these sections as follows:

## Getting ready

This section tells you what to expect in the recipe, and describes how to set up any software or any preliminary settings required for the recipe.

## How to do it...

This section contains the steps required to follow the recipe.

## How it works...

This section usually consists of a detailed explanation of what happened in the previous section.

## There's more...

This section consists of additional information about the recipe in order to make you more knowledgeable about the recipe.

## See also

This section provides helpful links to other useful information for the recipe.

## Conventions

In this book, you will find a number of text styles that distinguish between different kinds of information. Here are some examples of these styles and an explanation of their meaning.

Code words in text, database table names, folder names, filenames, file extensions, pathnames, dummy URLs, user input, and Twitter handles are shown as follows: "Copy `MOMCertImport.exe` to the root of the C drive along with the `GWCert.pfx` file."

A block of code is set as follows:

```
#Add Operations Manager Data Access and Action Accounts to Local Admin
Write-Output "Adding required accounts to the local administrators
group"
([ADSI]"WinNT://$env:computername/Administrators,group").
Add("WinNT://$SCOMDASUser")
([ADSI]"WinNT://$env:computername/Administrators,group").
Add("WinNT://$SCOMAAUser")
```

Any command-line input or output is written as follows:

```
/EnableErrorReporting: [Never | Queued | Always]
```

**New terms** and **important words** are shown in bold. Words that you see on the screen, for example, in menus or dialog boxes, appear in the text like this: "Click on the **Download certificate** link."

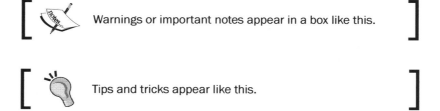

Warnings or important notes appear in a box like this.

Tips and tricks appear like this.

## Reader feedback

Feedback from our readers is always welcome. Let us know what you think about this book—what you liked or disliked. Reader feedback is important for us as it helps us develop titles that you will really get the most out of.

To send us general feedback, simply e-mail `feedback@packtpub.com`, and mention the book's title in the subject of your message.

If there is a topic that you have expertise in and you are interested in either writing or contributing to a book, see our author guide at `www.packtpub.com/authors`.

# Customer support

Now that you are the proud owner of a Packt book, we have a number of things to help you to get the most from your purchase.

## Downloading the example code

You can download the example code files from your account at `http://www.packtpub.com` for all the Packt Publishing books you have purchased. If you purchased this book elsewhere, you can visit `http://www.packtpub.com/support` and register to have the files e-mailed directly to you.

## Errata

Although we have taken every care to ensure the accuracy of our content, mistakes do happen. If you find a mistake in one of our books—maybe a mistake in the text or the code—we would be grateful if you could report this to us. By doing so, you can save other readers from frustration and help us improve subsequent versions of this book. If you find any errata, please report them by visiting `http://www.packtpub.com/submit-errata`, selecting your book, clicking on the **Errata Submission Form** link, and entering the details of your errata. Once your errata are verified, your submission will be accepted and the errata will be uploaded to our website or added to any list of existing errata under the Errata section of that title.

To view the previously submitted errata, go to `https://www.packtpub.com/books/content/support` and enter the name of the book in the search field. The required information will appear under the **Errata** section.

## Piracy

Piracy of copyrighted material on the Internet is an ongoing problem across all media. At Packt, we take the protection of our copyright and licenses very seriously. If you come across any illegal copies of our works in any form on the Internet, please provide us with the location address or website name immediately so that we can pursue a remedy.

Please contact us at `copyright@packtpub.com` with a link to the suspected pirated material.

We appreciate your help in protecting our authors and our ability to bring you valuable content.

## Questions

If you have a problem with any aspect of this book, you can contact us at `questions@packtpub.com`, and we will do our best to address the problem.

# 1

# Architecting System Center 2012 R2 Operations Manager

In this chapter, we will cover the following recipes:

- ▶ Introducing Operations Manager roles
- ▶ Understanding the business and its requirements
- ▶ Designing for high availability
- ▶ Sizing the environment

## Introduction

**System Center 2012 R2 Operations Manager** (**SCOM**) can be a very in-depth monitoring solution owing to its ability to gain an insight of various areas of an infrastructure. SCOM has the ability to start helping you understand your environment from the physical hardware of your network switches, SANs, and physical servers right through to the operating systems, whether they be Unix, Linux, or Windows operating systems, and the applications running either within your data centers or externally in public cloud solutions such as Microsoft Azure.

Because of the wide-reaching and powerful solution that System Center 2012 R2 Operations Manager delivers, it is very important before implementing it to understand what the various roles and features of SCOM are as well as how they function and, more importantly, relate to the business and its needs.

This chapter will help break down these areas to enable you to gain that knowledge as well as show you what areas of your design can be architected to provide high availability and how to size your environment.

# Introducing Operations Manager roles

The following information will help you understand the various roles found within System Center 2012 R2 Operations Manager.

## Getting ready

While in small or test environments you may consider installing all of the roles on a single server, large or production environments will often have the various roles spread across multiple servers for both performance and availability purposes.

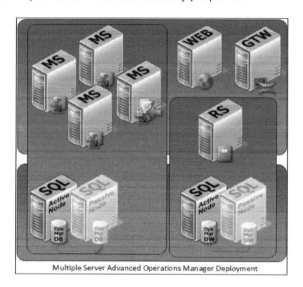

Multiple Server Advanced Operations Manager Deployment

## How to do it...

SCOM has various roles that need to be deployed and configured within an implementation. A breakdown of these roles is given in the following sections to help you understand roles within SCOM.

### Management server

The management server is the *brains* of SCOM. It is a role that coordinates management pack distribution, monitoring and rule application, as well as agent communication and the interface between the system and you, the admin, via the console.

Every deployment of SCOM will contain at least one management server, but adding more management servers will allow you to start to scale out the implementation for both performance and availability.

When implementing the first management server, SCOM creates what is known as a management group. This can be seen as a control boundary allowing you to select which servers are managed by this implementation of SCOM and, if required, to implement multiple management groups, each with their own sets of management servers, for different purposes.

## Operational database

The operational database is the database backend used by the management servers for short-term storage of data and processing of information related to the management packs implemented within your deployment and their rules, monitors, and overrides, which is the system configuration.

Every management group requires one unique operational database.

## Data warehouse database

The SCOM data warehouse consists of another SQL database but is used for long-term storage of data, the default period being 400 days. Data is written in parallel to the data warehouse while the data is simultaneously being written to the operational database, but over time the data in the data warehouse such as performance metrics is aggregated, rather than it being stored as raw data.

The data warehouse database is a required component for an SCOM management group, but it can be shared between different management groups, allowing for a centralized data warehouse to be implemented, providing you with a rolled-up and consolidated view of the health and performance of the different monitored areas of your environment.

Refer to the *Sizing the Environment* recipe in this chapter for further information on connected management groups.

## Reporting server

The reporting server, while an optional extra, is highly recommended as this is the role that provides access to the reporting features of SCOM. It requires a server with a dedicated **SQL Server Reporting Services** (**SSRS**) instance to be designated as the reporting server. SCOM requires a dedicated SSRS instance as it will modify its security to match that of the role-based access model used for SCOM, potentially removing access to any reports you might have previously had on the SSRS instance. It is not recommended or supported to use this SSRS instance for any purpose other than for SCOM reporting.

## Gateway server

A gateway server is used in two main scenarios, as a way to bridge security boundaries and to act as an agent traffic management point.

A gateway can be placed outside of the security boundary where the main management servers reside, such as within an isolated **Demilitarized Zone** (**DMZ**), workgroup, or domain environments, without trusts established.

A gateway within an Active Directory environment can communicate to agents and then act as the communication point from the untrusted environment back to the management group using certificates to secure the communication channel.

A gateway can also be used to manage non-domain joined devices and then all agents will communicate to the gateway using certificates, and the gateway in turn will communicate back to the management group via certificate-secured channels.

Agents can be set to communicate with the gateway instead of directly with the management servers. This is useful for low-bandwidth remote sites where instead of having multiple agents reporting data directly across the network link, they report their data to the gateway, which can then compress that data and send it in batches instead. The compression can be as much as 50 percent.

 While we refer to agents reporting to a gateway server, the agents themselves have no concept of a gateway and just see it as a management server.

## Web console server

SCOM offers users the ability to access a web-based version of the operator console using a Silverlight-rendered console. This role can either be deployed on a separate server or on an existing management server. However, it is worth noting that if installed on a separate server, a management role cannot be deployed to that same server after installation of the web console role.

Alongside the web-based operator console, the web portals for **Application Performance Monitoring** (**APM**) are also deployed as part of the web console role. These consoles give access to the rich diagnostic and performance monitoring that is gathered for .NET and Java applications.

## Audit Collection Services

**Audit Collection Services (ACS)** allows security events generated by audit policies applied to monitored systems to be collected to a central location for review and monitoring. When enabled within your environment, a service installed as part of the SCOM agent called ACS Forwarder will send all security events to the ACS Collector.

The ACS Collector is a role that is enabled on a management server and will then filter and write to the ACS Database any security events you define as being monitored. The ACS Database is a dedicated database for security events. Each ACS Collector will require its own individual database.

# How it works...

System Center 2012 R2 Operations Manager uses either Agent-based or Agentless communication to collect data from servers and devices. Servers with agents will push this data to the management servers or gateways that they have been assigned to, while agentless managed servers and devices, such as network switches, will generally have their information pulled from management servers.

The flow of information and/or connection points around the infrastructure can be visually represented as follows:

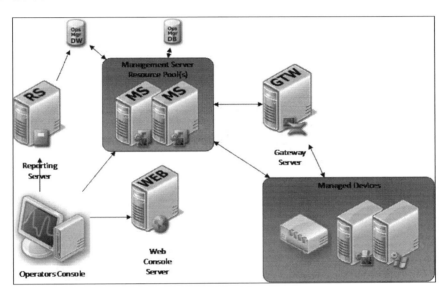

SCOM uses a mechanism known as management packs to control what type of information is collected and how to react to this information. These management packs are XML formatted files that define rules, monitors, scripts, and workflows for SCOM to use and essentially tell it how an aspect of your infrastructure should be monitored.

Most of these management packs will come from the suppliers of the software and devices used within your infrastructure, but there is nothing to stop you from creating your own management packs to fill a gap in monitoring if you find one. *Chapter 7, Authoring Custom Monitoring Solutions with System Center 2012 R2 Operations Manager,* will detail how to approach this.

You are also able to override predefined options within management packs to better tune the monitoring for your environment. Again, this is covered in more detail in *Chapter 4, Operating System Center 2012 R2 Operations Manager.*

## There's more...

While you've just been introduced to the main roles that will be encountered within almost all deployment scenarios of System Center 2012 R2 Operations Manager, there are a couple more, well, features rather than roles worth introducing.

With the release of Service Pack 1 for System Center 2012, Microsoft introduced a new feature known as **Global Services Monitoring** (**GSM**).

GSM allows you to configure a watcher node outside of your organization utilizing Microsoft's Azure platform, which can then be used to perform availability and performance monitoring of your externally accessible web-based application.

This allows you to gain a true 360 degree perspective on your environment with both internal monitoring happening from within your data center and a *customer* perspective from outside your network.

This information can then be surfaced through dashboards to see a visual representation of access to your services from different locations around the world.

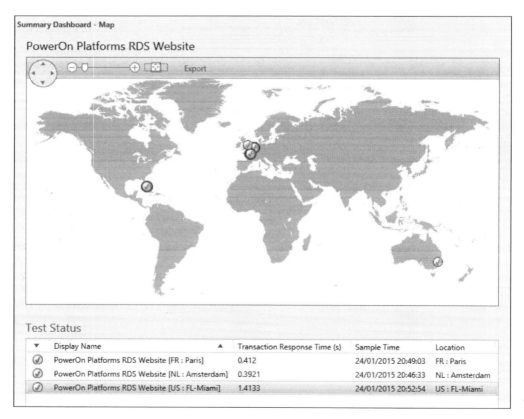

Another feature introduced fully with the 2012 R2 release is System Center Advisor integration. System Center Advisor is a standalone cloud-based service that helps in the proactive monitoring of the configuration of infrastructure systems and provides suggestions in line with best practices.

At the time of writing this, Microsoft had a preview of the replacement for Advisor in testing named Azure Operational Insights. This allows configuration information from SCOM to be uploaded into the cloud service and for the data to be analyzed for different purposes such as capacity planning, change tracking, and security. *Chapter 9, Integrating System Center 2012 R2 with Other Components*, for further information.

## RMS Emulator

In versions of Operations Manager prior to 2012, there was a role known as the **Root Management Server (RMS)**. This role was typically held by the first management server deployed into a management group and was responsible for running some distinct workflows such as AD assignment, notifications, and database maintenance.

This meant special attention was required when considering high availability with Failover Clustering and adding a layer of complexity. It also meant consideration of placement was required in relation to other components, such as the data warehouse or operator console access, owing to the SDK running on the RMS that scripts and consoles used to connect to SCOM.

The good news is this role requirement has been removed in the 2012 and later releases, but there is still a **RMS Emulator** (**RMSE**) component.

The RMSE is present to only provide backward compatibility for legacy management packs, which may still contain a workflow that specifically targets the RMS (for example, the Microsoft Exchange 2010 management pack). Most management packs, especially those from Microsoft, should now be re-released with the RMS requirement removed, but if you have any in-house management packs, it is recommended you check whether they are targeting the Root Management Server class instance (**Target="SC!Microsoft.SystemCenter. RootManagementServer"**).

You can identify which management server in your environment is running the RMSE by using the `Get-SCOMRMSEmulator` PowerShell command.

Running that command will display which management server is currently responsible for hosting and running the RMSE. In the event of a failure, however, the RMSE role will not fail over to another server, mainly as it isn't considered critical and should have limited impact on the environment.

If the RMSE does require to move to another management server in the event of a failure or just for proactive maintenance reasons, you can use this PowerShell command: `Set-SCOMRMSEmulator`.

To move the RMSE with a single PowerShell line, you would combine the command to get the details of the target management server with the `Set` command as in this example where the command would move the RMSE to a server named `POSNCOM01`:

```
Get-SCOMManagementServer –Name "PONSCOM01" | Set-SCOMRMSEmulator
```

## See also

The following are useful links to information related to the System Center 2012 Operations Manager roles and features:

- ▶ Microsoft TechNet—About Gateway Servers in Operations Manager: `http://technet.microsoft.com/en-us/library/hh212823.aspx`
- ▶ System Center Advisor: `https://www.systemcenteradvisor.com/`
- ▶ Microsoft TechNet—Global Service Monitor: `http://technet.microsoft.com/en-us/library/jj860368.aspx`

# Understanding the business and its requirements

In addition to understanding the various roles and how they are installed, as well as the performance, capacity sizing, and availability requirements for System Center 2012 R2 Operations Manager, it is equally important to understand what the business requires from its monitoring solution.

Without getting a clearly defined set of requirements, you could run the risk of not implementing high availability on the roles in highest demand, not implementing them at all, or focusing on monitoring areas of the business that provide no value.

## Getting ready

The following information should give you a good idea of the areas and questions that you can then take back to the business and seek answers from those involved in the decision-making processes.

## How to do it...

The following information will provide you with areas of thought when discussing the monitoring requirements with the business.

### Availability/percentage uptime required

Are you mandated to provide a five nines (99.999 percent) service or in reality can you provide a 98 percent uptime service? Most organizations like the sound of a five nines service, but in reality when they see the costs and controls associated with obtaining this uptime, requirements are often re-thought.

Try gathering information regarding your key systems and their priority. Once ranked, work with the business to agree on individual uptime percentages for each application rather than as a whole, as some may be less critical to the business and therefore shouldn't have the same amount of high availability and expense associated with them.

Rather than concentrating on only the time that an application should be up, again work with the business to correctly identify periods of time that the application is able to be taken out of service for planned maintenance. This can help maximize the percentage uptime by allowing you to schedule work around that application's maintenance window and track the different types of downtime to provide accurate metrics defining unplanned downtime, which lowers uptime, and planned downtime.

## Cost of downtime

The cost of downtime helps to get an understanding from the business with regard to what downtime of the application actually does cost the business.

Is it a financial loss such as a stock exchange or mining corporation may see if a critical system is down? Maybe, it's a loss of productivity or reputation or a loss of life in the case of systems used within hospitals.

Whatever the cost of downtime may be, knowing this in advance as you start designing your monitoring solution will enable you to focus on priorities and develop targeted reports that can represent the costs, highlighting areas doing well or others that need investments.

## Services within the monitoring scope

Alongside simply deciding to deploy agents to monitor servers, you must also consider what business services are within the scope of monitoring. As part of this, you need to ensure individual components (servers, network, applications, and so on) are accounted for and the solution scaled to support.

With these business services to be monitored, there also arises the questions regarding any specific SLAs for performance and availability that may need to be set up against the services, along with any reports that may be needed.

This requires you to take into account not only the scale but also the extra work involved in the creation and maintenance of your services.

## Financial penalties

Alongside knowing the cost of downtime, you should also know whether there are specific areas of the infrastructure that, if down, will cause business-specific financial penalties so that these can again be prioritized for monitoring.

## Resource metering – showback/chargeback

In addition to ensuring that you are monitoring key systems that may cause expenses to the business if problems aren't quickly identified, you may need to also capture areas within your business that earn revenue.

As multi-tenancy or even just the requirement to recoup costs from individual parts of the organization grows ever more important, you should start gathering information related to how much capital was expended on your infrastructure and how that can be equated to costs for individual resource usage of the components of that infrastructure.

Typically, you would assign costs to CPU, memory, storage, and networking utilization.

## Capacity planning

Not so much an area to gather specific information for, but to gain understanding from the business regarding at what level of utilization they require foresight into, for capacity planning and the purchasing of new equipment or redistribution of workloads.

For example, would the business like to know when the drive space is down to 20 percent or 40 percent of free space? Are they happy with the utilization of server memory at 80 percent or 95 percent?

Having this information on hand will help with the initial tuning of your new monitoring environment and the creation of any forecasting reports.

### How it works...

By gathering information from the outset before implementing your SCOM design, capacity planning allows you to understand exactly what the business is trying to achieve and how the SCOM implementation can best achieve that.

For example, if the business has no requirements to monitor access to files and systems, then implementing the ACS roles may be a waste of resources better served elsewhere. Again, if the business decides it has 50 applications that require extensive distributed apps for creating and monitoring, then be sure to scale the number of management servers appropriately.

Another area to consider is other systems and their integration. For example, does information regarding NetFlow data from another system need to be fed into SCOM or does SCOM need to output information into a Service Desk tool such as System Center 2012 R2 Service Manager?

These interactions, along with normal notifications and other subscriptions, can again place load on the solution and must be taken into consideration.

# Designing for high availability

SCOM can be deployed with high availability across the varying roles. This recipe will show you the various options for each role to allow you to implement SCOM with HA in mind.

### Getting ready

You should have already worked with the business using the previous recipe to gather information as to the business requirements.

## How to do it...

The following steps will guide you through the various high availability options you have when designing a SCOM infrastructure.

### Management servers

In previous versions of SCOM, high availability was achieved through the use of clustering owing to the reliance on a component known as the RMS. Starting with the 2012 release and carrying forward to the R2 release, the RMS role was deprecated, and therefore, it no longer requires clustering.

In SCOM now, high availability is achieved by deploying multiple management servers and grouping these into resource pools.

It is recommended, even in a simple deployment, to always deploy a minimum of two management servers, as this will provide failover of monitoring and access while simplifying the maintenance of your SCOM infrastructure.

As you scale out your infrastructure for larger monitoring deployments, you need to consider adding management servers that can be allocated to dedicated resource pools used for specific areas of monitoring.

The typical resource pools seen in implementations are *All Management Servers*, *Unix/Linux Servers* and *Network monitoring*.

All management servers will by default be added to the *All Management Servers* resource pool. It is recommended that once you have correctly sized your environment, if you need to dedicate management servers to monitoring, say, network devices, then you need to ensure you add these servers to the dedicated resource pool and remove them from the *All Management Servers* resource pool.

You must be aware that at least 50 percent of the servers in the *All Management Servers* resource pool need to be running in order for SCOM to fully function so you should always have, at a minimum, two servers remaining in this pool.

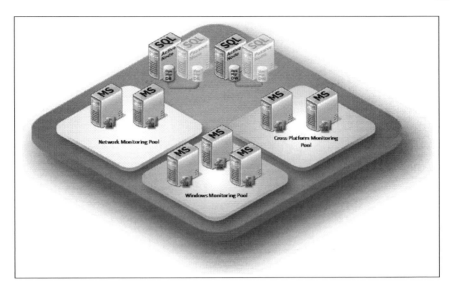

## Console connections

Basic implementations will see consoles connecting to a specifically named management server. If this server is offline, another server must be specified during the connection.

To provide high availability for console connections and to employ a more seamless connection method, **Network Load Balancing** can be implemented across the management servers used to provide console (or even SDK access for systems like the System Center 2012 R2 Service Manager connectors) and the DNS name allocated to the virtual IP address used, instead of a specific management server.

## Operational and Data Warehouse SQL databases

Since SCOM relies on the SQL databases in order to function, these should at a minimum be provided with high availability.

Normal SQL high availability scenarios apply here with the use of either standard failover clustering or the newer SQL Server 2012 AlwaysOn availability groups.

## Reporting server

SCOM uses **SQL Server Reporting Services (SSRS)** as the reporting mechanism and this cannot be made highly available. The underlying database for SSRS can be made highly available by utilizing either a traditional SQL Cluster or SQL 2012 Always-On.

Nevertheless, it is possible to quickly restore as long as the main SQL and SCOM components are still intact.

## Audit Collection Services

In a default deployment, ACS will usually be installed with a single ACS Collector and ACS Database pair. You can then implement multiple ACS Forwarders that point to this collector, but if the collector goes offline, the Security Event Log on the forwarder will effectively become a queue for the backlog until it can reconnect to a collector.

Using this configuration has the benefit of simplicity, and if the original ACS Collector can be brought back online within the Event Retention Period or the ACSConfig.xml file restored to a new ACS Collector, then potentially there would be no loss or duplication of data.

> ACS Collectors use a configuration file named ACSConfig.xml, which is stored in %systemroot%\System32\Security\AdtServer.
>
> This configuration file, which is updated every 5 minutes, keeps track of each forwarder communicating with the collector and a sequence number corresponding to the **EventRecordID**. This allows the collector to be aware of which events have been collected.

Using this simple configuration, however, does leave open the possibility for loss of data (Security Events not captured) if the ACS Collector is offline for longer than the retention period (the default is 72 hours) or duplication of data in the database if the original ACSConfig.xml file is not restored.

Another option would be to implement multiple ACS Collector/ACS Database pairs. This would allow you to specify a failover ACS Collector when deploying an ACS Forwarder and would provide you with automatic failover in case of an outage.

However, while this does provide automatic failover, it is important to note that each ACS Collector/ACS Database pair is independent, and after a failover, it would mean that Security Event data is spread across databases making it harder to query when reporting. It would also mean duplication of data after a failover as the ACSConfig.xml file on the failover ACS Collector would not be aware of the **EventRecordID** sequence the other ACS Collector was at.

This will provide automatic failover with no data loss and minimal data duplication while maintaining a single database for ease of reporting.

## Web console server

The SCOM web console can be made highly available and scalable by utilizing the normal Network Load Balancing technique used with most IIS websites.

This could either be through the use of dedicated hardware-based network load balancers or the built-in Windows Network Load Balancing role.

## Agents

Agents don't specifically have or need high availability at the client level as that would defeat the objective of monitoring to see whether the server went offline even if the agent was able to continue working. But you can implement multihoming, which allows the client to communicate with up to four management groups per agent. This is ideal for obtaining data from live systems in both test and production SCOM environments.

## Gateway servers

Multiple gateway servers can be deployed and agents pointed at both a primary server and multiple failover gateway servers to provide high availability.

To do this, use PowerShell to designate the primary and failover(s) servers and then set the agent configuration using the `Set-SCOMParentManagementServer` command with the `-Agent` switch.

For example, to set Failover Management Server (**PONSCOMGW02**) on Agent (**PONDC01**), use the following command:

```
Set-SCOMParentManagementServer -Agent (Get-SCOMAgent -DNSHostName
"PONDC01.PowerON.local") -FailoverServer (Get-SCOMManagementServer
-Name "PONSCOMGW02.PowerON.local")
```

The gateway servers themselves can also be pointed at multiple management servers as both primary and failovers. This technique uses the same PowerShell command, but with the `-Gateway` switch.

## How it works...

At the base layer, all the relevant databases for SCOM should reside on a highly available SQL instance. This may either be a traditional cluster or utilizing the new Always-On features of SQL 2012.

It would make sense, even for a very small deployment, to have at least two management servers, as this allows for easier maintenance with reduced downtime and you can then scale from there.

## See also

Detailed information for the various HA options can be found here:

- ▶ Modifying Resource Pool Membership—http://technet.microsoft.com/en-us/library/hh230706.aspx#bkmk_modifyingresourcepoolmembership
- ▶ Microsoft TechNet Documentation SQL Server 2012 Always On—http://technet.microsoft.com/en-us/library/jj899851.aspx
- ▶ Configure an agent for Gateway failover—https://technet.microsoft.com/en-us/library/hh212733.aspx
- ▶ Configure a Gateway for management server failover—https://technet.microsoft.com/en-us/library/hh212904.aspx

# Sizing the environment

While most areas of a System Center 2012 R2 Operations Manager environment can be scaled out later, there are several advantages to correctly sizing and implementing that design from the outset.

It will also certainly help mitigate the need to go back to the business and ask for more storage and compute resources further down the line.

## Getting ready

This recipe will show you how make use of the SCOM Sizing Helper that can be downloaded from http://www.microsoft.com/en-us/download/details.aspx?id=29270.

This sizing helper should only be used as an indicative guide, as your final sizing and design will require further thought around your requirements, and this is discussed more at the end of the recipe.

## How to do it...

The following steps will show you how to use the sizing calculator in order to gain an understanding of the hardware requirements for your environment:

1. Open **Sizing Helper** and enable editing and macro usage if prompted by your version of Excel. For this recipe, the screenshots show the **Sizing Helper** being used in Excel 2013.

2. Click the button under the **2. Standard Deployment** heading:

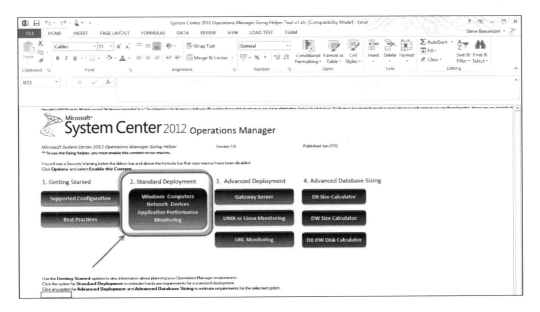

3. Use the drop-down selectors to choose **500** Windows Computers, **100** Network Devices, and set the APM as **Enabled** and click **Submit**:

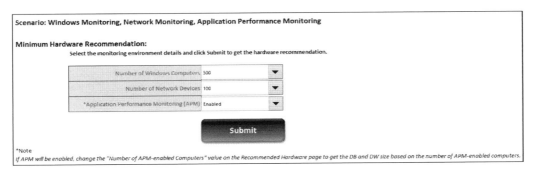

4. You will obtain a basic sizing output based on this scenario requiring 6 servers with 16 GB of memory and 4 cores each;

  ❑ One Management Server to support the selected number of agents, plus one to add high availability

  ❑ One Management Server to support the selected number of network devices, plus one to add high availability to create a resource pool dedicated to network monitoring

  ❑ One SQL server for the operational database

  ❑ One SQL server each for the data warehouse, SQL Reporting, and Web Console

The output will also calculate the disk space required for the SQL databases. What is important to note, however, is that as we choose to enable APM in this scenario, it defaults to calculating APM sizing for all of the 500 Windows computers that we chose.

It is highly unlikely that you will monitor application performance across every server so adjust this accordingly.

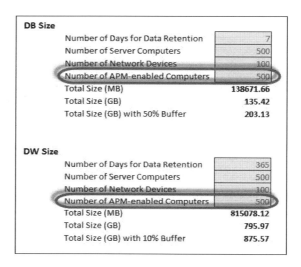

5. For this recipe, adjust the number of APM-enabled computers down to 20 for both the **DB Size** and **DW Size** sections and notice the reduction in the disk space requirements:

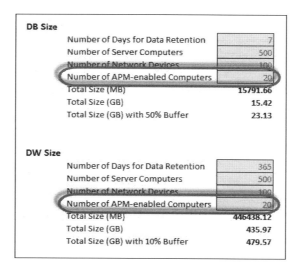

## How it works...

The **Sizing Helper** can be used to get a basic idea of the size of servers and disk space required for an environment of your size but must be used in conjunction with a more detailed plan of the infrastructure topology required for your environment.

For example, the preceding recipe includes no gateway servers, no resource pools dedicated to Unix or Linux monitoring, and no high availability across the SQL servers while also sharing the SQL server used for the data warehouse for the Web Console.

While there are no specific sizing fields to use to calculate for Unix or Linux, you can use the **Network Devices** fields as these will roughly calculate to the same values. It is worth exploring the other scenario tabs within the sizing calculator to see what other options you have and how they affect your sizing.

## There's more...

While the sizing helper is useful and good as a quick reference guide, there are some things you need to consider.

### Disk space requirements

One area you may have immediately zoomed in on is the disk space requirements for the SQL databases. While it is important to stress how critical it is to correctly size the databases and even more so to ensure there is enough free disk space always available for normal operation and maintenance tasks, the sizing helper can be a little on the generous side when calculating the requirements.

This is due to the complexity that would be involved in trying to model and account for every management pack you may wish to run, the rules and collections scoped for your devices, the overrides you may put in place, the distributed applications you may build, and so on.

We have seen some environments where the calculator has estimated 200 GB for the data warehouse, yet the environments haven't grown past 80 GB after a couple of years of full use.

However, this is not to say that you can simply ignore the recommendations, as your mileage may vary and the authors cannot stress just how important it is to ensure you have enough free disk space on the volumes used for your SQL databases.

### Why maintain free space?

System Center 2012 R2 Operations Manager has its own set of internal SQL maintenance tasks for its SQL Databases. The main operational database, for example, has regular schedules to re-index and defragment the tables. This means there is a hard requirement to ensure there is always at least 40 percent free space within the database for these maintenance tasks to operate.

A contingency must also be in place for the possibility of an event storm. If a large influx of alerts were to occur within your environment, causing the database to dramatically grow in size in a short period of time, not having the free disk space to allow for this could potentially make your monitoring system go offline before you've had a chance to use it to identify the root cause.

## Multiple management groups

Each management group can support up to 15,000 agents, so a single management group should be sufficient for most environments.

However, SCOM does allow for multiple management groups to be implemented within an environment, along with the ability for these separate management groups to share a single data warehouse.

Multiple management groups may need to be considered for a couple of reasons. The first is the fact that the number of supported agents, namely 15,000, reduces significantly in relation to the number of open console connections. For example, this number of supported agents is based on 25 open consoles. With 50 open consoles, this supported number drops to 6,000 agents.

 This is not something to consider lightly. Implementations on this scale are likely to already have very large data warehouses and adding more management groups is just going to increase the size and performance strain further.

These are still relatively high numbers for supported agents when considering just server monitoring, but can be quickly reached when also monitoring workstation class devices and must therefore be taken into account.

Another reason would be political reasons where **Role-based Access Control (RBAC)** cannot cover scoping of the console or where highly rigorous change control processes are in place across different parts of the infrastructure, which would make the normal deployment of management packs, overrides, and changes more challenging.

In addition to being able to deploy multiple management groups so that they share a single data warehouse, you have the option of connecting the individual management groups together in a *connected* method. This allows you to view and interact with alerts and discovery data in a consolidated view from a single console while also being able to run tasks on the monitored devices from other management groups.

Connected groups are joined together in a peer-to-peer relationship with a top-level *local group* in the hierarchy that has data fed from the other management groups, while groups have no visibility of each other, thus maintaining separation.

This is ideal for test or pre-production scenarios where typically you don't need a shared data warehouse and for them to remain separate, but with easy access from the console.

## See also

Detailed information for the recipes covered can be found here:

- ▶ Sizing Helper Download: `http://www.microsoft.com/en-us/download/details.aspx?id=29270`
- ▶ Kevin Holman's Blog: What SQL Maintenance Plans to use with SCOM? `http://blogs.technet.com/b/kevinholman/archive/2008/04/12/what-sql-maintenance-should-i-perform-on-my-opsmgr-databases.aspx`

# 2
# Deploying System Center 2012 R2 Operations Manager

In this chapter, we will cover:

- ► Implementing SQL high availability
- ► Scripting the deployment
- ► Deploying gateway servers

## Introduction

**System Center 2012 R2 Operations Manager** (**SCOM**) has a fairly mature wizard-driven GUI installation available for use. Assuming you have decided on the architecture for your deployment, performing the installation should be fairly straightforward with the use of this wizard, and therefore, this chapter won't cover a standard installation.

This chapter, nevertheless, will delve deeper into areas such as how to implement high availability at the SQL layer before you deploy SCOM. It will also explore prerequisites needed before installation and how to script the automation of deployments that will allow you to scale your infrastructure easier at a later date.

# Implementing SQL high availability

The following recipe will guide you through the steps required to set up SQL Server with high availability for use with System Center 2012 R2 Operations Manager.

For this recipe, we will be implementing the SQL Server 2012 AlwaysOn Availability Groups feature. You could also use the well-known method of **Windows Failover Clustering** (**WFC**) and SQL Server **Failover Clustered Instance** (**FCI**). These are well-understood methods with plenty of documentation, while AlwaysOn Availability Groups is still a relatively new method, but it is becoming the Microsoft preferred method of providing high availability.

 Another benefit of SQL Server 2012 AlwaysOn over traditional clustering is the fact that it doesn't require costly shared storage.

## Getting ready

For this recipe, you will require the following:

▸ Two virtual machines with Microsoft SQL Server 2012 Enterprise pre-installed

▸ A normal installation of SQL, not a SQL Server FCI installation

▸ Ensure during the installation that the SQL Service is set up with a domain account rather than using Local System

For installations of SQL that will hold SCOM-specific databases, you will require the following SQL features as shown in the following screenshot:

▸ Operational Database—Database Engine Services and Full-Text Search

▸ Data Warehouse—Database Engine Services and Full-Text Search

▸ Report Server—Reporting Services – Native

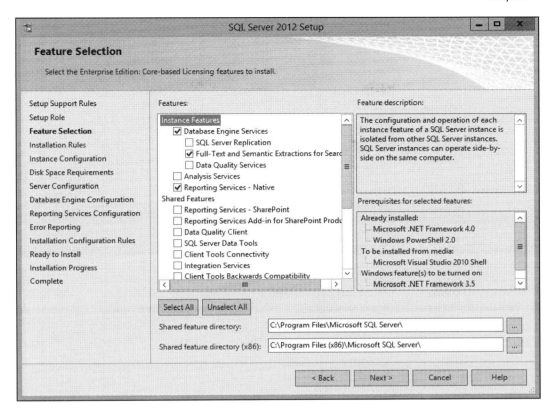

If using firewalls on your servers, ensure that TCP 1433, UDP 1434, and TCP 5022 ports are open. If using a named SQL instance, it is advisable to change that to a static port ensuring that the port is also open on the firewall and to allow inward-bound UDP 1434 on the management servers.

SQL Server collation settings for all databases must be one of the following as no other collation settings are supported:

- `SQL_Latin1_General_CP1_CI_AS`
- `Latin1_General_100_CI_AS, // EN, IT, DE, PT-BR, NE, PT-PT`
- `French_CI_AS; French_100_CI_AS`
- `Cyrillic_General_CI_AS; Chinese_PRC_CI_AS`
- `Chinese_Simplified_Pinyin_100_CI_AS, // CN simplified`
- `Chinese_Traditional_Stroke_Count_100_CI_AS, // CN traditional, CN-HKJapanese;_CI_AS`
- `Japanese_XJIS_100_CI_AS`
- `Traditional_Spanish_CI_AS`
- `Modern_Spanish_100_CI_AS`
- `Latin1_General_CI_AS`
- `Cyrillic_General_100_CI_AS,` // RU
- `Korean_100_CI_AS; Czech_100_CI_AS`
- `Hungarian_100_CI_AS`
- `Polish_100_CI_AS`
- `Finnish_Swedish_100_CI_AS`

For this recipe, we will be using `SQL_Latin1_General_CP1_CI_AS`, as this is the most widely supported setting across the System Center 2012 R2 components.

You must also have the rights within Active Directory to create the **Cluster Name Object** (**CNO**) that will be created during this recipe by the installation wizard. An account with domain admin rights or an account that is delegated to create computer objects will be sufficient.

The final thing you require is two file shares. Since we are using SQL AlwaysOn Availability Groups to negate the requirement for shared storage, we will be using a file share for the cluster quorum witness and will also require one for initial backups to initialize the databases in the Availability Group.

# How to do it...

Log on to one of the two virtual machines that will be used for the SQL Server 2012 AlwaysOn Availability Group and follow the steps in this recipe to configure it as required:

1.  Log on to your first server that has SQL installed with administrative rights. In this recipe, the first SQL server will be referred to as SQL01.

2.  Open **Server Manager** and click **Manage** in the top right and navigate to **Add Roles and Features**:

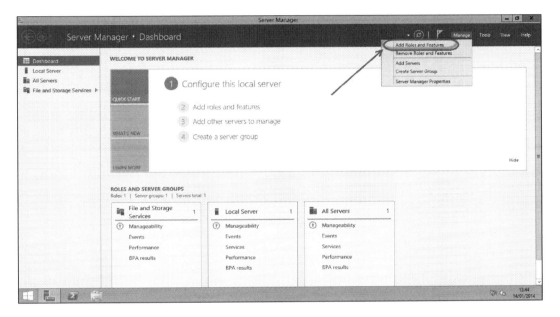

3.  On the **Before you begin** screen of the wizard, click **Next**.

4.  Choose **Role-based or feature-based installation** | **Next**.

5.  Choose **Select a server from the server pool**, select your server from the list (**SQL01** or **SQL02** in this recipe), and click **Next**.

6.  Click **Next** on the **Select server roles** screen of the wizard without selecting anything.

7. Scroll down on the list of features to find **Failover Clustering** and place a tick in the box next to it. Click **Add Features** when prompted about additional features required and then click **Next**.

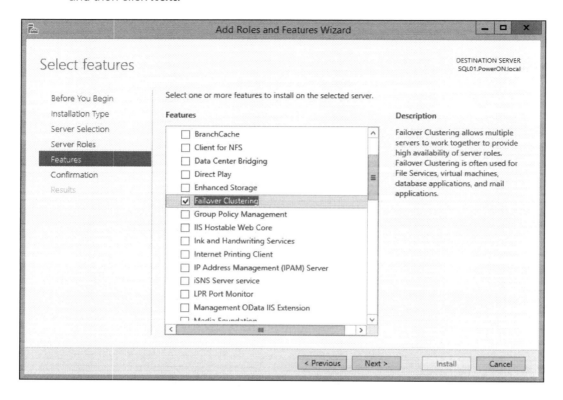

8. Click **Install** on the **Confirm installation selections** screen of the wizard.

9. Log on to your second server. The second SQL server is referred to as SQL02 in this recipe.

10. Repeat steps 2 through 8.

Perform the following steps to create a cluster; you can perform these from either SQL01 or SQL02:

1. Open **Server Manager** (if not already open) and click **Tools** in the top right and then click **Failover Cluster Manager**.

2. Click **Action | Create Cluster** and then click **Next**.

3. Enter the name of your first server and click **Add**.

4. Enter the name of your second server and click **Add**.

5. Wait for the wizard to verify the settings of the servers and click **Next** when ready.

6. The **Create Cluster Wizard** window will inform you at this point that the validation tests have not been run. Ensure **Yes** is selected and click **Next**.

7. The **Validate a Configuration Wizard** window will open. Now, click **Next** on the first screen.

8. Ensure **Run all tests (recommended)** is selected and click **Next**.

9. Click **Next** on the **Confirmation** screen and let the tests run.

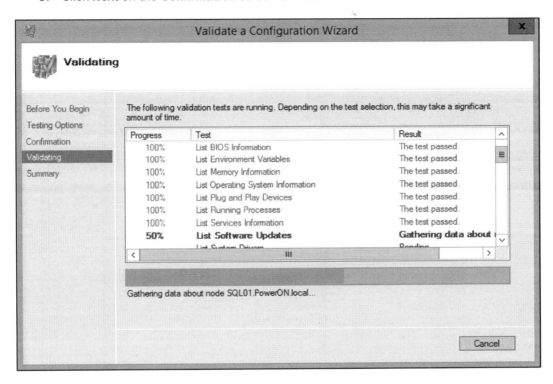

10. When the tests finish, click the **View Report** button and review any errors.

It's likely you will have warnings about storage, but these can be ignored since we won't be using shared storage. Depending on your server hardware configuration, you may have warnings about the network, usually due to one adapter.

It's recommended to have another network adapter in the server since we are trying to provide high availability, and a single network adapter in a cluster would be a single point of failure.

11. When ready, click **Finish**.

12. Back on the **Create Cluster Wizard** screen, supply a name for the **SQL AlwaysOn** cluster. This will be the name supplied during the setup for Operations Manager and for general connections to the SQL database. In this recipe, we will use SCOMSQL.

13. Type an IP address that will be used for connecting to the cluster:

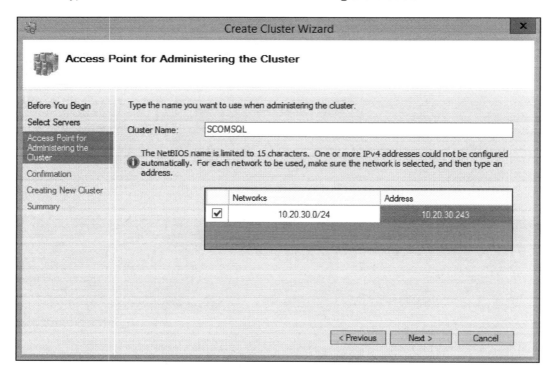

14. Click **Next**.

15. Review the information on the **Confirmation** screen and click **Next**.

16. Wait for the cluster to be formed and then click **Finish**.

17. Open **Failover Cluster Manager** if not already open.

18. Click **Action | More Actions | Configure Cluster Quorum Settings...**.

19. When the **Configure Cluster Quorum Wizard** window opens, click **Next**.

20. Choose **Advanced quorum configuration** and click **Next**.

21. Choose **All Nodes** and click **Next**.

22. Choose **Configure a file share witness** and click **Next**.

23. Click **Browse** and navigate to your file share that you will use for the quorum witness.

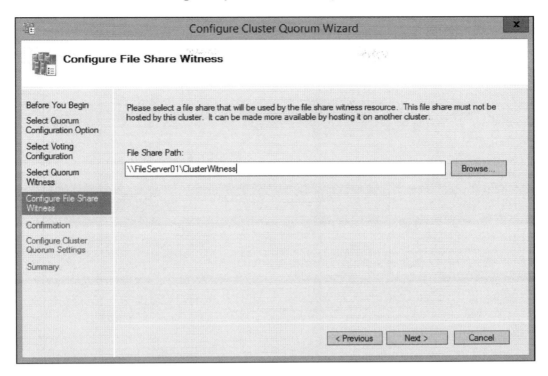

24. Click **Next**.
25. Review the information on the **Confirmation** screen and click **Next**.
26. Review the information on the **Summary** screen and click **Finish**.
27. Close **Failover Cluster Manager**.
28. Log on to your first SQL server (SQL01).
29. Open **SQL Server Configuration Manager**.
30. Underneath **SQL Server Configuration Manager (Local)**, click on **SQL Server Services**.
31. Right-click on **SQL Server (MSSQLSERVER)** and navigate to **Properties**.

 If you installed SQL with a named instance, then the text (**MSSQLSERVER**) will reflect the name you gave the instance instead.

32. Select the **AlwaysOn High Availability** tab on the **Properties** window.
33. Tick the box next to **Enable AlwaysOn Availability Groups**.

34. Click **OK**.

35. You will be prompted with a warning that the changes will be saved but will not take effect until the service is restarted. Now click **OK**:

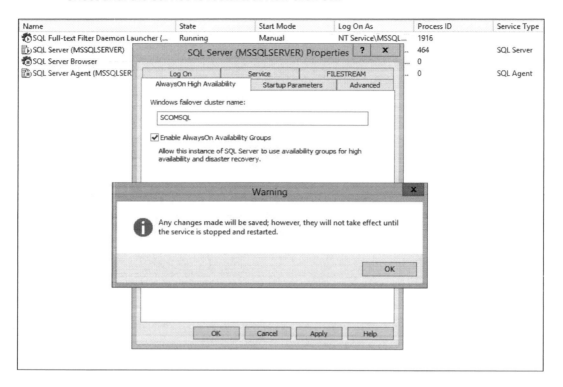

36. Right-click on the **SQL Server (MSSQLSERVER)** service and click on **Restart**.

37. Log on to your second SQL server (SQL02) and repeat steps 29 to 36.

38. Open **SQL Server Management Studio**.

39. Connect to the **Database Engine** of your SQL server (SQL01).

40. Right-click on **Databases** and navigate to **New Database...**.

41. Provide a database name of **TempSCOM** and click **OK**.

42. Expand **Databases** and right-click on the **TempSCOM** database and navigate to **Tasks | Back Up...**.

43. Click **OK** to back up to the default location.

44. Click **OK** when notified that the backup has completed.

45. Right-click on **AlwaysOn High Availability** and navigate to **New Availability Group Wizard...**.

46. Click **Next**.

47. Type **SCOMAG** as the name of the Availability Group and click **Next**.

48. Tick the box next to the **TempSCOM** database and click **Next**.

49. Tick the option for **Automatic Failover (Up to 2)**.

50. Click **Add Replica**.

51. Enter the name of the second SQL server (**SQL02**) and click **Connect**.

 If you get an error relating to connection problems, ensure that TCP 1433 and UDP 1434 are open on any firewalls on the SQL servers.

52. Tick the option for **Automatic Failover (Up to 2)**.

53. Leave the options for **Readable Secondary** as **No**, unless you specifically plan to do reporting from the secondary replicas directly and your SQL licensing allows you to have two active databases:

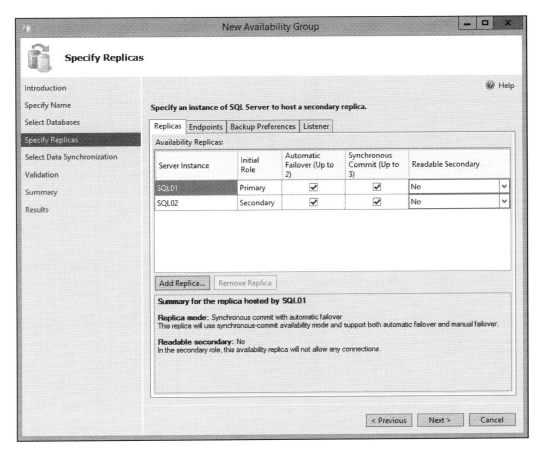

54. Click on the **Listener** tab.

55. Select the option to **Create an availability group listener**.

56. Type SCOMAGListener as the **Listener DNS Name**.

57. Type 5678 as the **Port**.

58. Choose **Static IP** as the **Network Mode**.

59. Click **Add**.

60. Enter an available IP address and click **OK**.

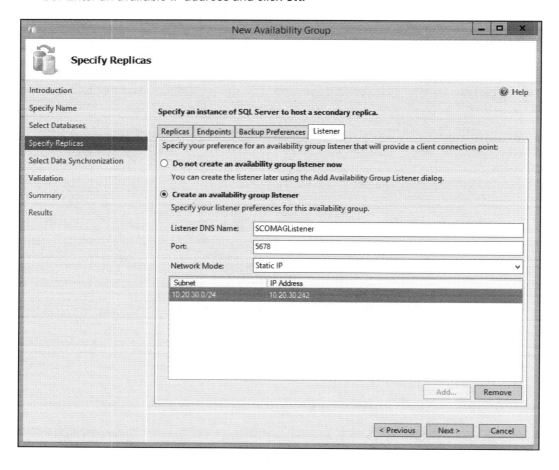

61. Click **Next**.

62. Ensure the **Full** option is selected for data synchronization. Browse for, or type, the file share that you will use for initial synchronization; the SQL Service account that will be used for SQL instances must have write permissions.

63. Click **Next**.

64. When the validation completes successfully, click **Next**.
65. Review the information on the **Summary** screen and click **Finish**.
66. When the wizard completes successfully, click **Close**.

Once the steps in this recipe are complete, you will see an AlwaysOn High Availability configuration as shown in the following screenshot:

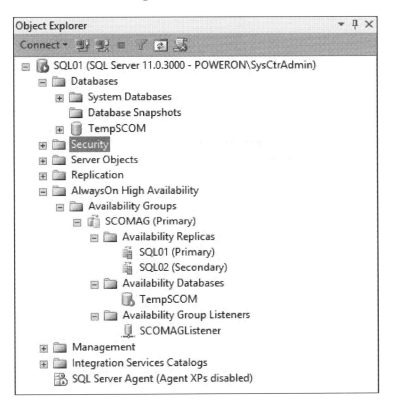

## How it works...

SQL Server 2012 AlwaysOn Availability Groups use the underlying technology of **Windows Server Failover Clustering** (**WSFC**) to monitor the SQL Services and inform SQL when a failure of a server hosting a SQL database makes it unavailable. It does not use it in the same way as when using a SQL Failover Cluster instance because there is no shared storage that the multiple SQL servers have access to concurrently.

Once WSFC was set up, we enabled **AlwaysON High Availability** on the SQL Server Services. This allows SQL to interact with WSFC and create the necessary registry keys that are contained as subkeys of WSFC, which allows the WSFC to monitor the health of the servers in the replica groups and manage their configuration metadata.

We then created a new database called **TempSCOM**. This is needed as you cannot create an Availability Group without a database and you require the Availability Group and Listener to be up and running before installing Operations Manager.

A full backup of the database was then taken as SQL will utilize the backup to perform a restore on the replica server.

An Availability Group was then created with the servers included that will hold a replica of the database with the options to allow for automatic failover and fully synchronous committing of data selected to ensure SCOM automatically fails over and does not miss any data in the event of a problem (or planned maintenance).

The Listener is in effect similar to the SQL Server **Failover Cluster Instance** (**FCI**) and WSFC cluster object names. It is the end point that will be referred to by SCOM when connecting to the database and it directs the application to the SQL server that is actively serving the database.

SQL Server 2012 AlwaysOn offers the following advantages:

▸ It provides a more granular approach to high availability while using a method based on tried and trusted technologies

▸ It uses the WSFC APIs to perform the failovers and yet doesn't require the shared storage element

▸ It utilizes database mirroring for the data transfer over TCP with the ability for synchronous data without needing SAN-level block replication

▸ It allows you to provide up to four replicas, which can be readable if needed to offload tasks such as backup and reporting from your primary database

## There's more...

This recipe shows how to set up a SQL Server 2012 AlwaysOn Availability Group for use with SCOM, but you still need to install and configure SCOM to use this high availability solution.

## Configuring Operations Manager

During the installation of SCOM, when you are prompted by the wizard to enter a **Server name and instance name** on the **Configure the operational database** screen, instead of specifying the name of the SQL server hosting the SQL instance, enter the name of the SQL AlwaysOn Listener you created earlier—**SCOMAGListener**—and the port—**5678**.

This will install the SCOM databases onto the server holding the active replica set for the Availability Group and add the databases into **Availability Groups**. Enter the same information for the `Data Warehouse` database details.

 While this recipe uses the default installation locations, it is not best practice, and individual drives or mount points should be configured for the various SQL files.

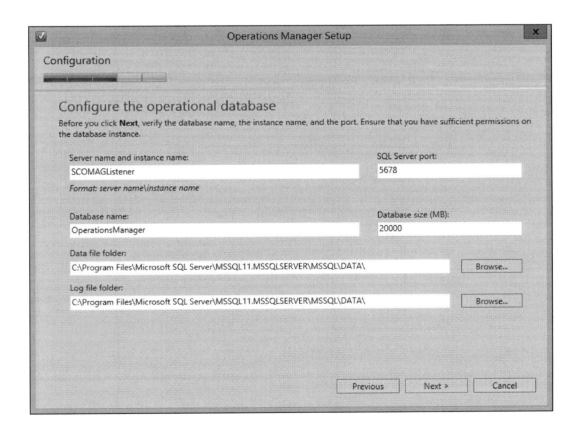

Once SCOM has finished installing, the database recovery model should be changed to the **Full Recovery** model. Do this by opening **SQL Server Management Studio**, right-clicking on the **OperationsManager** database, and navigating to **Properties | Options**. Then use the recovery model list box to change from **Simple** to **Full**:

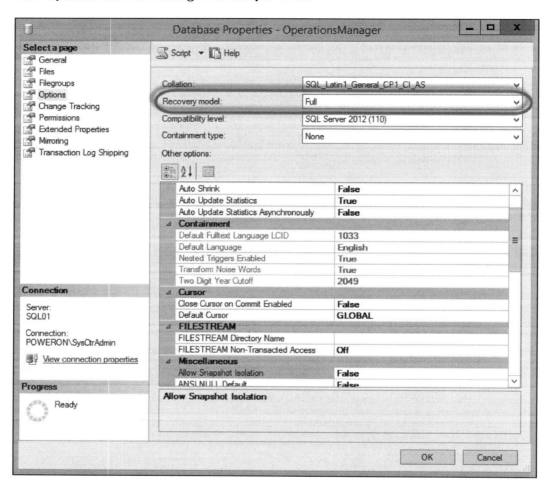

Repeat the same procedure for the Data warehouse database (the default is **OperationsManagerDW**).

Once the recovery model has been changed to **Full**, perform a full backup of both databases. Once the databases have been backed up, perform the following to add them to the Availability Group:

1. Log on to the SQL server hosting the SCOM databases.
2. Open SQL Server Management Studio.
3. Connect to the SQL instance hosting the SCOM databases.
4. Expand **AlwaysOn High Availability**.
5. Expand **Availability Groups**.

 If the Availability Group (**SCOMAG** in this recipe) does not currently have the wording **(Primary)** after it, right-click on it and select **Failover**. Step through the wizard to perform a manual failover to have the **Availability Groups** use the SQL server with the SCOM databases as the primary replica.

6. Right-click on the Availability Group (**SCOMAG** in this recipe) and navigate to **Add Database** and then click **Next**.
7. Tick the boxes for both the **OperationsManager** and the **OperationsManagerDW** databases and then click **Next**.
8. Choose the option for **Full** and ensure the file share path is the same as the one created earlier that both nodes can access as well as the SQL Service account and then click **Next**.
9. If prompted to connect to existing replicas, click **Connect...** and choose the other SQL server (SQLO2) and then click **Next**.
10. Review the validation information and click **Next**.
11. Review the summary information and click **Finish**.

The **TempSCOM** database that was created during the first steps of the recipe can now be removed from the Availability Group and deleted from SQL, as follows:

1. Log on to the SQL server hosting the SCOM databases.
2. Open SQL Server Management Studio.
3. Connect to the SQL instance hosting the SCOM databases.
4. Expand **AlwaysOn High Availability**.
5. Expand **Availability Groups**.
6. Right-click on the **TempSCOM** database and navigate to **Remove Database from Availability Group...** and then click **OK**.
7. Expand **Databases**.
8. Right-click on the **TempSCOM** database and navigate to **Delete** and then click **OK**.

## Additional Security and SQL Messages

The installation of SCOM will setup the first SQL node with the relevant security and will also modify the Master database with some additional configuration.

These changes do not get replicated automatically for you and therefore must be configured manually post installation.

Firstly you will need to add the following accounts used during installation of SCOM to any SQL servers used for replication for the relevant database:

| Database | Account | User Mapping |
|----------|---------|--------------|
| Operational | Data Writer | ConfigService |
| | | db_accessadmin |
| | | db_datareader |
| | | db_datawriter |
| | | db_ddladmin |
| | | db_securityadmin |
| | | sdk_users |
| | | sql_dependency_subscriber |
| Data Warehouse | Data Reader | db_datareader |
| | | OpsMgrReader |
| | | apm_datareader |

Finally, after a failover, errors (EventID 18054) will be written to the application event log.

This is due to custom SQL error messages that are configured during the SCOM installation residing in the Master DB of the primary SQL node, but not on secondary replicas.

To fix this, find the BUILD_MOM_DB_ADMIN.SQL file in the \Setup\AMD64 folder on the source media and find the line that starts with -- MOMv3 messages are 77798xxxx --.

Copy the full section into a new query (which ends just after -- Deployment: 77798-0500 to 77798-0550 -- at around line 6808 just before the * Management Group connect / disconnect / permission errors section starts) and run it against the Master database on all replica servers.

## Multi-site AlwaysOn Availability Groups

If you use different subnets across different sites and want to locate an AlwaysOn Replica server at these sites, you would need to add IP addresses from each of the different ranges used at these sites to the Listener.

This will create multiple DNS entries to allow for applications to create multiple connections simultaneously to the replicas to aid with efficient failover.

However, SCOM doesn't use the `multisitefailover` property in its connection string. This means SCOM will connect to each of the IP addresses in sequence that can cause timeout errors within SCOM's workflows.

To avoid this, you need to change the properties of the cluster so that it only registers the IP address of the primary active replica. It is also a good idea to reduce the time to live for the DNS record so that once a failover occurs, the DNS entry is updated and the management servers get the new IP address of the Listener in an appropriate timescale.

To alter the required parameters, the following PowerShell commands can be used.

Replace the variables with the information relevant for your environment. I have used the Availability Group name (`SCOMAG`) and the Listener name (`SCOMAGListener`) that we created earlier in the recipe. The parameters are altered as follows:

```
$AvailabilityGroup="SCOMAG"
$AGListener="SCOMAGListener"

If (!(Get-Module FailoverClusters)) {Import-Module
FailoverClusters}

Get-ClusterResource "$AvailabilityGroup`_$AGListener" | Set-
ClusterParameter RegisterAllProvidersIP 0

Get-ClusterResource "$AvailabilityGroup`_$AGListener" | Set-
ClusterParameter HostRecordTTL 300
```

As shown in the following screenshot, the settings are applied but the cluster role will need a restart before they take effect. Failing over the replica should be sufficient.

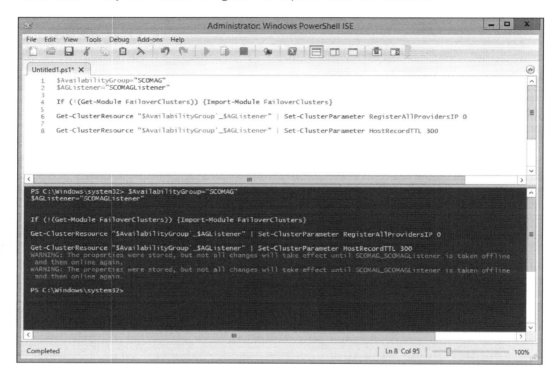

## See also

The following are useful links to information related to the recipe:

▶ Microsoft TechNet—Prerequisites, Restrictions, and Recommendations for AlwaysOn Availability Groups (SQL Server): `http://technet.microsoft.com/en-us/library/ff878487.aspx`

▶ Microsoft TechNet—Relationship of SQL Server AlwaysOn Components to Windows Server Failover Clustering: `http://technet.microsoft.com/en-us/library/79d2ea5a-edd8-4b3b-9502-96202057b01a#AlwaysOnWsfcRelationship`

▶ Microsoft TechNet—Overview of AlwaysOn Availability Groups: `http://technet.microsoft.com/en-us/library/ff877884.aspx`

▶ Microsoft TechNet—Using SQL Server 2012 AlwaysOn with SCOM: `http://technet.microsoft.com/en-us/library/jj899851.aspx`

# Scripting the deployment

This recipe will help you develop a series of scripts that can be used to deploy the main roles and features of System Center 2012 R2 Operations Manager:

- ▶ Management Servers
- ▶ Data Warehouse
- ▶ Reporting Server
- ▶ Gateways

While deploying some of the base infrastructure is usually a one-time operation, having these scripts will enable you to adopt a more scalable approach to Operations Manager with the ability to easily scale out your deployment as your monitoring needs expand.

## Getting ready

For this recipe, you will require some virtual machines on which to test the deployment of SCOM and a PowerShell editor, such as the PowerShell ISE that is supplied with Windows.

You will need to copy the SCOM installation files from the DVD or ISO image to a file share that you will have access to from the server and as the user that you will run the script as.

## How to do it...

The following code requires either typing into a PowerShell code editor such as the ISE or try downloading it from the Packt Publishing website:

```
Param (
    #Mandatory Parameters
    [Parameter(Mandatory=$true)]
    [string]$SCOMDASUser,
    [Parameter(Mandatory=$true)]
    [string]$SCOMDASPassword,
    [Parameter(Mandatory=$true)]
    [string]$SCOMAAUser,
    [Parameter(Mandatory=$true)]
    [string]$SCOMAAPassword,
    [Parameter(Mandatory=$true)]
    [string]$SCOMDRUser,
    [Parameter(Mandatory=$true)]
    [string]$SCOMDRPassword,
    [Parameter(Mandatory=$true)]
    [string]$SCOMDWUser,
    [Parameter(Mandatory=$true)]
```

```
    [string]$SCOMDWPassword,
    [Parameter(Mandatory=$true)]
    [string]$ManagementGroupName,
    [Parameter(Mandatory=$true)]
    [string]$Domain,
    [Parameter(Mandatory=$true)]
    [ValidateScript({Test-Path $_ -PathType 'Container'})]
    [string]$SourceFiles,
    [Parameter(Mandatory=$true)]
    [string]$SQLOpsDBServer,
    [Parameter(Mandatory=$true)]
    [string]$SQLDWDBServer,
#Optional Parameters with default Values
    [Parameter(Mandatory=$false)]
    [switch]$SCOMFirst=$false,
    [Parameter(Mandatory=$false)]
    [switch]$SCOMAdditional=$false,
    [Parameter(Mandatory=$false)]
    [switch]$SCOMWeb=$false,
    [Parameter(Mandatory=$false)]
    [switch]$SCOMConsole=$false,
    [Parameter(Mandatory=$false)]
    [string]$InstallDir="C:\Program Files\Microsoft System Center 2012
R2\Operations Manager",
    [Parameter(Mandatory=$false)]
    [string]$DatabaseName="OperationsManager",
    [Parameter(Mandatory=$false)]
    [Int]$DatabaseSize=30000,
    [Parameter(Mandatory=$false)]
    [string]$DatabasePath,
    [Parameter(Mandatory=$false)]
    [string]$DatabaseLogPath,
    [Parameter(Mandatory=$false)]
    [Int]$SqlInstancePort="7980",
    [Parameter(Mandatory=$false)]
    [string]$DWDatabaseName="OperationsManagerDW",
    [Parameter(Mandatory=$false)]
    [Int]$DWDatabaseSize=50000,
    [Parameter(Mandatory=$false)]
    [string]$DWDatabasePath,
    [Parameter(Mandatory=$false)]
    [string]$DWDatabaseLogPath,
    [Parameter(Mandatory=$false)]
    [Int]$DWSqlInstancePort="7981",
    [Parameter(Mandatory=$false)]
    [string]$WebSiteName="Default Web Site",
    [Parameter(Mandatory=$false)]
```

```
      [ValidateSet("Mixed","Network")]
      [string]$WebConsoleAuthorizationMode="Mixed",
      [Parameter(Mandatory=$false)]
      [switch]$WebConsoleUseSSL=$false,
      [Parameter(Mandatory=$false)]
      [ValidateSet(0,1)]
      [Int]$UseMicrosoftUpdate=0,
      [Parameter(Mandatory=$false)]
      [ValidateSet(0,1)]
      [Int]$SendCEIPReports=0,
      [Parameter(Mandatory=$false)]
      [ValidateSet("Never","Queued","Always")]
      [String]$EnableErrorReporting="Never",
      [Parameter(Mandatory=$false)]
      [ValidateSet(0,1)]
      [Int]$SendODRReports=0
      )


#Command setup and validation

$Features=""
If (($SCOMFirst) -and ($SCOMAdditional)) {Write-Output "You cannot
install the first management server and an additional management
server on the same server.  Please correct and try again.";break}
If (($SCOMFirst) -or ($SCOMAdditional)) {$Features=" OMServer"}
If ($SCOMWeb) {$Features=$Features+",OMWebConsole"}
If ($SCOMConsole) {$Features=$Features+",OMConsole"}
If ($Features -ne "") {
    $Features=$Features.SubString(1)
    } Else {Write-Output "No features specified, nothing to
install";break}


$InstallArgs="/install /silent /components:$Features
/SqlServerInstance:$SQLOpsDBServer /InstallPath:`"$InstallDir`"
/ActionAccountUser:`"$Domain\$SCOMAAUser`"
/ActionAccountPassword:$SCOMAAPassword
/DASAccountUser:`"$Domain\$SCOMDASUser`"
/DASAccountPassword:$SCOMDASPassword
/DataReaderUser:`"$Domain\$SCOMDRUser`"
/DataReaderPassword:$SCOMDRPassword
/DataWriterUser:`"$Domain\$SCOMDWUser`"
/DataWriterPassword:$SCOMDWPassword
/UseMicrosoftUpdate:$UseMicrosoftUpdate
/SendCEIPReports:$SendCEIPReports
/EnableErrorReporting:$EnableErrorReporting
/SendODRReports:$SendODRReports /AcceptEndUserLicenseAgreement:1"


If ($SCOMFirst) {
```

```
        $InstallArgs=$InstallArgs+"
/ManagementGroupName:$ManagementGroupName
/DWSqlServerInstance:$SQLDWDBServer /DatabaseName:$DatabaseName
/DatabaseSize:$DatabaseSize /DWDatabaseName:$DWDatabaseName
/DWDatabaseSize:$DWDatabaseSize"
    }
If ($SCOMWeb) {
    $InstallArgs=$InstallArgs+" /WebSiteName:`"$WebSiteName`"" /WebCons
oleAuthorizationMode:$WebConsoleAuthorizationMode"
    If ($WebConsoleUseSSL) {
        $InstallArgs=$InstallArgs+" /WebConsoleUseSSL"
        }
    Write-Output "Adding required Windows Features for the
Operations Manager Web Console"
    Add-WindowsFeature Web-WebServer,Web-Default-Doc,Web-Dir-
Browsing,Web-Http-Errors,Web-Static-Content,Web-Http-Logging,Web-
Request-Monitor,Web-Stat-Compression,Web-Filtering,Web-Windows-
Auth,Web-App-Dev,Web-Net-Ext,Web-Net-Ext45,Web-Asp-Net,Web-Asp-
Net45,Web-ISAPI-Ext,Web-ISAPI-Filter,Web-Mgmt-Console,Web-
Metabase,NET-Framework-45-ASPNET,NET-WCF-HTTP-Activation45,WAS-
Process-Model,WAS-Config-APIs,Windows-Identity-Foundation
    }
if ($SqlInstancePort -ne "") {
    $InstallArgs=$InstallArgs+" /SqlInstancePort:$SqlInstancePort"
    }
if ($DWSqlInstancePort -ne "") {
    $InstallArgs=$InstallArgs+" /DWSqlInstancePort:$DWSqlInstancePort"
    }
if ($DatabasePath -ne "") {
    $InstallArgs=$InstallArgs+" /DatabasePath:$DatabasePath"
    }
if ($DatabaseLogPath -ne "") {
    $InstallArgs=$InstallArgs+" /DatabaseLogPath:$DatabaseLogPath"
    }
if ($DWDatabasePath -ne "") {
    $InstallArgs=$InstallArgs+" /DWDatabasePath:$DWDatabasePath"
    }
if ($DWDatabaseLogPath -ne "") {
    $InstallArgs=$InstallArgs+"
/DWDatabaseLogPath:$DWDatabaseLogPath"
    }


#Add Operations Manager Data Access and Action Accounts to Local
Admin
Write-Output "Adding required accounts to the local administrators
group"
$SCOMUser=$SCOMDASUser
```

```
$LocalGroup =
[ADSI]"WinNT://$env:ComputerName/Administrators,group"
$members =""
$members = $LocalGroup.psbase.Invoke("Members") | Foreach-Object
{$_.GetType().InvokeMember("Name", 'GetProperty', $null, $_,
$null) }

if($members -contains $SCOMUser) {
    Write-Output "$SCOMUser is already member"
    } else {
        Write-Output "Adding: $SCOMUser"
        ([ADSI]"WinNT://$env:computername/Administrators,group").
Add("WinNT://$Domain/$SCOMUser")
    }


$SCOMUser=$SCOMAAUser
$members =""
$members = $LocalGroup.psbase.Invoke("Members") | Foreach-Object
{$_.GetType().InvokeMember("Name", 'GetProperty', $null, $_, $null) }

if($members -contains $SCOMUser) {
    Write-Output "$SCOMUser is already member"
    } else {
        Write-Output "Adding: $SCOMUser"
        ([ADSI]"WinNT://$env:computername/Administrators,group").Add("
WinNT://$Domain/$SCOMUser")
    }



#Install Operations Manager
Write-Output "Installing System Center 2012 R2 Operations Manager"
Add-WindowsFeature WAS-NET-Environment
Start-Process -FilePath "$SourceFiles\setup.exe" -Wait
-NoNewWindow -PassThru -ArgumentList $InstallArgs

If (!(Test-Path -Path "C:\Program Files\Microsoft System Center 2012
R2\Operations Manager")) {
  Write-Error "Installation Failed"
  } Else {
  Write-Output "Installation Complete"
  }
```

Save the script as Install-SCOM.ps1.

## How it works...

The script can be broken down into four logical blocks:

- ▶ Gathering parameters
- ▶ Setting up and validating variables
- ▶ Preparing Operations Manager prerequisites
- ▶ Deploying Operations Manager

### Gathering parameters

When deploying SCOM from the GUI, you are prompted to input a series of information relating to your environment. Therefore, the first thing the script must do is gather this information.

The script has the following two distinct sets:

- ▶ Mandatory parameters
- ▶ Optional parameters

The mandatory parameters are listed in the following table:

| Parameter | Use | SCOM install command-line mapping |
| --- | --- | --- |
| $Domain | Specifies the domain that the service accounts are located in. | Used as a prefix to the various service account switches. |
| $SCOMDASUser | Service account name for the Data Access Service account. | /DASAccountUser: |
| $SCOMDASPassword | Password for the Data Access Service account. | /DASAccountPassword: |
| $SCOMAAUser | Service account name for the Action account. | /ActionAccountUser: |
| $SCOMAAPassword | Password for the Action account. | /ActionAccountPassword: |
| $SCOMDRUser | Service account name for the Data Warehouse Reader account. | /DataReaderUser: |
| $SCOMDRPassword | Password for the Data Warehouse Reader account. | /DataReaderPassword: |
| $SCOMDWUser | Service account name for the Data Warehouse Writer account. | /DataWriterUser: |
| $SCOMDWPassword | Password for the Data Warehouse Writer account. | /DataWriterPassword: |

| Parameter | Use | SCOM install command-line mapping |
|---|---|---|
| $ManagementGroupName | Name of the SCOM management group that will be created. | /ManagementGroupName: |
| $SQLOpsDBServer | Name of the server or server and instance that will host the operational database.<br><br>If specifying a named instance, use the format Server\Instance. | /SqlServerInstance: |
| $SQLDWDBServer | Name of the server or server and instance that will host the Data Warehouse database.<br><br>If specifying a named instance, use the format Server\Instance. | /DWSqlServerInstance: |
| $SourceFiles | Location of the Operations Manager installation source files. | Used to locate setup.exe and the prerequisite files copied to the directory during the *Getting ready* section of the recipe. |

Even if not marked as mandatory within the script, and although you can run the script without error if not specified, one of the following parameters should be specified:

| Parameter | Use |
|---|---|
| $SCOMFirst | Installs the first SCOM management server in the deployment |
| $SCOMAdditional | Installs additional management servers for load balancing and/or resource pools |
| $SCOMWeb | Installs the SCOM web console |
| $SCOMConsole | Installs the full operator console |

Each parameter is a switch, so simply specifying it will change the value from false to true. You cannot specify SCOMFirst at the same time as SCOMAdditional, and specifying none of them will result in nothing being installed.

The optional parameters allow you to customize the installation more to your requirements, such as changing the name and initial size of the database, whether to enable SSL for the web console or to enable participation in the Customer Experience program.

All of them are set to use the default values that are present within a GUI installation, and normally the only ones that are required to be specified are the database initial sizes and, possibly, the SQL ports if using a named instance without the SQL Browser service running.

The optional parameters are listed in the following table:

| Parameter | Use | Default Value | SCOM Install Command-line Mapping |
|---|---|---|---|
| `$InstallDir` | Specifies the directory in which to install the SCOM components. | `C:\Program Files\ Microsoft System Center 2012 R2\Operations Manager` | `/InstallPath` |
| `$DatabaseName` | Specifies the name of the operational database. | `OperationsManager` | `/DatabaseName:` |
| `$DatabaseSize` | Specifies the initial size of the operational database. | `1000` | `/DatabaseSize:` |
| `$DatabasePath` | Specifies the location of the operational database files. | None. Leaving it blank will result in the files being installed in the default database path specified by SQL. | `/DatabasePath:` |
| `$DatabaseLogPath` | Specifies the location of the operational database log files. | None. Leaving it blank will result in the files being installed in the default database path specified by SQL. | `/DatabaseLogPath:` |
| `$SqlInstancePort` | Specifies the port used by the SQL instance hosting the operational database. | `1433` | `/SqlInstancePort:` |
| `$DWDatabaseName` | Specifies the name of the Data Warehouse Database. | `Operations ManagerDW` | `/DWDatabaseName:` |
| `$DWDatabaseSize` | Specifies the size of the Data Warehouse Database. | `1000` | `/DWDatabaseSize:` |
| `$DWDatabasePath` | Specifies the location of the Data Warehouse Database files. | None. Leaving it blank will result in the files being installed in the default database path specified by SQL. | `/DWDatabasePath:` |

| Parameter | Use | Default Value | SCOM Install Command-line Mapping |
|---|---|---|---|
| `$DWDatabase LogPath` | Specifies the location of the Data Warehouse Database log files. | None. Leaving it blank will result in the files being installed in the default database path specified by SQL. | `/DWDatabaseLogPath:` |
| `$DWSqlInstance Port` | Specifies the port used by the SQL instance hosting the Data Warehouse Database. | `1433` | `/DWSqlInstancePort:` |
| `$WebSiteName` | Specifies the existing IIS website to use for the web console. | `Default Web Site` | `/WebSiteName:` |
| `$WebConsole Authorization Mode` | Specifies the authentication mode for the web console. `Mixed` will attempt to use logged on credentials. The network will prompt for the username and password. | `Mixed` | `/WebConsole Authorization Mode:` |
| `$WebConsoleUseSSL` | Will install the web console with SSL bindings. | `false` | `/WebConsoleUseSSL` |
| `$UseMicrosoft Update` | Specifies whether to use Microsoft Update or not. | `0` | `/UseMicrosoft Update:` |
| `$SendCEIPReports` | Specifies whether to enable participation in the Customer Experience program or not. | `0` | `/SendCEIPReports:` |
| `$EnableError Reporting` | Specifies whether to enable sending of error reports or not to Microsoft. | `Never` | `/EnableError Reporting:` |
| `$SendODRReports` | Specifies whether to enable sending of operational data reports or not to Microsoft. | `0` | `/SendODRReports:` |

## Setting up and validating variables

For the script to be able to successfully install Operations Manager, we need to correctly verify that a correct combination of switches has been chosen. If these switches make up a validated combination, set the appropriate variable for role installation.

We cannot, for example, allow the choice of installing the first management server and an additional management server at the same time:

```
$Features=""
If (($SCOMFirst) -and ($SCOMAdditional)) {Write-Output "You cannot
install the first management server and an additional management
server on the same server.  Please correct and try again.";break}
If (($SCOMFirst) -or ($SCOMAdditional)) {$Features=$Features+",OMServ
er"}
If ($SCOMWeb) {$Features=$Features+",OMWebConsole"}
If ($SCOMConsole) {$Features=$Features+",Console"}
If ($Features -ne "") {
    $Features=$Features.SubString(1)
    } Else {Write-Output "No features specified, nothing to
install";break}
```

The script validates that both the SCOMFirst and SCOMAdditional switches have not both been specified at the same time, and if so, quits the script:

```
If (($SCOMFirst) -and ($SCOMAdditional)) {Write-Output "You cannot
install the first management server and an additional management
server on the same server.  Please correct and try again.";break}
The next block of code sets the installation arguments that are
applicable to all roles.
$InstallArgs="/install /silent /components:$Features /SqlServerInstan
ce:$SQLOpsDBServer /InstallPath:`"$InstallDir`" /ActionAccountUser:`
"$Domain\$SCOMAAUser`" /ActionAccountPassword:$SCOMAAPassword /DASAcc
ountUser:`"$Domain\$SCOMDASUser`" /DASAccountPassword:$SCOMDASPasswo
rd /DataReaderUser:`"$Domain\$SCOMDRUser`" /DataReaderPassword:$SCOMD
RPassword /DataWriterUser:`"$Domain\$SCOMDWUser`" /DataWriterPasswor
d:$SCOMDWPassword /UseMicrosoftUpdate:$UseMicrosoftUpdate /SendCEIPRe
ports:$SendCEIPReports /EnableErrorReporting:$EnableErrorReporting /
SendODRReports:$SendODRReports /AcceptEndUserLicenseAgreement:1"
```

If the SCOMFirst switch has been specified, then the script sets the installation arguments that are specific to installing the first management server for a new management group as follows:

```
If ($SCOMFirst) {
    $InstallArgs=$InstallArgs+" /ManagementGroupName:$ManagementGroup
Name /DWSqlServerInstance:$SQLDWDBServer /DatabaseName:$DatabaseName
/DatabaseSize:$DatabaseSize /DWDatabaseName:$DWDatabaseName /
DWDatabaseSize:$DWDatabaseSize"
    }
```

The SCOMAdditional switch doesn't apply any extra command-line arguments.

The SCOMWeb switch applies the relevant arguments to install the web console, checks whether SSL must be enabled, and installs the required **Internet Information Services** (**ISS**) features, all of which proceeds as follows:

```
If ($SCOMWeb) {
    $InstallArgs=$InstallArgs+" /WebSiteName:`"$WebSiteName`" /WebCons
oleAuthorizationMode:$WebConsoleAuthorizationMode"
    If ($WebConsoleUseSSL) {
        $InstallArgs=$InstallArgs+" /WebConsoleUseSSL"
        }
    Write-Output "Adding required Windows Features for the Operations
Manager Web Console"
    Add-WindowsFeature Web-WebServer,Web-Default-Doc,Web-Dir-
Browsing,Web-Http-Errors,Web-Static-Content,Web-Http-Logging,Web-
Request-Monitor,Web-Stat-Compression,Web-Filtering,Web-Windows-
Auth,Web-App-Dev,Web-Net-Ext,Web-Net-Ext45,Web-Asp-Net,Web-Asp-
Net45,Web-ISAPI-Ext,Web-ISAPI-Filter,Web-Mgmt-Console,Web-Metabase-
,NET-Framework-45-ASPNET,NET-WCF-HTTP-Activation45,WAS-Process-
Model,WAS-Config-APIs,Windows-Identity-Foundation
    }
```

The remaining optional parameters for SQL ports and file paths are then processed as follows:

```
if ($SqlInstancePort -ne "") {
    $InstallArgs=$InstallArgs+" /SqlInstancePort:$SqlInstancePort"
    }
if ($DWSqlInstancePort -ne "") {
    $InstallArgs=$InstallArgs+" /DWSqlInstancePort:$DWSqlInstancePort"
    }
if ($DatabasePath -ne "") {
    $InstallArgs=$InstallArgs+" /DatabasePath:$DatabasePath"
    }
if ($DatabaseLogPath -ne "") {
    $InstallArgs=$InstallArgs+" /DatabaseLogPath:$DatabaseLogPath"
    }
if ($DWDatabasePath -ne "") {
    $InstallArgs=$InstallArgs+" /DWDatabasePath:$DWDatabasePath"
    }
if ($DWDatabaseLogPath -ne "") {
    $InstallArgs=$InstallArgs+" /DWDatabaseLogPath:$DWDatabaseLogPath"
    }
```

## Preparing Operations Manager prerequisites

The following code block first adds the SCOM Data Access Service and Action Account Service accounts to the local administrators group:

```
#Add Operations Manager Data Access and Action Accounts to Local Admin
Write-Output "Adding required accounts to the local administrators
group"
([ADSI]"WinNT://$env:computername/Administrators,group").
Add("WinNT://$SCOMDASUser")
([ADSI]"WinNT://$env:computername/Administrators,group").
Add("WinNT://$SCOMAAUser")
```

Second, it installs the SQL Report Viewer 2012 component after its prerequisite SQL CLR types:

```
#Install Pre-Reqs
Write-Output "Installing Prerequisited"
Start-Process -FilePath "msiexec.exe" -Wait -NoNewWindow
-PassThru -ArgumentList "/i $SourceFiles\Prerequisites\SQL2012CLR\
SQLSysClrTypes.msi /QN ALLUSERS=2"
Start-Process -FilePath "msiexec.exe" -Wait -NoNewWindow -PassThru
-ArgumentList "/i $SourceFiles\Prerequisites\RV2012\ReportViewer.msi /
QN ALLUSERS=2"
```

## Deploying Operations Manager

Finally, the following code block starts the installation process for SCOM using the arguments created from the gathered parameters:

```
#Install Operations Manager
Write-Output "Installing System Center 2012 R2 Operations Manager"
Start-Process -FilePath "$SourceFiles\setup.exe" -Wait -NoNewWindow
-PassThru -ArgumentList $InstallArgs
Write-Output "Installation Complete"
```

## There's more...

The preceding recipe provides a PowerShell script that can be used to automate the deployment of the Operations Manager Management Server, Web Console, and Operator Console roles. There are various ways this can be utilized and/or extended upon.

### Installing the reporting role

The script in this recipe does not presently deploy the reporting role. This is mainly due to the requirement to have **SQL Server Reporting Services** (**SSRS**) installed and partially configured before the reporting role can be installed.

If that requirement is already complete, then the following code could be added to the script to enable the installation.

Another parameter should be added within the mandatory parameter block to capture the intention to install the reporting role:

```
[Parameter(Mandatory=$false)]
[switch]$SCOMReporting=$false,
```

Another parameter should be added within the optional parameter block to capture the SQL SSRS instance on which to install the reporting role:

```
[Parameter(Mandatory=$false)]
[string]$SRSInstance,
```

We then need to check the switches and build the list of features for installation. Add the following check for the `SCOMReporting` role:

```
If ($SCOMReporting) {$Features=$Features+",OMReporting"}
```

Finally, introduce the section that adds the arguments for the SQL SSRS instance to use:

```
If ($SCOMReporting) {
    $InstallArgs=$InstallArgs+" /SRSInstance:$SRSInstance"
    }
```

This will then deploy the SCOM reporting role to a server if the switch is used and the SSRS instance specified. However, no checks are done to ensure SSRS is installed or configured, and it must be on the same server as you deploy the SCOM role.

## Validation checking

While the script in this recipe has basic checking to ensure that a role is chosen for deployment and that the `SCOMFirst` and `SCOMAdditional` switches are not specified at the same time, no further validation checks are in place. This means that you could run the script and specify that the first management server for a management group is to be deployed but not specify a management group name or SQL server for the databases, resulting in a failed deployment.

You could either code additional checks or investigate the use of PowerShell Parameter Sets.

## When to automate

The script in this recipe isn't designed to be used for just quick installations on a one-time basis. The GUI is just as quick for deploying the first management server, for example, at the beginning of your deployment.

This script is designed to be utilized in conjunction with automation technologies such as those provided with System Center.

For example, this script could be quite easily dropped into a runbook within System Center 2012 R2 Orchestrator that could then be linked into a Service Request within System Center 2012 R2 Service Manager to allow for requests to be placed to scale the infrastructure, when required, without the manual task of someone logging on to a server and installing Operations Manager.

Using this script within System Center 2012 R2 **Service Management Automation** (**SMA**) is another example, and could then be utilized by tenants within a service provider model to allow customers to deploy their own Operations Manager infrastructures very easily.

This script is also perfectly placed to deploy SCOM using a service template within Virtual Machine Manager.

## See also

The following are useful links to information related to the recipe:

▶ Microsoft TechNet—Installing Operations Manager by Using the Command Prompt Window: `http://technet.microsoft.com/en-us/library/hh416216.aspx`

▶ Microsoft TechNet—PowerShell Advanced Parameters: `https://technet.microsoft.com/en-us/library/hh847743.aspx`

# Deploying gateway servers

The following recipe will guide you through the steps required to deploy Gateway Management Servers for use with System Center 2012 R2 Operations Manager.

Gateways are predominately used to provide communications between segments of networks that are not trusted or have bandwidth constraints.

Rather than employing clients with agents reporting directly across the network on mass to the main management servers, by implementing a gateway server, you provide a local point for the agents to report to that will then compress and forward the collected information back to the main management server. This allows for better control of network bandwidth usage and provides the ability to restrict communication to a single endpoint IP address and port while using certificates for authentication purposes, negating the need for cross-forest or domain trusts.

## Getting ready

For this recipe, you will require the following:

▶ Deployment of at least one SCOM management server with it being a member of a resource pool

▶ A **Public Key Infrastructure** (**PKI**) solution within your environment if the gateway is to be deployed in an untrusted environment

▶ Ensure that port 5723 is not blocked on any firewalls between the server to be used for the gateway and the SCOM management server

▶ Ensure that both the gateway and the SCOM management server you are going to designate can resolve each other's **fully qualified domain name** (**FQDN**)

## How to do it...

1. Open the SCOM console.

2. Navigate to **Administration | Security**.

   Change the option from **Reject new manual agent installations** to **Review new manual agent installations in pending management view**:

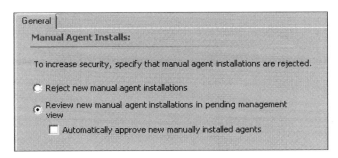

3. The following code requires either typing into a PowerShell code editor such as the Windows PowerShell ISE or downloading from the Packt Publishing website:

```
Param (
    #Mandatory Parameters
    [Parameter(Mandatory=$true)]
[string]$ManagementServer,
    [Parameter(Mandatory=$false)]
[string]$ManagementGroupName,
    [Parameter(Mandatory=$true)]
    [ValidateScript({Test-Path $_ -PathType ''Container''})]
[string]$SourceFiles
    )


#Command setup and validation
$InstallArgs=""/i `""$SourceFiles\Gateway\AMD64\MOMGateway.msi`""
/qn ADDLOCAL=MOMGateway MANAGEMENT_GROUP=$ManagementGroupName IS_
ROOT_HEALTH_SERVER=0 ROOT_MANAGEMENT_SERVER_DNS=$ManagementServer
ROOT_MANAGEMENT_SERVER_PORT=5723 ACTIONS_USE_COMPUTER_ACCOUNT=1
AcceptEndUserLicenseAgreement=1""
```

```
#Install Operations Manager
Write-Output ""Installing System Center 2012 R2 Operations
Manager""
Start-Process -FilePath ""msiexec.exe"" -Wait -NoNewWindow
-PassThru -ArgumentList $InstallArgs

If (!(Test-Path -Path ""C:\Program Files\System Center Operations
Manager\Gateway"")) {
  Write-Error ""Installation Failed""
  } Else {
  Write-Output ""Installation Complete""
  }
```

4.  Once you have the code written and have saved and verified the FQDN resolution, run
    the script on the server you are going to use as a SCOM gateway.

## How it works...

This code is much simpler than the code in the previous recipe (*Scripting the deployment*) as
the gateway is not much more than a *Super* agent.

The script specifies to the installation, and therefore the gateway configuration, the values
for the management server that it will connect back to when sending data and receiving
configuration.

Running the installation from the GUI is just as simple, and it prompts for the management
group name and the designated management server you want to connect to.

Gateway servers are then responsible for both deploying configuration (**Management Packs**)
onto clients and receiving data from clients before compressing the data and forwarding it to
the assigned management servers.

Gateway servers allow you to have a single contact point between monitored servers and the
core SCOM infrastructure, ideal in situations where firewalls or security boundaries (different
forests) are in place.

Gateways are also helpful in reducing bandwidth across WAN links by providing a single,
compressed traffic flow rather than all agents sending data across the WAN.

## There's more...

While the previous script will deploy the SCOM gateway, there are a couple of further steps
that need to be completed to allow the clients and gateway servers to communicate with each
other and the management servers.

If a gateway cannot communicate using Kerberos authentication with the SCOM management server you designated, for example, if the gateway server is within an untrusted domain or a workgroup server, you need to set up SSL certificates to secure the communication.

You will also need to ensure that the root **Certificate Authority** (**CA**) certificate and chain from the CA used to generate the certificate for your gateway server are downloaded and imported into the Trusted Root Certification Authorities certificate store on your gateway server.

## Creating the PKI certificate template

A **PKI** is a private certificate service run within your infrastructure that allows for the issuing, validation, and management of certificates that are used to secure communication between services.

The following steps will show how to create a template that holds the required configuration of the certificates used by Operations Manager:

1. Open **Certificate Templates** by clicking **Start** and navigating to **Run**. On the command line, type mmc and click **OK**.

2. Click the **File** menu and navigate to **Add/Remove Snap-in**.

3. Under **Add Available Snap-ins**, choose **Certificate templates | Add | OK**.

4. Right-click on **Certificate Templates** and navigate to **Connect to another writeable domain controller ...**:

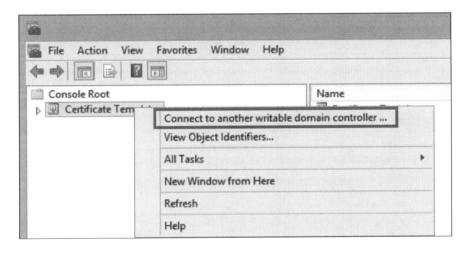

5. Enter the name of your CA and click **OK**.

6. Expand **Certificate Templates** and right-click on the **Computer** template and navigate to **Duplicate Template**.

7. Ensure the version is selected as **Windows Server 2003** on the **Compatibility** tab or if prompted by a pop-up window.

8. On the **General** tab, type `SCOMGateway` as the **Template display name:**.

9. On the **Request Handling** tab, select **Allow private key to be exported**.

10. On the **Subject Name** tab, select the **Supply in the request** option and, if prompted, click **OK** to acknowledge the recommendation.

11. On the **Security** tab, ensure only **Domain Admins**, **Domain Computers**, and **Enterprise Admins** have **Enroll** permissions.

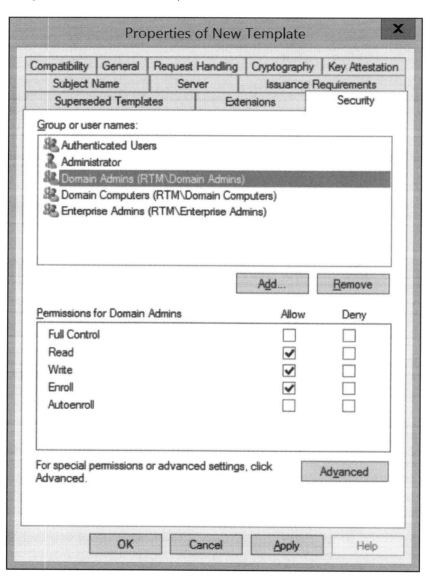

> If you have a dedicated security group for accounts that you would like to allow to request SCOM gateway certificates, add those groups as well.
>
> You could also replace **Domain Computers** with a group containing only the SCOM gateway servers if domain joined to increase the security by ensuring no rogue devices enroll for the gateway certificate, only the servers specifically in the group that you specify.

12. Close the **Certificate Templates** mmc.

13. Open **Certificate Templates** by clicking **Start** and navigating to **Run**. On the command line, type mmc and click **OK**.

14. Click the **File** menu and navigate to **Add/Remove Snap-in**.

15. Under **Add Available Snap-ins**, choose **Certification Authority | Add**.

16. Select **Another computer: | Browse |** choose the PKI server | **OK | Finish | OK**.

17. Add the new template to the CA by expanding **Certification Authority** | <PKI Server> and navigating to **Certificate Templates | New | Certificate Template to Issue**:

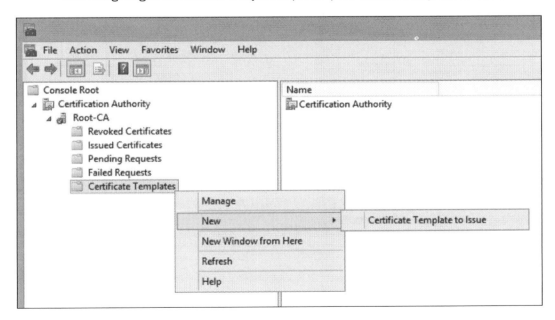

18. Choose the template you just created (SCOMGateway) and click **OK**.

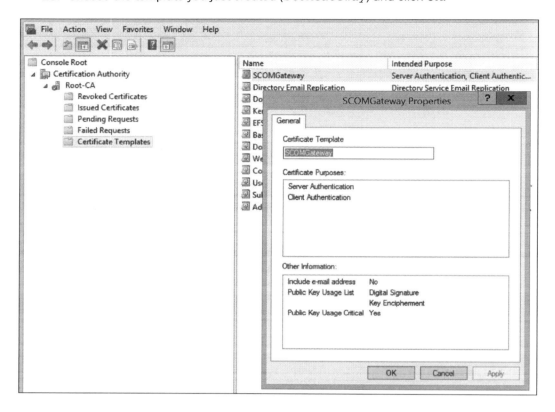

19. Verify that the new template appears in the **Details** pane under **Certificate Templates**. Right-click on the template and navigate to **Properties** and verify that **Server Authentication** and **Client Authentication** appear under **Certificate Purposes:**.

## Requesting and applying the certificate

To request a certificate for the gateway server, the following steps must be performed:

1. Log on to the server to be used as the SCOM gateway server.

2. Open Notepad and type in the following:

```
[NewRequest]
Subject="CN=<FQDN>"
Exportable=TRUE
KeyLength=2048
KeySpec=1
KeyUsage=0xf0
MachineKeySet=TRUE
```

3. Replace <FQDN> with the fully qualified domain name of your gateway server.

4. Save the file as GWCertRequest.inf.

5. Open a PowerShell session elevated as an administrator.

6. Type certreq -new -f GWCertRequest.inf GWCert.req and press *Enter*.

7. From a domain-based computer, log on to http://<PKIServer>/certsrv and click **Request a certificate**:

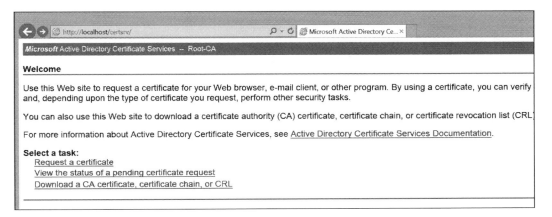

8. Click on **advanced certificate request**.

9. Click on **Submit a certificate request by using a base-64-encoded CMC or PKCS #10 file, or submit a renewal request by using a base-64-encoded PKCS #7 file**.

10. Paste the contents of the GWCert.req file you created previously into the box.

11. Under the **Certificate Template** section, select the **SCOMGateway** template and click **Submit**:

12. Select **Base 64 encoded**.

13. Click on the **Download certificate** link.

14. Save the downloaded certificate as `GWCert.cer`.

15. Copy the `GWCert.cer` file to the SCOM gateway server.

16. Open a PowerShell session elevated as an administrator.

17. Type `certreq -Accept -Machine GWCert.cer` and press *Enter*.

18. Type `certutil.exe -privatekey -exportpfx <FQDN of GW Server> C:\GWCert.pfx nochain` and press *Enter*.

19. Type in a password again to confirm it.

20. Copy `MOMCertImport.exe` to the root of the C Drive along with the `GWCert.pfx` file.

 The `MOMCertImport.exe` tool can be found in the `Support Tools` folder of the Operations Manager installation media.

21. Type `C:\MOMCertImport.exe C:\GWCert.pfx` and then press *Enter*.

22. Enter the password you typed earlier when exporting the `pfx` file and press *Enter*.

23. Open **Services** by clicking **Start** and navigating to **Run**. On the **Run** command line, type `services.msc` and click **OK**.

24. Find and click **Microsoft Monitoring Agent** to highlight it.

25. Right-click on it and navigate to **Restart**.

26. Repeat steps 20 to 25 again on the management server you selected for the gateway to communicate with.

27. From the source media `\SupportTools` folder, copy the Microsoft. EnterpriseManagement.GatewayApprovalTool.exe to the SCOM installation directory on the management server.

28. Open an elevated command prompt and type: `M`.

## See also

The following is a useful link to information related to the recipe:

► Microsoft TechNet—About Gateway Servers in Operations Manager: `http://technet.microsoft.com/en-us/library/hh212823.aspx`

# 3
# Configuring System Center 2012 R2 Operations Manager

In this chapter, we will be providing recipes on how to configure the base installation for your Microsoft System Center 2012 R2 Operations Manager implementation. These recipes will cover topics such as:

- ▶ Configuring resource pools
- ▶ Configuring active directory agent assignment
- ▶ Deploying agents for Windows operating systems
- ▶ Deploying agents for UNIX/Linux based operating systems
- ▶ Options for deploying the Admin console

## Introduction

After installing System Center 2012 R2 Operations Manager, you will have the platform deployed but no monitoring yet. You will need to further configure SCOM to monitor your infrastructure.

This chapter will help break down the areas needed to configure SCOM to enable it to start monitoring your environment and for you to configure SCOM so that monitoring is performed in the most efficient manner.

# Configuring resource pools

When working with Windows operating systems that report directly to management servers, the agents will automatically fail over to other management servers in the event of a failure unless specifically configured for primary and failover management servers via PowerShell or Active Directory integration.

UNIX/Linux operating systems and network devices, however, do not have the ability to fail over automatically to any available management server and instead rely on resource pools to define the management servers that are involved in supporting communications with these types of devices.

Adding management servers to these resource pools allows you to dedicate specific servers to dedicated device monitoring types, and multiple management servers in a resource pool provide failover capabilities to support high availability.

## Getting ready

You need to have prepared at least one management server to dedicate to the resource pool.

## How to do it...

1. Open the SCOM console and click on the **Administration** section tab.
2. Navigate to **Administration | Resource Pools**.
3. On the **Tasks** pane, click **Create Resource Pool**.
4. In the **Create Resource Pool** wizard, on the **General Properties** page, enter a name and, optionally, a description for the resource pool and then click **Next**.
5. On the **Pool Membership** page, click **Add...**.
6. If you click **Search** without entering anything in the filter field, all available management servers will be displayed.

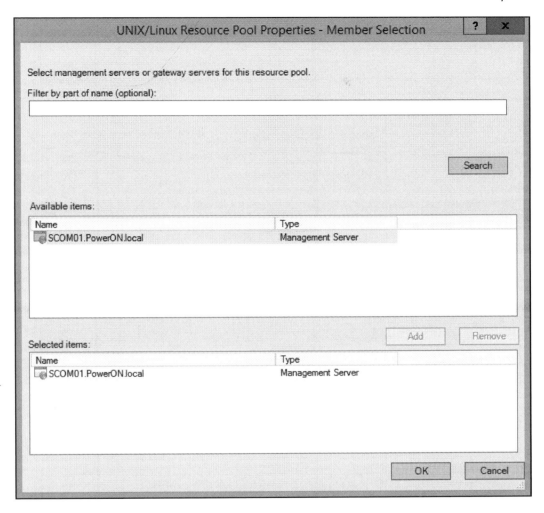

7. In the **Available items:** section, select the management servers you require in the resource pool and click **Add** and then click **OK**.

8. Click **Next**.

9. Click **Create**.

10. Click **Close**.

## How it works...

When you deploy agents to Unix/Linux devices or discover network devices, you are prompted to specify a resource pool. This resource pool should contain the management servers that you intend to dedicate to performing this type of monitoring.

For UNIX/Linux devices, the relevant certificates for these management servers will then be transferred to the agents to allow communications to be secured and to continue communication, should a management server be unavailable.

For network devices, while a specific management server (specified during the discovery wizard) will be used for the discovery of network devices, the management servers within the resource pool will be used for monitoring, thus ensuring high availability.

Resource pools can also be used for **Watcher Nodes** to again ensure high availability for Web Application monitoring.

By default, there are three resource pools after installation:

 ▸ A **Notifications Resource Pool** runs the workflows for notifications and is useful, for example, if you have a hardware SMS device attached to a server where having the notification workflows for sending text messages running on a server, without it attached, would be pointless.

 ▸ An **AD Assignment Resource Pool** is used to target management servers that will run the **Active Directory** (**AD**) Integration workflows.

 ▸ The **All Management Servers Resource Pool** is the default "catch all" resource pool where most of the older RMS specific instances and workflows are now targeted at this resource pool unless specifically targeted at another pool that you create.

When setting up dedicated resource pools for monitoring areas such as UNIX/Linux or network devices, you should also remove those dedicated servers from the All Management Servers Resource Pool.

However, this is not something that can be performed from the console, as this resource pool is set to Automatic membership and must be changed first using PowerShell to Manual membership.

This can be done by running the following command:

```
Get-SCOMResourcePool -Name "All Management Servers Resource Pool" | Set-
SCOMResourcePool -EnableAutomaticMembership $false
```

This should be performed on the AD Assignment and Notifications Resource Pools as well.

You should then remove the servers you have dedicated to your custom resource pool by modifying the properties of the resource pool and removing those management servers.

However, you must ensure there are at least two management severs left within these default resource pools if you intend to have at least a minimum level of high availability in place.

Alongside removing a management server from the All Management Servers Resource Pool, you will also need to ensure that any Run As accounts that were targeting that resource pool are also modified to still be distributed to those management servers that were removed. Otherwise, you may see an issue where removing management servers from the All Management Servers Resource Pool causes the server to become grayed out.

On initial installation, the two accounts affected by this are the Data Warehouse Action Account and the Data Warehouse Report Deployment Account.

To change these accounts, perform the following steps:

1. Open the SCOM console and click on the **Administration** section tab.

2. Navigate to **Administration** | **Run As Configuration** | **Accounts**.

3. Right-click on the **Data Warehouse Action Account** and choose **Properties**.

4. Click the **Distribution** tab.

5. Click **Add....**

6. Drop the **Option:** list down and choose **Search by resource pool**.

7. Click **Search**.

8. Choose the resource pool that contains the management servers you removed from the **All Management Servers Resource Pool** and click **Add**:

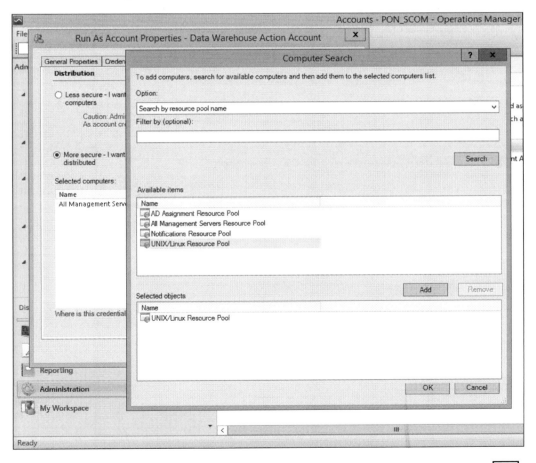

9. Click **OK** twice.

10. Repeat these steps again for the **Data Warehouse Report Deployment Account**.

## There's more...

When using more than one management server for the UNIX/Linux resource pool, you need to pre-stage the certificates that will be used for server/client communication.

For each management server in the resource pool, you need to export or import the root certificate from every management server in the resource pool.

For example—Resource Pool "**UNIX/Linux Resource Pool**" contains the following management servers: SCOM01, SCOM02, and SCOM03.

SCOM01 must import the certificates from SCOM02 and SCOM03. SCOM02 must import the certificates from SCOM01 and SCOM03, and SCOM03 must import the SCOM01 and SCOM02 certificates.

Thankfully, there is a command line that can be run to do this.

To export the certificates, run the following:

```
%ProgramFiles%\Microsoft System Center 2012 R2\Operations Manager\Server\
scxcertconfig.exe - export <Path and filename>
```

To import the certificates, run the following:

```
%ProgramFiles%\Microsoft System Center 2012 R2\Operations Manager\Server\
scxcertconfig.exe -import <Path and filename>
```

The following is a script example that can be used to automate the process of exporting the certificates from each member of the resource pool and then importing each certificate into each server.

Before running this script, you will need to ensure that WinRM is configured on your management servers either via group policy, or by running WinRM /qc from a command prompt on each server.

```
Param (
    [Parameter(Mandatory=$true)]
    [String]$SCOMManagementServer,
    [Parameter(Mandatory=$true)]
    [String]$ResourcePoolName,
    [Parameter(Mandatory=$true)]
    [ValidateScript({Test-Path $_})]
```

```
    [String]$CertStorePath,
    [Switch]$Export,
    [Switch]$Import
    )

If (!(Get-Module OperationsManager)) {Import-Module
OperationsManager}
If ($CertStorePath[-1] -ne "\") {$CertStorePath+="\"}
New-SCOMManagementGroupConnection -ComputerName
$SCOMManagementServer

$ResourcePool=Get-SCOMResourcePool | Where-Object DisplayName -EQ
$ResourcePoolName
If ($ResourcePool -eq $null) {
    Write-Output "Resource Pool cannot be found, please check
and run again"
    break
    }

#Export Certificates
If ($Export) {
    $ResourcePool.Members | ForEach-Object {
        Invoke-Command  -ComputerName $_.DisplayName -ScriptBlock
{ Param ($CertStorePath)
            Write-Output "Exporting Certificate for
$env:COMPUTERNAME"
            $path=(Get-ItemProperty -path
"HKLM:\SOFTWARE\Microsoft\Microsoft Operations Manager\3.0\Setup"
-name InstallDirectory).InstallDirectory
            & ($path+'scxcertconfig.exe') -export
($CertStorePath + $env:COMPUTERNAME + "." + ([System.Net.
NetworkInformation.IPGlobalProperties]
::GetIPGlobalProperties()).domainName +'_SCOM.cer')
            } -ArgumentList $CertStorePath
        }
    }


#Import Certificates
If ($Import) {
    $ResourcePool.Members | ForEach-Object {
        Invoke-Command  -ComputerName $_.DisplayName -ScriptBlock
{ Param ($CertStorePath)
            Write-Output "Certificate Imports being performed for
$env:COMPUTERNAME"
```

```
        $path=(Get-ItemProperty -path "HKLM:\SOFTWARE\Microsoft\
Microsoft Operations Manager\3.0\Setup"
-name InstallDirectory).InstallDirectory
        Get-ChildItem $CertStorePath -Include "*_SCOM.cer" -
recurse | ForEach-Object {
            Write-Output "   Importing Certificate
$($_.FullName)"
            & ($path+'scxcertconfig.exe') -Import $_.FullName
            }
        } -ArgumentList $CertStorePath
    }
}
```

This process should be repeated whenever you add a new server to the resource pool.

## See also

More information on resource pools can be found in these links:

▶ Modifying Resource Pool Membership—http://technet.microsoft.com/en-us/library/hh230706.aspx#bkmk_modifyingresourcepoolmembership

▶ Removing Management Servers from the All Management Servers Resource Pool causes the server to become grayed out—http://support.microsoft.com/kb/2853431

# Configuring active directory agent assignment

Unlike UNIX/Linux agents and network devices, Windows operating systems don't use resource pools to specify the management servers that they can report to.

If you deploy an agent from the console, you will specify a management server during installation, and this will become the primary management server for that agent.

The agent is still able to fail over to another management server in the event of its primary becoming unavailable. However, if you have a preferred server that you would like to use as a secondary, you would have to manually specify this using PowerShell.

However, using Active Directory integration allows manually installed agents to automatically assign the primary management server and enables you to configure rules to group servers together and match them to specific primary and secondary management servers.

This also allows you to better handle manually installed agents as well as agents deployed via System Center 2012 R2 Configuration Manager or as part of an operating system deployment.

## Getting ready

Before you start this recipe, you will need to create an Active Directory Security Group containing SCOM administrators that you would like to be able to manage the AD Integration as per how you want it to proceed. This group must also be a member of the SCOM administrator role.

You will also need to create an Active Directory user that will be used by SCOM as a Run As account that will have permissions to read, write, and delete objects within the AD Container that SCOM uses for the integration. These permissions will be set during the process of creating the container.

You will then need to run the MOMADAdmin.exe tool to create the required container in Active Directory.

The MOMADAdmin.exe tool can be found in C:\Program Files\Microsoft System Center 2012 R2\Operations Manager\Server if SCOM is installed in the default location.

The syntax for the tool is as follows:

**MOMADAdmin.exe <ManagementGroupName> <MOMAdminSecurityGroup> <RunAsAccount> <Domain>**

For this recipe, we will use following details:

| | |
|---|---|
| **Management Group Name** | PON_SCOM |
| **AD Security Group** | OM-AD-Integration-Admins |
| **Run As Account** | SVC_SCOMADINT |
| **Domain** | PowerON.local |

Create the container by running the following command from an elevated PowerShell console with the directory location changed to the path of MOMADAdmin.exe:

```
\MOMADAdmin.exe PON_SCOM OM-AD-Integration-Admins PowerON\SVC_SCOMADINT
PowerON.local
```

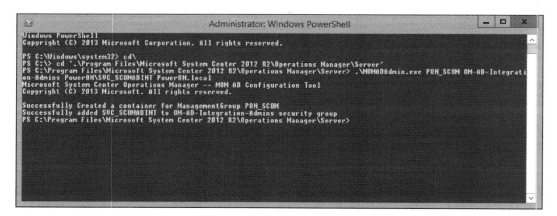

The command should complete successfully so that you are able to see the created **OperationsManager** container with a sub-container for your management group within.

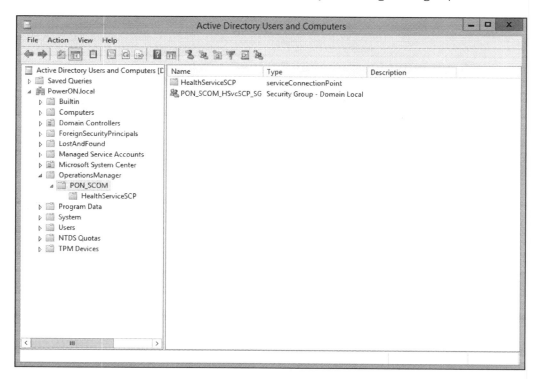

## How to do it...

The following recipe will show you how to configure **Active Directory** (**AD**) Integration for SCOM.

### Assigning the Run As account to the AD Profile

The following steps are performed in the SCOM console to provide credentials with which to interact with Active Directory:

1. Open the SCOM console and click on the **Administration** section tab.

2. Navigate to **Administration** | **Run As Configuration** | **Accounts**.

3. From the **Actions** pane to the right of the screen, choose **Create Run As Account...**.

4. If the **Introduction** page is displayed, click **Next**.

5. Choose **Windows** as the Run As account type.

6. Enter Active Directory Integration Account as the display name and click **Next**.

7. Enter the **User name** and **Password** for the account you set up previously and used, when running the MOMADAdmin.exe tool:

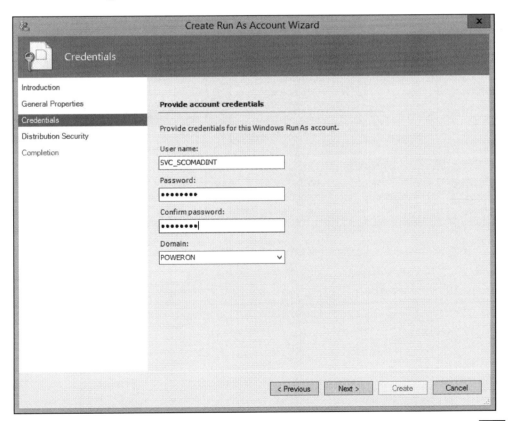

8. Click **Next**.

9. Leave the option for **More secure** selected as we will manually choose the **AD Assignment Resource Pool** later to distribute these credentials and click **Create**:

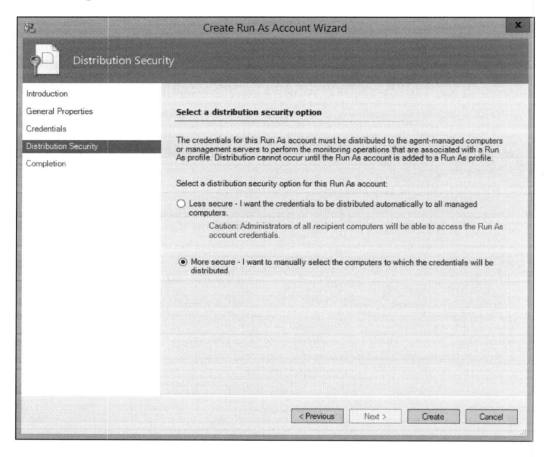

10. Read the success summary screen and click **Close**.

11. Right-click on the newly created account and choose **Properties**.

12. Click on the **Distribution** tab and then click **Add....**

13. Change the **Option** to **Search by resource pool name** and click **Search**.

14. Choose the **AD Assignment Resource Pool** and click **Add**.

15. Click **OK** twice.

16. Navigate to **Administration | Run As Configuration | Profiles**.

17. Right-click on **Active Directory Based Agent Assignment Account** and choose **Properties**.

18. Click **Next** twice to show the **Run As Accounts** screen and click **Add....**

19. Drop the list down and choose the **Active Directory Integration Account** that you created previously.

20. Leave the setting as **All targeted objects** and click **OK**.

21. Click **Save** and then **Close**.

## Assigning managed computers to a primary and secondary management server

The following steps are performed in the SCOM console to assign agents to management servers:

1. Open the SCOM console and click on the **Administration** section tab.

2. Click on the top-level **Administration** node that will show the **Administration Overview** content on the main window pane.

3. Click on **Configure Active Directory (AD) Integration** under the **Optional Configuration** section.

4. Select the management server that you would like to configure the agents to assign to it as their primary management server and click **Add...** under the **Auto Agent Assignment** section.

5. Review the introduction screen and click **Next**.

6. Choose the domain that your monitored computers with agents reside in, from the drop-down list.

7. Tick the option to **Use a different account to perform agent assignment in the specified domain** and choose the **Run As Profile** for **Active Directory Based Agent Assignment Account** from the drop-down list and then click **Next**.

## How it works...

The MOMADAdmin.exe tool when run creates a top-level container in the root of Active Directory for the domain specified at runtime and then creates a sub-container for the management group specified.

It also sets the security on the management group container to allow the security group and Run As account specified to create security groups and **Service Connection Point** (**SCP**) objects.

When you use the console to configure the AD Integration, the configuration is captured as a rule within SCOM, and when it runs, it creates SCP's and security groups within the container.

An SCP is created for each management server configured for assignment and the accompanying security groups contain agent servers that are allowed to discover the appropriate management server for assignment by granting them read access to the SCP.

Each SCP created will be in the format of *<ManagementServerName>*_SCP, while the security groups will be named *<ManagementServerName>*_PrimarySG_*<randomnumber>* or *<ManagementServerName>*_SecondarySG_*<randomnumber>* depending on their role of controlling discovery of primary or secondary management servers.

# Deploying agents for Windows operating systems

One of the key configuration steps for System Center 2012 R2 Operations Manager is to decide which systems you would like to monitor and then enable them to be monitored.

There are two options for monitoring which systems are Agentless or Agent-based.

This recipe will focus on deploying agents to Windows operating systems for Agent-based monitoring, as this is the richest form of monitoring, but Agentless monitoring is another option.

## Getting ready

You will need to identify an appropriate device that you want to monitor using agent-based deployment and need an account with local administrative rights to that device.

For this recipe, we will be using a device named DC01 with a Microsoft Windows Server 2012 R2 Operating System.

## How to do it...

1. Open the SCOM console and click on the **Administration** section tab.
2. Right-click on **Device Management | Discovery Wizard...**:

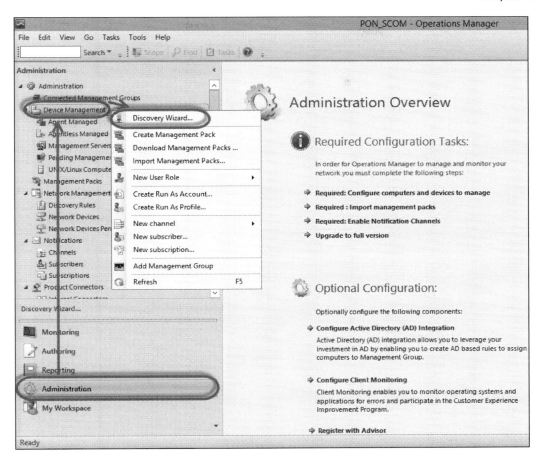

3. Ensure **Windows computers** is selected and click **Next**.

4. Ensure **Advanced discovery** is selected, along with **Servers and Clients**, and for now leave the management server at its default and click **Next**.

5. Choose **Browse for, or type-in computer names** and type the name of the device to deploy the agent to, DC01 in this recipe, and click **Next**.

6. Choose **Other user account** and supply the credentials for an account that has administrative rights on the device you are deploying the agent to and click **Discover**.

 If you don't have a domain user account that has local administrative privileges on the device you are targeting, then you can choose the option below the credentials section, **This is a local computer account, not a domain account**. However, you must ensure that you change the computer name to reflect that of the device you are deploying to.

7. Once the discovery has completed and if it was successful, you can then select the device you want to deploy the agent to by placing a check next to its name and then click **Next**.

8. Leave the installation details and **Agent Action Account** options at their defaults and click **Finish**.

9. This will then start the deployment of the agent and an **Agent Management Task Status** window will be shown. Closing this window will not interrupt the deployment and will allow you to continue with other tasks.

> If you close the **Agent Management Task Status** window and the installation fails, an alert will be raised with SCOM, and you can view it from the **Monitoring | Alerts** view.
>
> You can also view the tasks submitted by the discovery wizard via the **Monitoring | Task Status** view.

10. If you still have the **Agent Management Task Status** window open and the deployment has succeeded, click **Close**.

11. Click **Monitoring | Windows Computers** and the newly monitored device will be present.

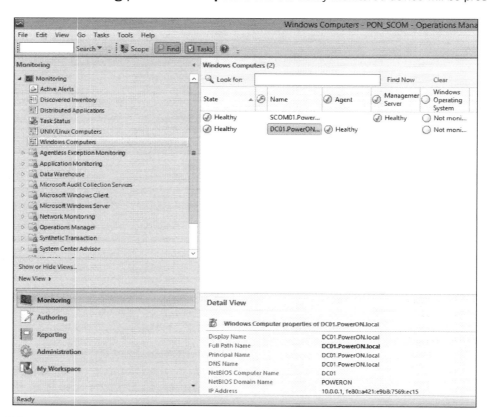

## How it works...

System Center 2012 R2 Operations Manager has a unified agent that is also shared with the **Azure Operational Insights** online service or used standalone to provide support for its use with Visual Studio as an IntelliTrace collector. It also combines what used to be the separate **Application Performance Monitoring (APM)** agent.

The agent is now known as the **Microsoft Monitoring Agent** rather than the Operations Manager Agent.

Once installed, the agent will run as a service and process its configuration as handed out by the SCOM management servers that it reports to. The management servers the agent reports to are either defined when deploying the agent via the console during the discovery wizard, as part of the command line used to install the agent, via a script or a software deployment solution such as Configuration Manager, or via information read from Active Directory if the integration has been set up.

It is also possible to manually select the management servers for the client to use by employing the **Control Panel** applet.

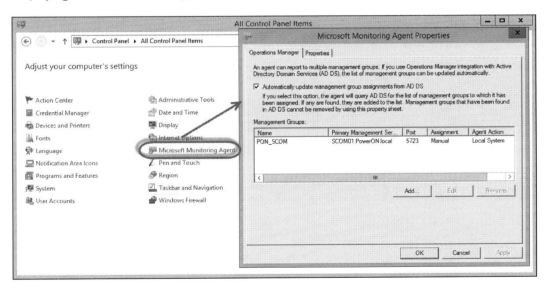

You can also set an additional management server that belongs to a different management group entirely from this control panel applet, which is referred to as multihoming of the agent. This is useful for Test/Dev scenarios and migration strategies.

## There's more...

While pushing agents from the SCOM console is certainly the easiest method for deploying agents, there will be times that the deployment process needs to either be automated or built into other deployment processes and tools used within your organization.

The following command can be used either from a command line (or script) or within a deployment tool such as System Center 2012 R2 Configuration Manager.

```
%WinDir%\System32\msiexec.exe /i <Path to Agent files>\MOMAgent.msi /
qn USE_SETTINGS_FROM_AD=0 MANAGEMENT_GROUP=PON_SCOM MANAGEMENT_SERVER_
DNS=PONSCOM01.PowerON.local SECURE_PORT=5723 ACTIONS_USE_COMPUTER_
ACCOUNT=1 AcceptEndUserLicenseAgreement=1
```

This command will install the agent, with the local system as its action account and connected to the PON_SCOM management group and reporting to PONSCOM01.PowerON.local on port 5723.

A full breakdown of the installation switches can be found here: http://technet.microsoft.com/en-us/library/hh230736.aspx

## See also

The following are useful links to information related to the System Center 2012 Operation Manager Agents:

▶   Microsoft support—recommended operating system hotfixes and updates to best support SCOM agents: http://support.microsoft.com/kb/2843219

# Deploying agents for Unix- or Linux-based operating systems

One of the key configuration steps for System Center 2012 R2 Operations Manager is to decide which systems you would like to monitor and then enable them to be monitored.

There are two options for monitoring that are Agentless or Agent-based.

This recipe will focus on deploying agents for Agent-based monitoring, as this is the richest form of monitoring, but Agentless monitoring is another option.

Agents can be deployed to devices running both Microsoft Windows and UNIX/Linux operating systems.

## Getting ready

You will need to identify an appropriate device for which you want to monitor using agent-based deployment and have an account with local administrative rights to that device.

For this recipe, we will be using a device named Linux01 with Ubuntu Server as the operating system.

Before we attempt to deploy agents to UNIX/Linux devices, there are some prerequisite configuration tasks that need to be performed.

### Management packs

You will need to download and import the UNIX/Linux management packs that are relevant for the operating systems you plan to monitor. The latest versions can be downloaded from this URL: `http://www.microsoft.com/en-us/download/details.aspx?id=29696`.

Download the MSI files, run the installation, and then use the console to import the management packs. See *Chapter 5, Maintaining System Center 2012 R2 Operations Manager*, for more information.

### WinRM

SCOM utilizes WinRM to connect and establish CIM sessions to the UNIX/Linux devices, but since these systems are unlikely to be using Kerberos for authentication, it is required to set WinRM to use basic authentication.

The preferred long-term method is to use a group policy targeted at the SCOM management servers, but for quick use in this recipe, use the following command:

```
Winrm set winrm/config/client/auth @{Basic="true"}
```

### Run As accounts

You could attempt to use the root account to connect to the device during discovery at or even for monitoring. However, in most installations, the root account will not have access to the device via **Secure Shell** (**SSH**), so we will look to use an unprivileged account and sudo to elevate the installation.

Looking forward, for ongoing monitoring and maintenance, it's best practice to use the principle of least privileges, and it is therefore recommended to set up account information within SCOM for specific roles.

You, therefore, need to identify accounts that can be configured within your UNIX/Linux devices to provide support for the following:

| SCOM Account Profile | Usage |
|---|---|
| UNIX/Linux Action Account | Low-privilege account used for normal monitoring |
| UNIX/Linux Privileged Account | Account to use for sudo elevation when monitoring requires access to protected resources that require higher privileges |
| UNIX/Linux Agent Maintenance Account | Account to use for sudo elevation when performing agent maintenance tasks such as upgrades, repairs, or uninstalls |

You can associate multiple accounts with each profile, but it is recommended to simplify and consolidate the number of accounts where possible, but maintain separation between the different usages.

For this recipe, we will be using the following accounts:

| Account Display Name | Description | Account Name |
|---|---|---|
| Ubuntu Low Privilege | Low-privilege account used for monitoring | SCOMLP |
| Ubuntu High Privilege | High-privilege account used for monitoring | SCOMHP |
| Ubuntu Agent Maintenance | High-privilege account used for agent maintenance tasks | SCOMAM |

To create these accounts in SCOM, we perform the following steps:

1. Open the SCOM console and click on the **Administration** section tab.

2. Navigate to **Administration | Run As Configuration | UNIX/Linux Accounts**.

3. From the **Actions** pane to the right of the screen, choose **Create Run As Account...**.

4. Choose **Monitoring account** and click **Next**.

5. Enter a name and description for the account. Refer to the following example:

   **Display Name**—Ubuntu Low Privilege

   **Description**—Low-privilege account used for monitoring

6. Enter the **User name** and **Password** for the account.

7.  If the account is to be used for the high-privilege monitoring, change the option for **Do you want to use elevation for privileged access?** to elevate this account using sudo for privileged access. Otherwise, select the default option of **Do not use elevation with this account**:

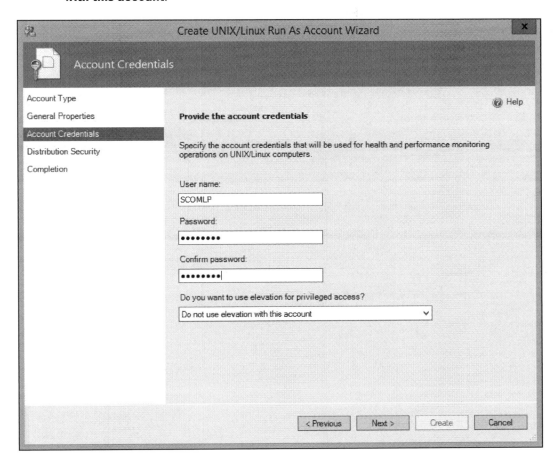

8.  Click **Next**.

9.  Leave the option for **More secure** selected as we will manually choose the resource pool containing the UNIX/Linux devices later to distribute these credentials too and click **Create**.

10. Read the success summary screen and click **Close**.

11. Right-click on the newly created account and choose **Properties**.

12. Click **Next** twice to get to the **Distribution Security** section and then click **Add....**

13. Change the **Option** to **Search by resource pool name** and click **Search**.

14. Choose the **UNIX/Linux Resource Pool** you created earlier and click **Add**.

15. Click **OK**.

16. Click **Save** and then click **Close**.

Repeat steps 3 to 16 for high-privilege monitoring and the agent maintenance accounts.

When creating the **Run As** account to be used for the agent maintenance tasks, make sure you select the **Agent Maintenance** account in the wizard instead of the **Monitoring** account.

Also, unless you specifically use an SSH key, choose **User name** and **Password** and supply the credentials for the account.

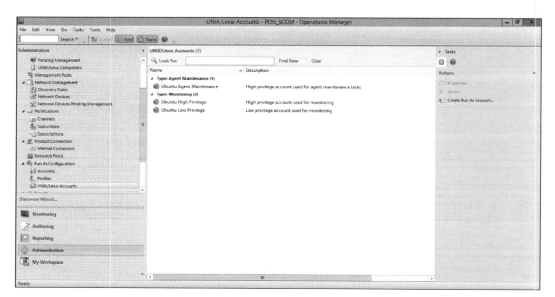

# Run As profiles

The following steps will show you how to create a **Run As** profile to associate a **Run As Account** to:

1. Within the SCOM console, navigate to **Administration | Run As Configuration | Profiles**.

2. From the list, find the **UNIX/Linux Action Account**, right-click on it, and navigate to **Properties**.

3. Click **Next** twice to show the **Run As Accounts** section and click **Add...**.

4. Drop the list selection down and choose the **Low Privilege** account you created earlier and click **OK**.

5. Click **Save** and then **Close**.

Repeat steps 1 to 5 for the UNIX/Linux Privileged Account and UNIX/Linux Agent Maintenance Account profiles but adding the relevant Run As account you created earlier. The following table shows the Run As account and matching profiles used for this recipe:

| Run As Profile | Account Display Name | Description | Linux Account Name |
|---|---|---|---|
| **UNIX/Linux Action Account** | Ubuntu Low Privilege | Low-privilege account used for monitoring | SCOMLP |
| **UNIX/Linux Privileged Account** | Ubuntu High Privilege | High-privilege account used for monitoring | SCOMHP |
| **UNIX/Linux Agent Maintenance Account** | Ubuntu Agent Maintenance | High-privilege account used for agent maintenance tasks | SCOMAM |

## How to do it...

1. From within the SCOM console, click on the **Administration** section tab.

2. Right-click on **Device Management** and navigate to **Discovery Wizard...**:

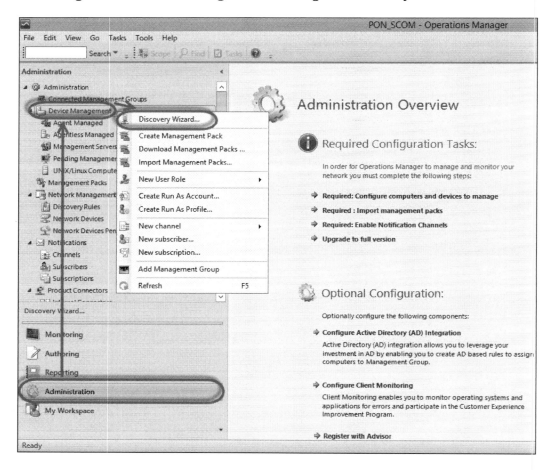

3. Ensure **UNIX/Linux computers** is selected and click **Next**.

4. Click **Add...** to open the **Discovery Criteria** screen.

5. In the **Discovery Scope** column, enter the name of the UNIX/Linux device to discover. For this recipe, we will use **Linux01**.

6. Since we will be pushing the agent to the device, leave the **Discovery Type** at its default of **All computers**.

7. Click the **Set credentials...** button.

8. Choose the username and password and enter the credentials that you used for the Agent maintenance account earlier.

9. Choose **This account does not have privileged access** from the drop-down and then click on the **Elevation** tab to the left of the window.

10. Ensure **Use 'sudo' elevation** is selected and click **OK**.

11. Click **Save**.

12. Under **Select target resource pool:**, use the drop-down to select the **UNIX/Linux Resource Pool** you created earlier.

13. Click **Discover**.

14. Once the discovery completes and successfully finds your Linux server, ensure it is selected and click **Manage** to deploy the agent:

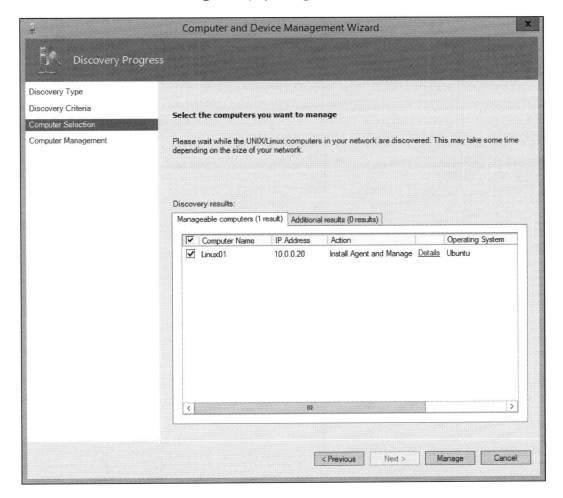

15. Once the deployment has completed, click **Done**.

## There's more...

Two main common problems are encountered when we try to discover and deploy UNIX/Linux agents—name resolution and permissions.

All UNIX/Linux devices must be resolvable via their hostnames to an IP address. If there is not already a DNS record matching the hostname of the UNIX/Linux system, create one manually and point it at the device accessible IP address. If you are unable to add one to DNS, create an entry in the management server's HOSTS file.

 To find the hostname of the UNIX/Linux server, type the command `hostname` in the UNIX/Linux command shell.

To set up the UNIX/Linux accounts within the operating system for monitoring, refer to the information for your UNIX/Linux Operating System, along with the information that can be found at `http://social.technet.microsoft.com/wiki/contents/ articles/7375.configuring-sudo-elevation-for-unix-and-linux-monitoring-with-system-center-2012-operations-manager.aspx`.

## See also

The following are useful links to information related to the System Center 2012 Operation Manager UNIX/Linux monitoring:

► Microsoft TechNet—Supported UNIX/Linux Operating System versions: `http://technet.microsoft.com/en-us/library/jj656654.aspx#BKMK_ RBF_UnixAgent`

► Microsoft TechNet—Update Rollup 2 Monitoring Pack for UNIX/Linux Operating Systems: `http://www.microsoft.com/en-us/download/details. aspx?id=29696`

► Microsoft TechNet Wiki—Troubleshooting UNIX/Linux Agent Discovery: `http://social.technet.microsoft.com/wiki/contents/ articles/4966.troubleshooting-unixlinux-agent-discovery-in-system-center-2012-operations-manager.aspx`

# Options for deploying the Admin console

While the administration console for SCOM is usually installed as part of the management server deployment, it is not recommended to log on to the management server to perform administrative tasks. Therefore, deployment of the console to workstations or a Remote Desktop Services farm is highly recommended.

While mounting an ISO or accessing the source files and running the setup wizard is certainly one possible option, doing this repeatedly for multiple people can be inefficient.

This recipe will show you how to deploy the console from the command line so that you can use this method either within scripts or via a software deployment tool such as System Center **Configuration Manager** (**ConfigMgr**).

## Getting ready

You will need access to the SCOM source files and the PowerShell ISE to complete this recipe.

## How to do it...

The following steps will show you how to deploy the SCOM admin console from the command line by creating a PowerShell script to help automate the deployment:

1. Open the PowerShell ISE.
2. Type the following code:

```
Param (
    [ValidateSet(0, 1)]
    [int]$SendCEIPReports = 0,
    [ValidateSet(0, 1)]
    [int]$UseMicrosoftUpdate = 0,
    [ValidateSet("Never", "Queued", "Always")]
    [string]$EnableErrorReporting = "Never",
    [Parameter(Mandatory=$true)]
    [ValidateScript({ Test-Path $_ -PathType 'Container' })]
    [string]$SourceFiles
    )
$InstallArgs = "/silent /install /components:OMConsole
/EnableErrorReporting:$EnableErrorReporting
/SendCEIPReports:$SendCEIPReports
/UseMicrosoftUpdate:$UseMicrosoftUpdate"
Start-Process -FilePath "$SourceFiles\setup.exe" -Wait -
NoNewWindow -PassThru -ArgumentList $InstallArgs
If (!(Test-Path -Path "C:\Program Files\Microsoft System
Center 2012 R2\Operations Manager")) {
    Write-Error "Installation Failed"
    } Else {
    Write-Output "Installation Complete"
    }
```

3. Save the script as `Install-SCOMConsole.ps1`.

4. Run the following command from a PowerShell window with the directory set to where the script was saved: `\Install-SCOMConsole -SourceFiles "<PathtoSCOMfiles>"`

> Replace `<PathtoSCOMfiles>` with the location of your extracted SCOM installation files. For example, if they are stored in a directory called `OperationsManager` on a file share of `Apps` on the `PONDML` server, this would be `\\PONDML\Apps\OperationsManager`.

5. When the script finishes running and the **Installation Complete** message is shown, open the SCOM admin console from the **Start Menu**.

## How it works...

The SCOM admin console can be installed from the command line by running `setup.exe` with the relevant parameters.

The first mandatory parameters to achieve an unattended installation of the console are:

`/Silent /Install /Components:OMConsole`

These tell the setup process to run an unattended (`/Slient`) installation (`/Install`) of only the admin console (`/Components:OMConsole`).

All of the following switches dictate the behavior of the uploading of error or usage information to Microsoft and the use of Microsoft Update for SCOM:

`/EnableErrorReporting: [Never | Queued | Always]`

`/SendCEIPReports [0 | 1]`

`/UseMicrosoftUpdate: [0 | 1 ]`

The script first defines some parameters with default values in place to disable the use of error reporting and Microsoft updates, but these can be overridden by appending the switch to the script, for example, to turn on Microsoft updates:

```
\Install-SCOMConsole -UseMicrosoftUpdates 1 -SourceFiles
"<PathtoSCOMfiles>"
```

The script then builds the command-line arguments for deploying the console with the selected options and then passes these parameters to the `setup.exe` process.

The script contains a check for the source files location to ensure it exists and is also set as mandatory.

If you update the script to hard code the location of the source files by changing the line to `[st ring]$SourceFiles="<PathtoSCOMfiles>"` and `Parameter(Mandatory=$true)]` to `Parameter(Mandatory=$false)]`, the script would become completely parameter free and would deploy an unattended installation of the SCOM admin console by merely running:

```
\Install-SCOMConsole
```

## There's more...

While the console can be installed from the setup wizard or the command line by adding some parameters, the script in this recipe is an example of making it easier, as in as far as making it a single script to click or command to type.

However, this does still require a level of manual interaction and access to the SCOM installation source files.

For a truly enterprise-level, unattended, self-service deployment method, a solution such as ConfigMgr should be used.

Using the principles in this recipe, a new application should be created with the relevant application name, supplier, version, and so on, and a new deployment type created, as can be seen in the following image from ConfigMgr:

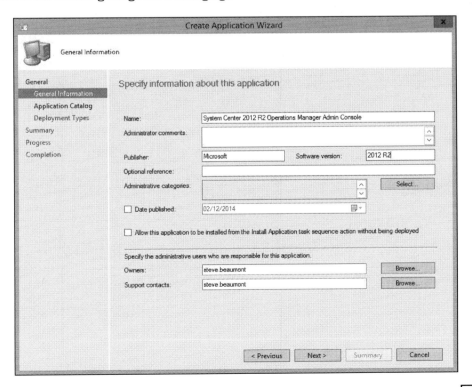

This deployment type should use the following as the installation command:

```
Setup.exe /silent /install /components:OMConsole /
EnableErrorReporting:Never /SendCEIPReports:0 /UseMicrosoftUpdate:0
```

The following should be used as the uninstallation command for x64 platforms:

```
Msiexec /x{041C3416-87CE-4B02-918E-6FDC95F241D3} /qn /norestart
```

The following should be used as the uninstallation command for x86 platforms:

```
Msiexec /x {175B7A24-E94B-46E5-A0FD-06B78AC82D17} /qn /norestart
```

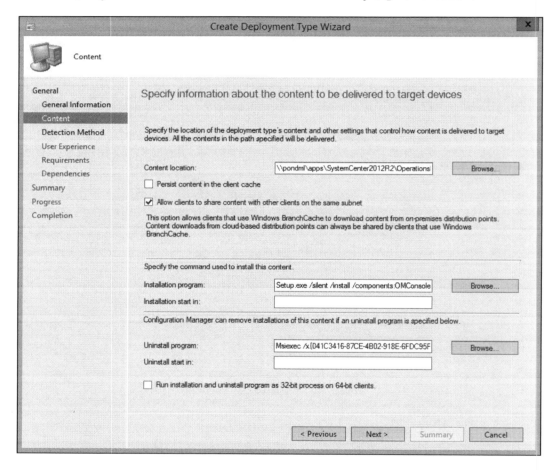

To finish off within Configuration Manager, you can also set the requirements for the deployment to ensure that it only installs on devices that can run it.

The following table shows the requirement matrix you can use for the various deployment types:

| Requirement | Value |
| --- | --- |
| Memory | Greater than 2 GB |
| Disk type | NTFS Formatted Disk |
| Disk size | Greater than 512 MB |
| Operating system | Windows Server 2008 R2 SP1 |
| | Windows Server 2012 |
| | Windows Server 2012 R2 |
| | Windows 7 |
| | Windows 8 |
| | Windows 8.1 |
| Miscellaneous | No Pending Reboot |
| | Device is Active Directory Domain Joined |

The admin console also has a dependency on the following software that can be modeled to deploy if not already present in Configuration Manager:

▶ PowerShell 2.0

▶ Windows Installer 3.1

▶ Microsoft Report Viewer 2012 Runtime

# 4

# Operating System Center 2012 R2 Operations Manager

In this chapter, we will provide recipes for configuring overrides and tuning, and review recovery tasks, and the use of PowerShell for administrative tasks in SCOM. These recipes will cover topics such as:

- ▶ Implementing tuning and best-practice recommendations
- ▶ Understanding self-tuning thresholds and baselining
- ▶ Configuring self-tuning thresholds
- ▶ Using PowerShell for administration tasks
- ▶ Setting up recovery tasks

## Introduction

The previous chapter reviewed best practices for configuring **System Center Operations Manager** (**SCOM**). The recipes in this chapter will take those concepts a step further by exploring best-practice recommendations for performing initial tuning as part of SCOM deployment as well as for working with monitors and rules, configuring self-tuning thresholds and baselines, and automating administration and configuration tasks in SCOM with PowerShell.

# Implementing tuning and best-practice recommendations

After going through the recipes for configuring SCOM in *Chapter 3, Configuring System Center 2012 R2 Operations Manager*, you will now have a number of management packs installed in SCOM. While it is highly recommended that you install only the management packs that you need, many of the base management packs come with rules and monitors that also need to be tuned.

The initial tuning should be performed according to the following guidelines:

> ▸ Devise a strategy and identify the order in which you would like to review and tune management packs.

> ▸ Thoroughly review the management pack guide for each management pack. These guides provide valuable insight into how to best install, configure, and tune the management packs.

> ▸ For each management pack that you plan to install, create an additional management pack in which to store overrides and name it `Management Pack_ Override`, where `Management Pack` is the name of the sealed management pack to which the overrides apply. For example, overrides to the management pack `Microsoft.SQLServer.2012.Monitoring.mp` would be saved to `Microsoft. SQLServer.2012.Monitoring_Overrides.xml`.

> ▸ Perform the testing and tuning in your pre-production environment before extending to production.

> ▸ Install a single management pack at a time to simplify the tuning process.

> ▸ Create an event view so that you can see all events that are captured in SCOM.

> ▸ Involve the service owner or application experts in understanding the alerts that are generated by each management pack, so as to most effectively tune the management packs.

> ▸ Use the built-in reports or review the alerts in the console to identify the monitors and the rules that are generating the most activity.

> ▸ For each management pack, determine what monitors and rules are generating the most activity and how best to resolve any alerts through, for instance, the use of overrides.

> ▸ Override the rule or monitor where necessary and disable the rule or monitor if the issue is not severe enough to necessitate an alert.

> ▸ After the initial tuning, continue to review management packs in your production environment and continue tuning to ensure that the management pack is optimally configured for your environment.

# Getting ready

As you install management packs, you will notice that some alerts get generated and show up in the console. Depending on your environment, these alerts will range in severity from critical to informational, and you will now need to investigate and address the alerts. Alert remediation and tuning can be done by overriding alerts to make them more meaningful for your environment.

The following screenshot shows alerts in the Operations Console.

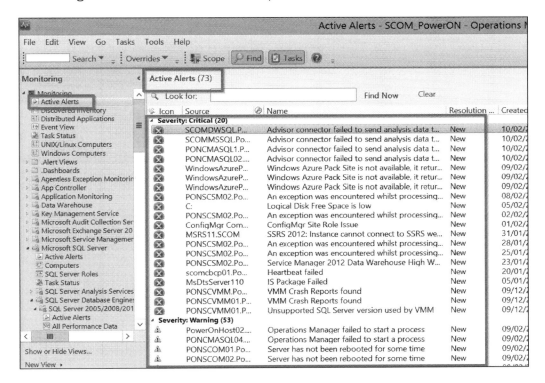

After installation, evaluate the behavior of the management pack to ensure that all components of the application have been discovered, and then review the alerts that get generated for that management pack.

# How to do it...

A suggested approach for management pack tuning is to tune each management pack on the basis of the underlying application components, such as the servers and services that comprise the application, and to tune alerts according to severity from the highest severity alerts and dependencies to the lowest. First, review the alerts in the console; then use the Health Explorer to gather more detailed information about the underlying problem.

While evaluating each rule, ask yourself the following:

▶ Is the generated alert actionable? An alert is actionable if it clearly identifies a problem and has suggestions on how to fix the problem. Consider disabling alerts that do not require any action.

▶ Is the alert a duplicate? There should be only one alert indicating that a specific issue has occurred. If more than one alert gets generated for a specific issue, consider tuning the rule or monitor to enable suppression.

▶ Is the alert valid? An alert is valid if you can confirm that the underlying issue that generated the alert actually occurred at the time the alert was generated.

## Creating an event view in SCOM

You can create an event view in SCOM to identify generated events as well as generating rules. Perform the following steps:

1. Open the SCOM console and click on the **Monitoring** workspace tab.

2. Right-click on **Monitoring** in the **Monitoring** pane, navigate to **New**, and select **Event View**. Name the view and optionally describe the view.

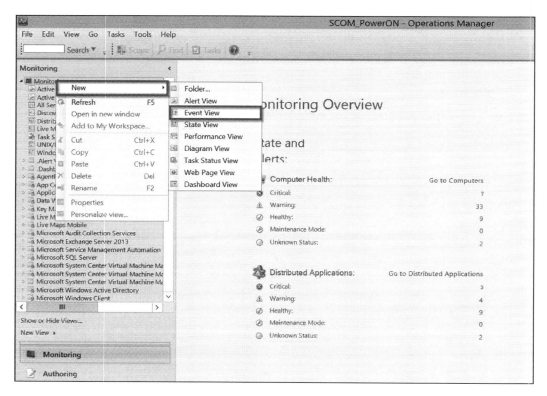

Review the newly created view to determine whether the captured events are relevant for your environment. This is recommended because the collected events take up storage in SCOM, and thus, you want to ensure that only relevant events get collected.

## Using the server approach for alert tuning

The server approach for alert tuning is as follows:

1. Open the SCOM console and click on the **Monitoring** workspace tab.

2. Navigate to **Windows Computers**.

3. Select a computer and right-click on it. Select open and navigate to **Open | Health Explorer** for that computer.

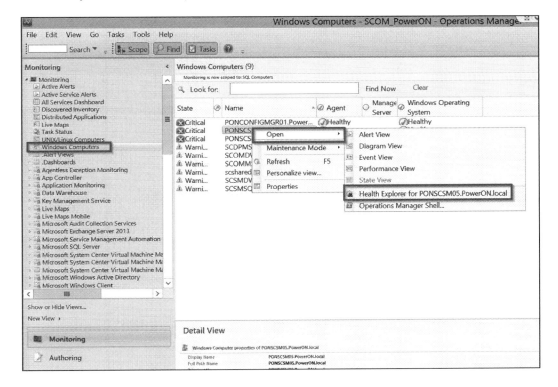

 The default view scope is for only unhealthy child monitors. This makes it easier to focus on the problems with the monitored components. You can change the scope to include all child monitors. The Health Explorer shows the state of the various monitored components as well as the rollup for the monitors. You can also override the monitor from the Health Explorer.

4. Click on the monitor of interest, right-click on the monitor, and then select **Monitor properties**.

5. Click on the **Configuration** tab to review the configuration for the monitor.

## How it works...

During the installation of SCOM, a number of management pack libraries get automatically imported. These libraries provide a foundation of object types on which all subsequent management packs depend. They also contain basic settings that SCOM requires for minimum functionality to manage the SCOM application itself. In addition to these management packs, you should import some additional management packs to monitor those applications used by your environment. Management packs for Windows Server Operating System and Active Directory are a good place to start.

After these management packs are installed (provided you have deployed agents to some servers in your environment), the object discoveries in the management packs will identify objects to be monitored, and the monitors and rules will direct the SCOM agents to track the state of various parts of a managed component, collect discovery and performance data, and generate alerts.

## There's more...

The knowledge pane in Health Explorer provides detailed information about the monitor, including issues that cause the monitor to change state, as well as suggestions for resolution. The state change events tab will show you the monitor's state change frequency and the historical overview of the times during which the events occurred. On the basis of these, you can check the properties of the monitor to ensure that the thresholds and monitor settings are relevant for your environment.

After you determine what monitors and rules are generating the most activity, you can tune the monitor or rule by either disabling it or creating an override to change the properties for the monitor or rule. You can override alerts and events in SCOM from the Operations Console. As recommended earlier, for each Management pack that you plan to install in SCOM, create an additional management pack for storing overrides.

## Creating alert overrides

To create alert overrides in SCOM:

1. Open the SCOM console and click on the **Monitoring** workspace.

2. Click on the alert, then right-click on the alert and open **Health Explorer**.

3. Click on the **Overrides** drop-down option in **Health Explorer**, select **Override the Monitor**, and then select the overridden target.

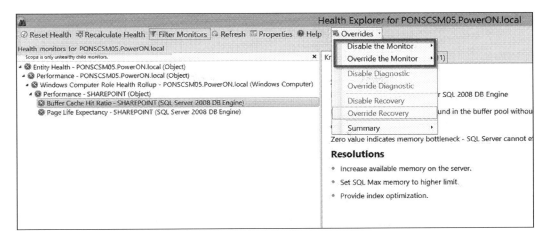

## Overriding an event in SCOM

To create event overrides in SCOM:

1.  Open the SCOM console and click on the **Monitoring** workspace.

2.  Click on **Event View** and navigate to the event view you created earlier.

3.  Right-click on **Overrides**, select **Override the Rule**, and then select your overrides target.

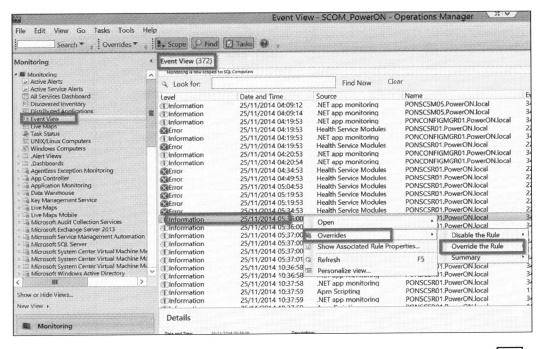

## See also

For more useful information related the tuning of System Center 2012 R2 Operations Manager, refer to the Microsoft TechNet article *Tuning Monitoring by using Targeting and Overrides* at the following link: `http://TechNet.microsoft.com/en-us/library/hh230704.aspx`.

# Understanding self-tuning thresholds and baselining

A self-tuning threshold monitor is a Windows Performance Counter monitor type that was introduced in System Center Operations Manager 2007. Unlike monitors that use a fixed threshold (static monitors), **self-tuning Threshold (STT)** monitors learn what is acceptable for a performance counter and, over time, update the threshold for the performance counter.

In contrast to STTs, static thresholds are simple monitor types and are based on predefined values and counters that are monitored for conformity within the predefined values. For instance, a static threshold could be used to monitor for specific thresholds, such as Available Megabytes of Memory. Static thresholds are very useful for various monitoring scenarios but have some drawbacks. Primarily, there's some acceptable variation in performance of servers even when they fulfil the same role, and as such, a performance value that may be appropriate for one server may not apply to another. STTs were therefore created as an option for monitoring in such instances.

Baselines in SCOM 2012 R2 are used to collect the usual values for a performance counter, which then allows SCOM to adjust alert thresholds accordingly. STTs are very useful for collecting performance counter baselines on the basis of what it has learned over time.

## Getting ready

To understand how STTs work, we will take a look at the basic components of an STT. To do so, we will create a self-tuning monitor using the wizard. The process for configuring an STT involves configuring the logic for the STT to learn. The configuration can be performed in the wizard for creating the performance counter monitor. To create a performance counter monitor in System Center Operations Manager, you will need to log on to a computer that has an Operations console, using an account that is a member of the Operations Manager Administrators user role, or Operations Manager Authors user role for your Operations Manager 2012 R2 management group.

Create a management pack for your custom monitor if you don't already have one.

## How to do it...

For illustration purposes, we will create a 2-state self-tuning threshold monitor.

### Creating a self-tuning threshold monitor

To create a self-tuning threshold monitor, carry out the following steps:

1. Log in to a computer with an account that is a member of the Operations Manager Administrators user role or Operations Manager Authors user role for the Operations Manager 2012 R2 management group.

2. In the Operations console, click on the **Authoring** button.

3. In the **Authoring** pane, expand **Authoring**, expand **Management Pack Objects**, click on **Monitors**, right-click on the **Monitors**, select **Create a Monitor**, select **Unit Monitor**, and then expand **Windows Performance Counters**.

4. Select **2-state Baselining**, select a **Destination Management Pack**, and then click on **Next**.

5. Name the monitor, select **Windows Server** as your monitor target, and then select the **Performance** parent monitor from the drop-down option.

6. In the **Object** field, enter processor, enter % Processor Time in the **Counter** field, enter _Total in the **Instance** field, and set the **Interval** to **1 minute**.

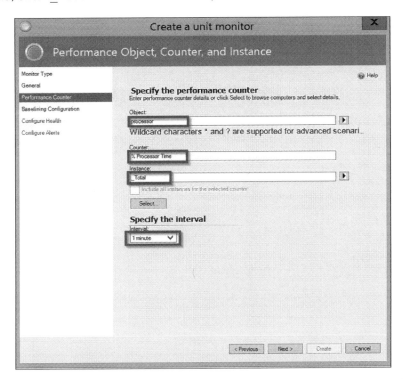

7.  Click on **Next** to **Configure business cycle**, which is the unit of time you would like to monitor. The default is 1 week, which is fine in general, but for the purpose of illustration, select **1 Day(s)**.

8.  Under **Alerting**, leave the default value of **1 business cycle(s) of analysis**.

9.  Move the **Sensitivity** slider to the left to select a low sensitivity value and then click on **Next**.

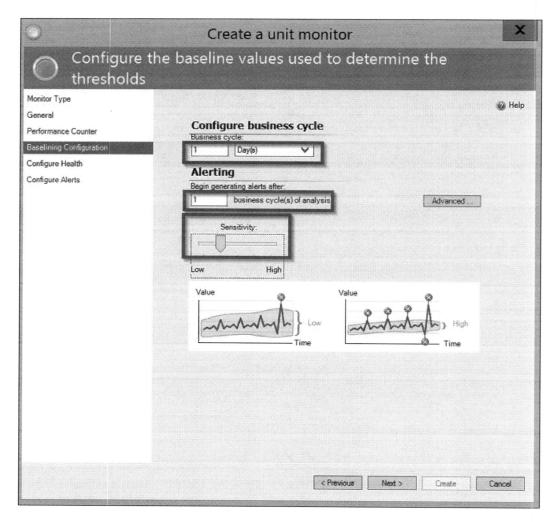

10. Leave the default values on the **Configure Health** screen and click on **Next**.

11. On the **Configure Alerts** screen, check the box **to generate alerts for the monitor** and click on **Create**.

# How it works...

A self-tuning threshold consists of two rules and a monitor. The performance collection rule collects performance counter data, and the signature collection rule establishes a signature. The monitor compares the value of the performance counter data with the signature. The signature is a numeric data provider that learns the characteristics of a business cycle. SCOM then uses the signature to set and adjust the thresholds for alerts by evaluating performance counter results against the business cycle pattern.

In this recipe, we effectively created a 2-state baselining self-tuning threshold monitor, as you can see in the following screenshot:

| Target | Type | Inherited Fr... | Manage... | Enabled by... |
|---|---|---|---|---|
| ▷ Security | Aggregate Rollup | Object | Health Li... | Yes |
| ◢ **Windows Server** | | | | |
| ◢ Entity Health | Aggregate Rollup | Object | Health Li... | Yes |
| ▷ Availability | Aggregate Rollup | Object | Health Li... | Yes |
| ▷ Configuration | Aggregate Rollup | Object | Health Li... | Yes |
| ◢ Performance | Aggregate Rollup | Object | Health Li... | Yes |
| PON % Processor Time Monitor | 2-state Baselining | (Not inherit... | PowerON... | Yes |
| APM Agent Health Rollup | Dependency Rollup | Windows C... | Operatio... | Yes |
| Hardware Performance Rollup | Dependency Rollup | (Not inherit... | Windows... | Yes |

You will find that this also created some rules such as performance collection and signature collection rules to collect performance and signature data, respectively. Data collection will occur at the frequency specified at the time the monitor was created, as you can see in the following screenshot:

| Name | Inherited from | Management ... | Created | En... |
|---|---|---|---|---|
| Performance Collection Rule for STT Monitor [PON % Processor Time Monitor] | Windows Server | PowerON.SCO... | 08/12/2014... | Ye... |
| ◢ **Type: Windows Server (2)** | | | | |
| Signature Collection Rule for STT Monitor [PON % Processor Time Monitor] | Windows Server | PowerON.SCO... | 08/12/2014... | Ye... |
| Performance Collection Rule for STT Monitor [PON % Processor Time Monitor] | Windows Server | PowerON.SCO... | 08/12/2014... | Ye... |

You will also notice that the collection frequency values can be changed, along with the sensitivity values for the monitor, as you can see in the following screenshot:

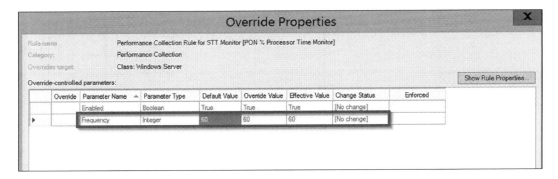

107

## There's more...

Monitors that use self-tuning thresholds are based on Windows performance counters and the business cycle setting. The business cycle establishes a time period of activity that SCOM will use to create a signature. The business cycle can be configured in either days or weeks, and the default is 1 week.

For example, the STT monitor for the `% Processor Time` counter that we created learns that processor activity for some database servers spikes between noon and 2 pm on Wednesdays. The threshold is adjusted to take that pattern into account. As a result, an alert would not be generated for a spike in processor activity at 12:30 pm on Wednesday. However, if similar processor activity spikes at the same time on Thursday, the monitor will generate an alert.

## See also

For detailed information on activities listed in this recipe, refer to the Microsoft TechNet article *Understanding Self-Tuning Threshold Monitors* in the following link: `http://TechNet.microsoft.com/en-us/library/dd789011.aspx`.

# Configuring self-tuning thresholds

In the previous recipe, we introduced self-tuning thresholds and sought to understand how they function. In this recipe, we will further configure self-tuning thresholds to expand on what we've done thus far.

To recap, a self-tuning threshold monitor uses a learning process to determine the usual values for a specified performance counter object, and on the basis of the learned values, it sets the threshold. During the period of learning, SCOM establishes a baseline representing the regular and expected activity of the computer. After the learning period has elapsed, SCOM logs all subsequent activity for the computer and compares it with the baseline.

Self-tuning monitors can be either 2-state or 3-state monitors. The following are the available self-tuning monitor types:

- **2-state Above**: This monitor establishes a baseline and generates a status change when the performance counter goes above the learned baseline.

- **2-state Below**: This is the opposite of the 2-state Above baseline. After the learning period and the baseline are established, a status change will get generated when the performance counter goes below the baseline.

- **2-state Baselining**: This monitor is similar to the 2-state Above monitor. It, however, records the baseline information for use in performance graphs.

► **3-state Baselining**: Given a baseline, there is an area above, below, and within the baseline. These three areas determine the health state of the monitor at any given time. A healthy state is defined as being in an area within the baseline, while an error state is defined as being either above or below the baseline. A counter that falls in any other area that is not defined as an error causes a warning state.

Given the propensity for STTs to be particularly noisy, owing to such factors as the default medium-high sensitivity settings of such monitors, it is important to configure and tune these monitors so that they are relevant for your environment.

## Getting ready

To configure a self-tuning threshold, you will need to log in to a computer that has the Operations Console, using an account that is a member of the Operations Manager Administrators user role, or Operations Manager Authors user role, for your Operations Manager 2012 R2 management group. In the previous recipe, we created a 2-state Baselining monitor for illustration, so we will focus on a 3-state Baselining self-tuning threshold monitor in this recipe. For illustration, we will create and configure an STT monitor and use the `SQL DB Engine`, `Lock Requests\sec`, and `_Total` as our Object, Counter, and Instance, respectively.

## How to do it...

To create a 3-state baselining self-tuning monitor, carry out the following steps:

1. Log in to a computer with an account that is a member of the Operations Manager Administrators user role or Operations Manager Authors user role for the Operations Manager 2012 R2 management group.

2. In the Operations console, click on the **Authoring** workspace.

3. In the **Authoring** pane, expand **Authoring**, expand **Management Pack Objects**, and then click on **Monitors**.

4. Right-click and select **Create a Monitor**, select **Unit Monitor**, and then expand **Windows Performance Counters**.

5. Select **3-state Baselining**, select a **Destination Management Pack**, and then click on **Next**.

6. Name the monitor. Select **Windows Server** as your monitor target and select the **Performance** parent monitor from the drop-down menu.

7. In the **Object** field, enter `SQL DB Engine`, enter `Lock Requests/sec` in the **Counter** field.

8. Enter _Total in the **Instance** field and set the **Interval** to **1 minute**.

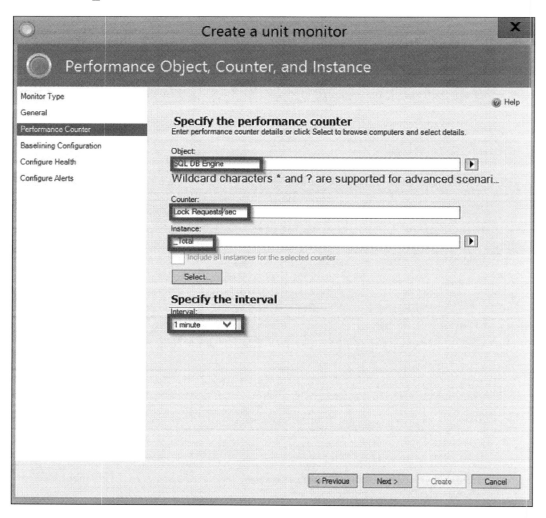

9. Click on **Next** to **Configure business cycle**, which is the unit of time you would like to monitor. The default is 1 week, which is fine in general, but for the purpose of illustration, select **1 Day(s)**.

10. Under **Alerting**, leave the default **1 business cycle(s)** of analysis. We will look at the advanced alerting configuration later.

11. Next, leave the **Sensitivity** slider at the default value and click on the **Advanced** button to configure sensitivity in more detail.

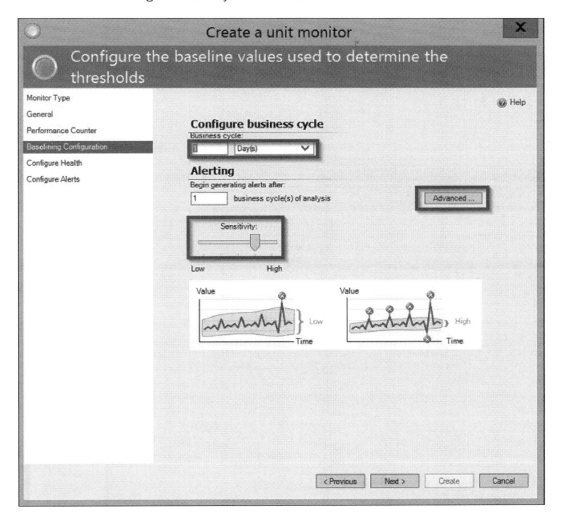

12. On the resulting **Baselining – Advanced** page, leave the default settings for the **Learning rate** and **Time sensitivity** settings, click on **OK** to close the **Baselining – Advanced** page, and click on **Next** on the **Baseline Configuration** page.

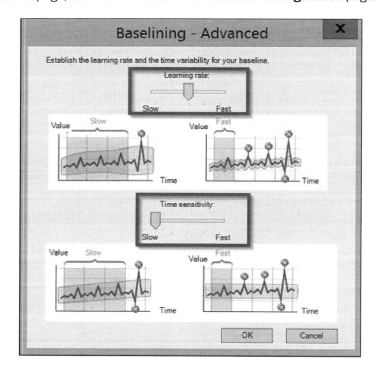

13. Leave the default values on the **Configure Health** screen and click on **Next**.

14. On the **Configure Alerts** screen, check the box to **generate alerts for the monitor**, optionally enter an alert description under the **Alert Properties**, **Alert description** field, and then click on **Create**.

## How it works...

As mentioned in the previous section, a self-tuning threshold consists of a performance collection rule, a signature collection rule, and a monitor. In the preceding example, a monitor and the corresponding rules are visible in the console as shown in the following illustrations.

| Target | Type | Inherited Fr... | Managem... | Enabled by... |
|---|---|---|---|---|
| **Windows Server** | | | | |
| Entity Health | Aggregate Rollup | Object | Health Libr... | Yes |
| Availability | Aggregate Rollup | Object | Health Libr... | Yes |
| Configuration | Aggregate Rollup | Object | Health Libr... | Yes |
| Performance | Aggregate Rollup | Object | Health Libr... | Yes |
| PON % Processor Time Monitor | 2-state Baselining | (Not inherit... | PowerON... | Yes |
| PON Lock Requests/sec 3-state Monitor | 3-state Baselining | (Not inherit... | PowerON... | Yes |

The following screenshot shows the collection rules that are created with the STT monitor:

In the preceding example, the performance collection rule collects lock requests/sec performance counter data, and the signature collection rule establishes the numeric data provider that learns the characteristics of the business cycle for the monitor. The monitor compares the value of the performance counter data with the signature. SCOM then uses the signature to set and adjust the thresholds for alerts by evaluating performance counter results against the business cycle pattern.

Recall that the **Configure Health** page during the creation of the monitor presented you with the option of specifying what health state should be generated for each condition that the self-tuning threshold monitor will detect. On the basis of the default values, a healthy state is defined as being in an area within the baseline, while an error state is defined as being in an area above the baseline, and a warning state is in an area below the baseline. These values can be configured to make the monitor relevant for your environment.

## There's more...

You can adjust self-tuning threshold monitors to be relevant for your environment.

### Adjusting self-tuning threshold monitors for your environment

Out of the box, self-tuning thresholds might have sensitivity thresholds that cause them to be very noisy and generate many unnecessary alerts. This can cause many a frustration, especially because the baseline numbers do not tell you much about the actual values. Therefore, as part of the initial configuration, we recommend turning off alerting for the monitors for several business cycles and keeping track of the behavior of the associated counter. This will enable you to get a better idea of the behavior of the counter in your environment, and give the monitor ample time to adjust the baseline for your environment.

If the counter displays frequent spikes and large variations, consider tuning the sensitivity by lowering the sensitivity settings on both the signature collection rule and the monitor. There exists an inverse relationship between the numerical value of the sensitivity threshold and the resulting alerting function, with higher numeric values indicating a lower sensitivity and consequently a lower number of alerts.

The inner sensitivity setting for the monitor must match the sensitivity setting of the signature collection rule. The outer sensitivity setting must also be larger than the inner sensitivity setting. The degree to which this is the case is not important because the inner sensitivity setting is the only setting that gets taken into account in generating the counter values. You can change these settings by creating overrides for the respective monitor and rule as shown in the following screenshot:

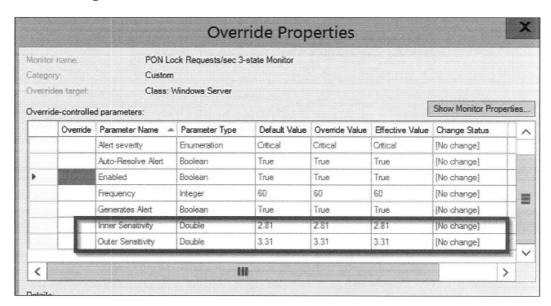

The following screenshot shows the parameter items for the STT monitor signature collection rule that can be overridden:

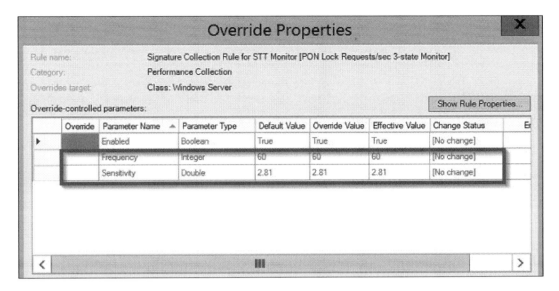

The default sensitivity values depend on the sensitivity setting selected during the creation of the monitor. One of five sensitivity settings is possible. It is recommended to adjust these settings upwards in increments that correspond to the settings in the SCOM user interface, for instance, from 2.81 to 3.31.

## To use or not to use self-tuning thresholds

While self-tuning thresholds are great for many monitoring scenarios in the real world, they should not be used for monitoring all performance counters. In the event that you deem a self-tuning threshold to not be appropriate for monitoring a specific performance counter, use a static threshold monitor in lieu of an STT.

## See also

For detailed information on information relating to configuring self-tuning thresholds in System Center Operations Manager 2012 R2, refer to the Microsoft TechNet article *How Self-Tuning Threshold Baseline is Computed* in the following link: `http://social.TechNet.microsoft.com/wiki/contents/articles/237.scom-how-self-tuning-threshold-baseline-is-computed.aspx`.

# Using PowerShell for administration tasks

PowerShell is Microsoft's command shell and scripting language that gives us a single and consistent method for automating our entire environment. It is essentially an automation engine that Microsoft has built into its major products, and its extensibility is a major strength that makes it an invaluable resource for any administrator of Microsoft products. Knowing and using PowerShell can enable you to automate many administration and configuration tasks in SCOM and save you a great deal of time and energy in the process. That is the beauty of automation.

This section will provide a brief introduction to PowerShell, review some frequently used and useful cmdlets, and provide some practical examples on how to use PowerShell for administration tasks in System Center 2012 R2 Operations Manager.

PowerShell comprises a number of features such as cmdlets, pipeline, providers, and the help system. These features make PowerShell a very powerful tool for administering Microsoft products.

## Cmdlet

Cmdlets are small, self-contained pieces of functionality that are used in Windows PowerShell. Cmdlets are named using a verb-and-noun name pair in Windows PowerShell. The verb identifies the action that is performed by a cmdlet, and the noun identifies the resource on which the cmdlet performs an action. For instance, the cmdlet, `Import-SCOMManagementPack`, comprises the verb import which identifies the action that will be performed on the noun resource, `SCOMManagementPack`.

## Help system

PowerShell includes a set of help files that are presented in the command-line shell when you use `Get-Help`. The `Get-Help` cmdlet can be used to find information about an individual cmdlet as well as PowerShell and the environment. Read further for more information on this.

## What's new in Operations Manager 2012 R2 PowerShell?

System Center Operations Manager 2012 R2 includes several cmdlets for performing various administration and configuration tasks. Most recently, SCOM 2012 R2 introduced several cmdlets for System Center Advisor, bringing the total number of cmdlets for SCOM to 173. We can confirm this by reviewing a count of all cmdlets in the Operations Manager PowerShell module, by using the following command:

```
(Get-Command -Module OperationsManager).count
```

## Getting ready

You will need to load the Operations Manager PowerShell module in order to access the cmdlets.

### Loading the operations manager PowerShell module

A **module** is a method of loading additional functionality into PowerShell. A module can contain several functions that are loaded into PowerShell, and provides functionality. The `Import-Module` cmdlet is used to add modules into PowerShell. To load the Operations Manager PowerShell module, open a PowerShell command prompt or the PowerShell **Integrated Scripting Environment** (**ISE**) and type the following command:

```
Import-Module OperationsManager
```

## How to do it...

The `Get-Help` and `Get-Command` PowerShell cmdlets are good resources for getting information about the various Operations Manager cmdlets.

### Using Get-Help and Get-Command

`Get-Help` is the PowerShell cmdlet that enables you to interact with the PowerShell help system. Typing `Get-Help` followed by a cmdlet name returns a brief set of information about the cmdlet, including:

- ▶ Name and description of the cmdlet
- ▶ Syntax description for the cmdlet
- ▶ Detailed description
- ▶ Other remarks and related links

`Get-Help` can be used with the full and detailed parameters to provide more information about the cmdlet.

`Get-Command` complements `Get-Help` and provides basic information about cmdlets and elements of other Windows PowerShell commands. `Get-Command` can come in very handy when, for instance, you want to work with SCOM agents but can't remember the cmdlets. You can type the following command:

```
Get-Command *Agent
```

The command outputs all cmdlets that contain the word `Agent` in them, as you can see in the following screenshot:

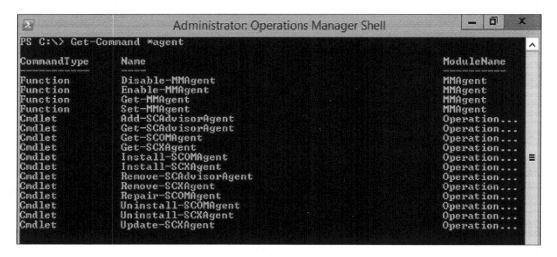

## Reviewing System Center 2012 R2 cmdlets

To confirm that the SCOM PowerShell module was properly imported, review the available cmdlets for SCOM by typing the following command:

```
Get-Command -module OperationsManager
```

## Setting your PowerShell execution policy

Scripts are very useful for automating various tasks and simplifying the process of administration, but in the wrong hands, they can be used with a detrimental effect. Windows PowerShell therefore has several built-in security features, which includes the execution policy. There are seven execution policy options in Windows PowerShell that determine whether scripts will be allowed to run in your environment, whether or not they need to be digitally signed, and whether configuration files can be loaded. To find out more about the execution policy options, type the following command in PowerShell:

```
Get-Help Set-ExecutionPolicy
```

To determine what execution policies apply to your machine, type the following in PowerShell:

```
Get-ExecutionPolicy -list
```

To set your execution policy to one of the execution policy types, such as `RemoteSigned`, use the following command:

```
Set-ExecutionPolicy RemoteSigned
```

## Connecting to the SCOM console

You can access and use SCOM cmdlets either directly through the SCOM shell on a computer that has the Operations console installed or remotely by initiating a connection to an SCOM management server via a machine that has at least PowerShell v2, even if the machine does not have the Operations console installed on it. To do this, you will make use of the `New-PSSession` cmdlet.

To remotely establish such a connection to the SCOM shell:

1.  Create a new session and initiate a remote connection to a server that has the SCOM module imported, using the following command:

    ```
    New-PSSession -ComputerName <SCOM Management Server FQDN> | Enter-
    PSSession
    ```

2.  Perform any SCOM action directly via the session. For instance, get a count of the number of agents in your management group:

    ```
    (Get-SCOMAgent).count
    ```

3.  To end the interactive session, type: `Exit-PSSession`.

4.  Get details such as the ID, name, state, configuration name, and availability of the interactive session: `Get-PSSession`.

5.  Close the Windows PowerShell sessions in the current session, end the `PSSession`, and release resources by using the following command:

    ```
    Remove-PSSession -Id <session Id>
    ```

## Using SCOM management group connections

There are two kinds of management group connections in SCOM 2012 R2: temporary and persistent connections.

## Working with temporary connections

Temporary connections are created when a cmdlet is run with the `-ComputerName` parameter, and the input is used only in that single connection. With this, you essentially initiate a connection to a management server to get some data, after which the connection is closed. For instance, remoting into a management server called `OMServerA` to retrieve a list of all SCOM agents in the management group in which `OMServerA` resides creates a temporary connection.

```
Get-SCOMAgent -ComputerName OMServerA.FQDN
```

After this one-liner returns the list of SCOM agents, the connection will get closed. The following table shows the cmdlets that can be used to manage SCOM management group connections:

| Cmdlet name | Description |
|---|---|
| Get-SCOMManagementGroupConnection | Retrieves all management group connections, including the IsActive state of these connections |
| Set-SCOMManagementGroupConnection | Sets the specified connection as the active connection |
| Remove-SCOMManagementGroupConnection | Removes a management group connection |

## Working with persistent connections

If you have an SCOM environment with multiple management groups, you will often have to initiate multiple connections and will therefore need to make use of persistent connections.

To create a persistent connection, run the New-SCOMManagementGroupConnection cmdlet:

```
New-SCOMManagementGroupConnection –ComputerName <SCOMMgmtServerName>
```

To review the properties of the persistent connection that you have created, type the following command:

```
Get-SCOMManagementGroupConnection | Select *
```

Now that you have the connection, you can pass it into a cmdlet and use it to get additional information from the management group to which you established the connection. For instance, if you were tasked with retrieving all new and critical alerts from a management group and sorting the output by name, you could accomplish this by first establishing a persistent connection to the management group and then passing that information into the Get-SCOMAlert cmdlet with various parameters with the following command:

```
$mgcon = Get-SCOMManagementGroupConnection –ManagementGroupName
"YourMgmtGroup"
```

```
Get-SCOMAlert –SCSession $mgcon –ResolutionState 0 –Severity 2 |
Sort-Object Name
```

To close the connection, you will need the ID of the active connection. Type the following:

```
Get-SCOMManagementGroupConnection | Select Id
```

```
Get-SCOMManagementGroupConnection –Id <your connection Id> | Remove-
SCOMManagementGroupConnection
```

## How it works...

As mentioned earlier in this section, the features of Windows PowerShell make a particularly compelling and useful tool for automation. In addition to the other features discussed, you must have noticed how extensively the pipeline gets used in PowerShell, as shown in the cmdlets used previously. The pipeline is a method of passing data from one command to another. The objects and resulting data pass along the pipeline, and this controls how they get processed by each cmdlet in the chain. For instance, refer to the following command:

```
Get-SCOMManagementGroup | Where-Object {$_.SkuForLicence -like
"Retail"} | Select-Object Name
```

The `Get-SCOMManagementGroup` cmdlet passes the SCOM management group data into the PowerShell pipeline. The `Where-Object` filters and selects the data that meets the condition `skuforlicence -like 'Retail'`. The result of this initial filter is then passed via the pipeline on to the `Select-Object` cmdlet, which returns the Name property from the data and outputs it.

## There's more...

There are many more cmdlets that the SCOM Administrator will find very useful for performing administration tasks.

### Managing agents

The agent-related cmdlets in SCOM enable you to perform all actions that relate to SCOM agents. Actions such as installing, uninstalling, repairing, and working with agent proxying can be performed using the various cmdlets available for these tasks.

To get information about SCOM agents, use the `Get-SCOMAgent` cmdlet. This will get the agent-managed computers in your management group. This cmdlet will also enable you to identify about 30 other SCOM agent properties that you might find useful to know. Properties such as the agent `patchlist`, `ProxyingEnabled`, `version`, `healthstate`, and `ManuallyInstalled` can all be queried using this cmdlet. For instance, if after updating your environment to UR4, you need to determine what if any agents did not get updated, you could type the following:

```
Get-SCOMAgent | Where-Object {$_.PatchList -notlike "*UR4*"} |
Select-Object Name
```

## Installing SCOM agents with PowerShell

To install SCOM agents, use the `Install-SCOMAgent` cmdlet. For instance, to install an SCOM agent on a machine called `TargetA`, using the management server `ServerB`, first enter credentials with permissions to install an agent on the target machine. This proceeds as follows:

```
$InstallAccount = Get-Credential

$PrimaryMgmtServer = Get-SCOMManagementServer -Name "ServerB.FQDN"

Install-SCOMAgent -Name "TargetA" -PrimaryManagementServer
$PrimaryMgmtServer -ActionAccount $InstallAccount -verbose
```

## Uninstalling SCOM agents

To uninstall an SCOM agent from a computer called `TargetA`, make use of the `Uninstall-SCOMAgent` cmdlet. Ensure that you have access to an account with the appropriate permissions and run the following:

```
Get-SCOMAgent -Name "TargetA.FQDN" | Uninstall-SCOMAgent -verbose
```

## Repairing SCOM agents

To repair an SCOM agent, make use of the `Repair-SCOMAgent` cmdlet. To repair an SCOM agent on `TargetA`:

```
Get-SCOMAgent -Name "TargetA.FQDN" | Repair-SCOMAgent -verbose
```

## Managing SCOM agent proxying

Enabling agent proxying in SCOM enables an agent to act as a proxy, and to discover objects and submit data on behalf of other objects. This is a very important setting because many management packs depend on this setting for functionality. To enable agent proxying, make use of the `Enable-SCOMAgentProxy` cmdlet. For instance, to identify all the agent-managed computers in your environment with agent proxying disabled, run the following command:

```
Get-SCOMAgent | Where-Object {$_.ProxyingEnabled.Value -eq $False} |
Enable-SCOMAgentProxy
```

## See also

The following are useful links to information related using PowerShell with SCOM 2012 R2, to the articles of Microsoft TechNet:

▶ *Operations Manager Cmdlet Reference*: `http://TechNet.microsoft.com/en-us/library/hh545244(v=sc.20).aspx`

▶ *Operations Manager Cmdlet Help Topics*: `http://TechNet.microsoft.com/en-us/library/hh920227(v=sc.20).aspx`

# Setting up recovery tasks

System Center 2012 R2 Operations Manager is a great monitoring tool for many reasons, among which is its ability to resolve problems when they arise. Through the use of automatic and on-demand tasks, you can greatly simplify the monitoring experience by automating the resolution of the most common and recurring issues in your infrastructure.

The SCOM features that enable you to diagnose issues and perform recoveries to remediate the issues are known as tasks. Tasks are contained in the SCOM management packs and can either be run automatically, or on demand. Other tasks can enable you to run administrative tasks from the Operations console.

When the state of a monitor changes, diagnostics and recoveries are run. The diagnostics tasks collect information about the detected problem, while the recoveries attempt to remediate the problem. Diagnostic and recovery actions allow you to run a script or a command whenever a particular monitor changes its health state from a healthy state to a warning or critical state.

A good example of diagnostic and recovery tasks that run in SCOM 20102 R2 are the tasks associated with the Health Service Heartbeat Failure monitor. When the Health Service Watcher detects a problem with a health service(s) that fails to heartbeat, the diagnostics and recovery tasks are executed in an attempt to fix the underlying issues that caused the health service heartbeat failure. Opening the properties of the Health Service Heartbeat Monitor shows the **Diagnostics and Recovery** tab as well as the various associated tasks.

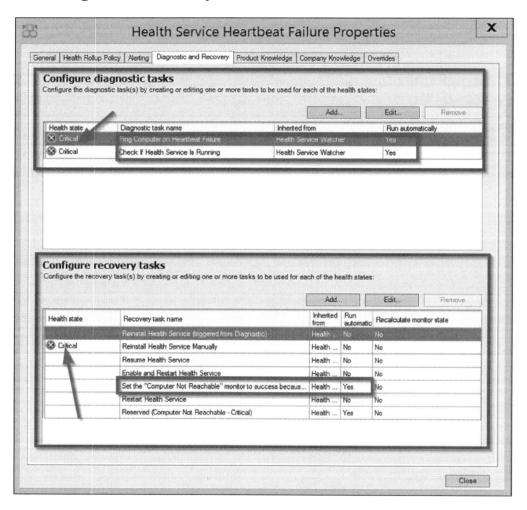

As seen in the preceding screenshot, the **Ping Computer on Heartbeat Failure** and **Check if Health Service is Running** diagnostic tasks are run automatically whenever the health state of the Health Service Heartbeat monitor changes to critical.

Also the **Set the "Computer Not Reachable" monitor to success because the "Ping Computer on Heartbeat Failure" diagnostic succeeded** recovery task will run automatically if the first diagnostic task successfully pings the affected computer.

You can also configure other diagnostic tasks to run automatically using overrides. You can also add and edit tasks in the **Diagnostic and Recovery** tab.

## Getting ready

To enable diagnostic and recovery tasks, log in to a computer that has the Operations Console, using an account that is a member of the Operations Manager Administrators user role, or Operations Manager Authors user role, for your Operations Manager 2012 R2 management group.

## How to do it...

1. Open the SCOM console and click on the **Authoring** workspace tab, expand **Management Pack Objects**, and click on **Monitors**.

2. Right-click on a monitor and click on **Properties**.

3. Click on the **Diagnostic and Recovery** tab, select the desired task(s) under the **Configure diagnostic tasks | Configure recovery tasks** sections, and then click on **Edit**.

4. In the resulting task properties window, click on the **Overrides** tab, click on the **Override** button, and select a specific object or all objects within a group.

In the resulting **Override Properties** dialog box, in the **Override-controlled parameters** section, select **Enabled** and change the override value to **True**, as shown in the following screenshot:

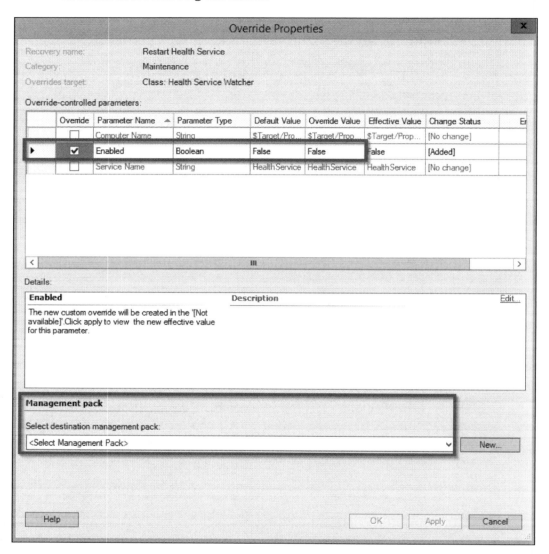

## Creating a Diagnostic or Recovery Task

1. Open the SCOM console and click on the **Authoring** workspace tab | expand **Management Pack Objects** and click on **Monitors**.

2. Right-click on a monitor and select **Properties**.

3. Click on the **Diagnostic and Recovery** tab under the **Configure diagnostic tasks** and/or **Configure recovery tasks** sections and click on **Add** to configure a diagnostic or recovery task. Then, choose between **Diagnostic for warning health state** and **Diagnostic for critical health state**.

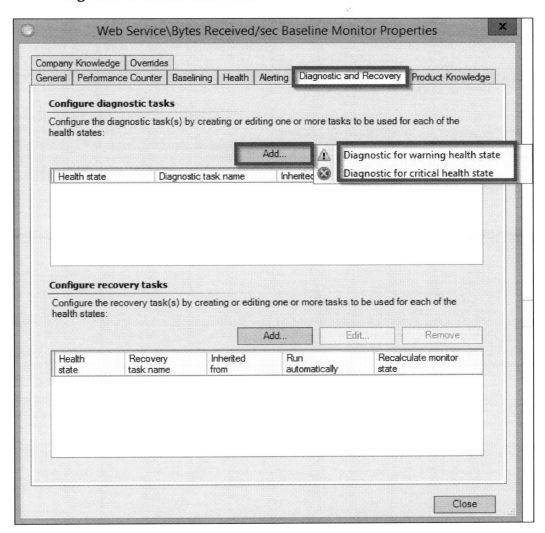

4. In the resulting **Create Diagnostic Task Wizard**, choose to either run a script or a command as a diagnostic task and either click on the **Select destination management pack** drop-down, or the **New** button to create a new unsealed management pack in which to save your task. Click on **Next**.

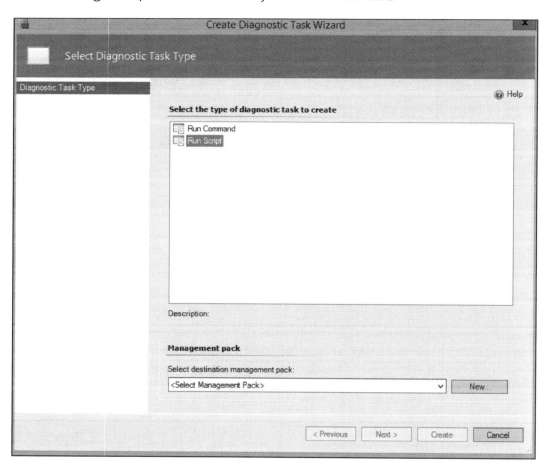

5. On the **Diagnostic/ Recovery Task Name and Description** window, enter the task name, description, and target. You can also have the task run automatically by checking the box for that option.

## How it works...

Diagnostics run after the state of a monitor changes from healthy to either warning or critical. The diagnostic then tries to collect additional information about the issue. If the diagnostic is set to run automatically, it will run when the monitor changes state. However, if it is not set to run automatically, the operator can run the diagnostic from a link in the console.

Recoveries are workflows that run after a monitor's state changes from healthy to either warning or critical. The recoveries attempt to remediate the issue and return the monitor to a healthy state. Similarly, the recovery will run automatically when the monitor's state changes from healthy, if the recovery's Run diagnostic automatically property is set to `true`.

Creating diagnostic and/or recovery tasks to automatically remediate the underlying problem that triggers the monitor state change from healthy to warning or critical obviates the need for your operator to address this issue, freeing up valuable time for them to focus on other tasks.

Note, however, that not all tasks should be run automatically. Certain tasks require operator intervention, and in such cases, such tasks should not be set to run automatically.

## See also

For more useful information on setting up recovery tasks in Operations Manager 2012 R2, refer to the Microsoft TechNet article *Diagnostics and Recoveries* at the following link: `http://TechNet.microsoft.com/en-us/library/hh705258.aspx`

# 5
# Maintaining System Center 2012 R2 Operations Manager

In this chapter, we will provide recipes for maintaining System Center 2012 R2 Operations Manager after installation, the common tasks that should be performed, and how to optimize for scale and performance. These recipes will cover topics such as:

- Running daily, weekly, monthly recommended tasks
- Maintaining and grooming the SCOM database
- Recovering Operations Manager
- Updating System Center 2012 R2 Operations Manager
- Optimizing for scale and performance

## Introduction

Maintaining your **System Center 2012 R2 Operations Manager** (**SCOM**) deployment is essential for the optimal performance of your SCOM environment.

This chapter will review the common tasks that should be performed periodically to keep your SCOM deployment running optimally.

# Running daily, weekly, and monthly recommended tasks

By default, SCOM performs daily maintenance tasks to enable the Operations Manager database to run optimally.

In addition to these tasks, other backup tasks should be run on a periodic basis to ensure that critical SCOM features are protected. Running daily, weekly, and monthly tasks will ensure that your SCOM infrastructure is recoverable, and data loss is minimized in the event of a catastrophic failure. The following tasks should be run daily:

  ▶ Performing an incremental backup of the operational database

  ▶ Monitoring your Management Group health

  ▶ Checking and remediating open alerts

Tasks that should be run weekly include the following:

  ▶ Performing an incremental backup of the data warehouse database

  ▶ Performing a full backup of the operational database

  ▶ Performing an incremental backup of the **Audit Collection Services** (**ACS**) database (only if you make use of this SCOM feature)

  ▶ Reviewing the data volume getting generated by your management packs, and workflows and instances

Tasks that should be run on a monthly basis include the following:

  ▶ Performing a full backup of the data warehouse database

  ▶ Backing up your custom management packs

  ▶ Performing a full backup of your ACS database

  ▶ Checking for updates to management packs

## Getting ready

You need to have a backup procedure in place for your SCOM infrastructure. This procedure should conform to your company's backup policy. Establishing a backup procedure is outside of the scope of this chapter, but if you do not already have a backup procedure established, refer to the guidelines for periodic maintenance tasks mentioned previously and consider using System Center 2012 R2 Data Protection Manager, which is included in your System Center 2012 R2 License, to protect your management group.

## How to do it...

The following topics will explain how to protect key SCOM features.

### Backing up SCOM features

The following table provides a suggested schedule for periodically backing up key features of your SCOM infrastructure.

| SCOM feature | Backup type |
|---|---|
| Operational database | Daily incremental backup |
| | Weekly full backup |
| Data warehouse database | Weekly incremental backup |
| | Monthly full backup |
| SQL Reporting database | Monthly full backup |
| Audit collection services database | Daily incremental backup |
| | Weekly full backup |
| Master database | Full backup after making any changes to SCOM database features and configurations |
| Msdb database | Full backup after initial installation of SCOM database features |
| | Monthly full backup |
| Custom reports and management packs and files | Daily full backup |

### Monitoring the management group health

The management group health view in SCOM enables you to view the health state of all SCOM management group functions in a single view. As shown in the following screenshot, the view displays the health state of your management servers, resource pools, and SCOM databases.

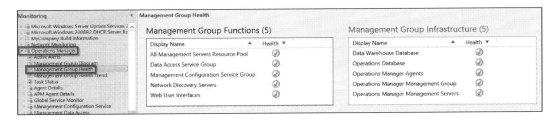

1. Open the SCOM console and click in the **Monitoring** workspace tab.

2. Navigate to the **Operations Manager** folder, expand the folder, and then select the **Management Group Health** view.

## Backing up custom management packs

Backing up your custom management packs ensures that your overrides and custom rules and monitors can be restored in the event of a disaster, with minimal data loss. You can back up (export) an unsealed management pack from the Operations console, or with the use of Windows PowerShell.

### Export custom management packs using the Operations console

To manually export custom management packs, perform the following steps from the Operations console:

1. Log in to a computer that has the Operations console with an account that is a member of the System Center 2012 R2—Operations Manager Administrators role for your SCOM management group.
2. In the Operations console, click **Administration**.
3. In the **Administration** pane, click **Management Packs**.
4. Select your target custom management pack, right-click the custom management pack, and then click **Export Management Pack**.
5. In the resulting **Save As** dialog box, enter the path and file name for the management pack file and click **Save**.

## Export unsealed management packs using Windows PowerShell

Run the following script, which accepts a management server name parameter. The script imports the Operations Manager PowerShell module so you can run it from a standard PowerShell environment.

```
param ($MgmtServer)
$Server = $MgmtServer
Ipmo OperationsManager
Get-SCOMManagementGroupConnection -ComputerName $Server | Set-
SCOMManagementGroupConnection
$CustomMps = Get-SCOMManagementPack | Where {$_.Sealed -eq $False}
foreach ($mp in $CustomMps)
{
Export-SCOMManagementPack -ManagementPack $mp -path "C:\SCOMBackups"
}
```

```
CustomMPExport.ps1  X
1    param ($MgmtServer)
2    $Server = $MgmtServer
3    Ipmo OperationsManager
4    Get-SCOMManagementGroupConnection -ComputerName $Server | Set-SCOMManagementGroupConnection
5    $CustomMps = Get-SCOMManagementPack | Where {$_.Sealed -eq $False}
6    foreach ($mp in $CustomMps)
7    {
8        Export-SCOMManagementPack -ManagementPack $mp -path "C:\SCOMBackups"
9    }
```

From a PowerShell prompt, type the following and enter the name of a management server for the MgmtServer parameter:

```
\CustomMPExport.ps1 -MgmtServer: <ComputerName>
```

## Update management packs

Updating your management packs will enable you to benefit from any additional monitoring functionality that's built into the updates. You can update your management packs by downloading updates available for installed management packs directly from the Operations console, or by downloading management pack updates from the System Center Marketplace.

## Review Imported Management packs in SCOM

To review imported management packs in SCOM, perform the following steps:

1.  Log in to a computer that has the Operations console with an account that is a member of the System Center 2012 R2 Operations Manager Administrators role for your SCOM management group.

2.  In the Operations console, click **Administration**.

3.  In the **Administration** pane, click **Management Packs**.

4.  Select a management pack and take note of the version number as shown in the following screenshot :

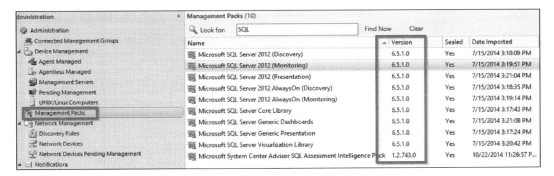

## Check for updates to management packs

After you note the version number(s) of your installed management pack(s), you can check for management pack updates directly from the Operations console or in the System Center Marketplace. To check for updates to installed management packs, perform the following steps:

1.  Log in to a computer that has the Operations Console with an account that is a member of the System Center 2012 R2—Operations Manager Administrators role for your SCOM management group.

2.  In the Operations console, click **Administration**.

3. In the **Administration** pane, click **Management Packs**, and right-click and select **Download Management Packs**.

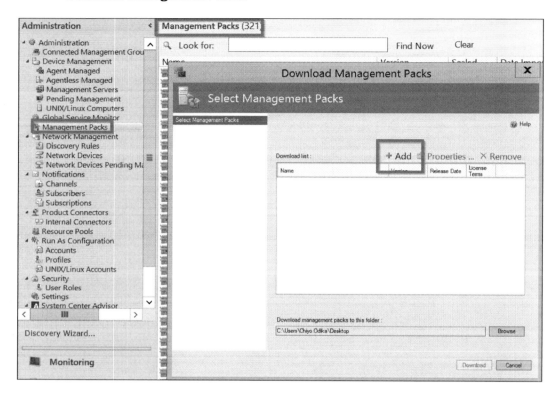

4. On the **Download Management Packs** window, click **Add**, click the **View** dropdown, select **Updates available for installed management packs**, and then click **Search** to find updates for any installed management packs with updates.

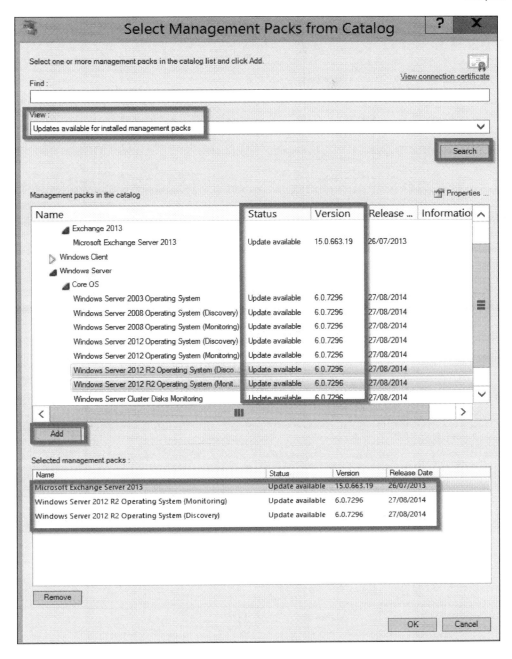

5. In the **Management packs in the catalog** field, select your management pack update(s), click **Add**, and then click **OK** to select and download the management pack update.

In some cases, management pack updates will not be available for download in the catalog and will have to be downloaded from the System Center Marketplace. To download management packs from the System Center Marketplace, perform the following steps:

1.  Open a web browser and navigate to the Microsoft Pinpoint System Center Market place (`http://go.microsoft.com/fwlink/?LinkId=82105`).

2.  Use the **Search Applications** field to locate the management pack that you would like to download.

3.  Review the details page of the management pack and take note of the management pack version and published date.

4.  Compare the management pack version with the version of the management pack you have installed in SCOM.

5.  Click the management pack you would like to download and click **Download** on the details page for the management pack.

6.  Select the download link for the management pack file and the management pack guide then click **Download** on the management pack download page.

7.  In the **File Download** dialog box, click **Save** to download the files without extracting the `.msi` files or **Run** to download and extract the management pack files.

## How it works...

Backing up key SCOM features is very important because SCOM does not include backup processes or tasks out of the box. It is important to closely follow the recommended backup schedule in the table covered previously so as to minimize data loss in the event of a failure of any of the key features of your SCOM infrastructure. The operational database is the most important database to back up, so having a daily backup for this database and other critical files that change often ensures that, in the event of a catastrophic failure, you will not lose data for more than 24 hours.

## There's more...

When downloading management packs, endeavor to download any available management pack guides along with the `.msi` files for the management pack. A best practice is to thoroughly review the management pack guides before importing the management pack into SCOM. Management pack guides provide detailed information about the features of the management pack, including but not limited to management pack object discoveries, attributes, monitors and rules, as well as run-as account and other configuration information. This information will enable you to better understand how the management pack works and what it can actually do for you.

Management pack guides are available when you download the management packs from the online catalog at the **Microsoft Download Center**, but are not available when you import management packs directly from the catalog in SCOM, so the former method of obtaining management packs is the recommended approach.

## See also

The following are useful links to information related to recommended tasks in System Center 2012 R2 Operations Manager:

▶ Microsoft TechNet—Complete and Incremental Backups in Operations Manager: `http://technet.microsoft.com/en-us/library/hh278857.aspx`

▶ Microsoft TechNet—How to Import an Operations Manager Management Pack: `http://technet.microsoft.com/en-us/library/hh212691.aspx`

▶ Microsoft TechNet—Microsoft Management Packs: `http://social.technet.microsoft.com/wiki/contents/articles/16174.microsoft-management-packs.aspx?PageIndex=4`

# Maintaining and grooming the SCOM databases

Managing data retention for your SCOM databases is strongly recommended for maintaining your SCOM databases. Data retention affects the size of your databases and can consequently also affect the performance of your databases. It is therefore important to ensure that your data retention settings are properly configured for your environment. SCOM has built-in grooming processes and rules that remove unnecessary data from the Operations Manager database in order to maintain performance. For each data type in the operational database, you can specify how much time will elapse before the data gets deleted. The SCOM Operations Console allows you to modify the retention settings for each data type in the operational database. The SCOM Operations console does not however provide a means for modifying the data retention settings for your data warehouse database. To modify the data retention settings for the SCOM data warehouse, you will need to edit specific tables inside the SCOM data warehouse database, or use the **Data Warehouse Data Retention Policy** (`dwdatarp.exe`) command-line tool.

## Getting ready

To make changes to the data retention settings in the SCOM Operations console, you will need to log in to a computer that has the Operations console, using an account that is a member of the Operations Manager Administrators user role for your Operations Manager 2012 R2 management group.

The server with `dwdatarp.exe` installed must have access to the **OperationsManagerDW** along with the user running the tool.

## How to do it...

You can groom the operational database and reporting data warehouse database in a number of ways, including manually, from the Operations console and SQL Management studio, respectively, and using PowerShell and the **DWDATARP** utility.

## Grooming the Operational database

The operational database can be groomed either manually from the Operations console, or with PowerShell.

### Manually Groom the Operational database

To manually modify data retention settings for the SCOM operational database, perform the following steps:

1.  Log in to a computer that has the Operations console with an account that is a member of the System Center 2012 R2 Operations Manager Administrators role for your SCOM management group.

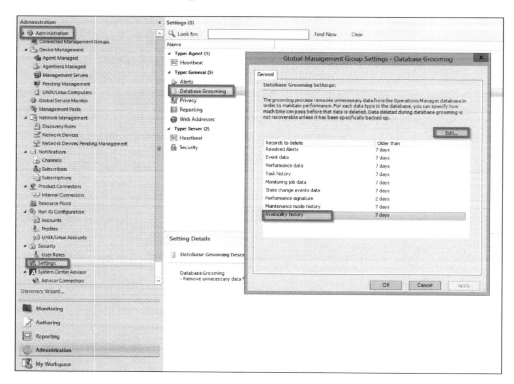

2.  In the **Operations Console**, click **Administration**.

3.  In the navigation pane, expand **Administration** and then click on **Settings**.

4. In the **Settings** pane, right-click **Database Grooming** and click on **Properties**.

5. In the **Global Management Group Settings – Database Grooming** dialog box, select a **Records to delete** type and then click on **Edit**.

6. In the dialog box for the selected **Records to delete** type, specify **Older than** days and click on **OK**.

7. Repeat the preceding steps for any other record type you would like to modify.

## Groom the SCOM Operational database using PowerShell

To modify data retention settings for the SCOM Operational database using PowerShell, you will need to make use of the `Set-SCOMDatabaseGroomingSetting` cmdlet. This cmdlet accepts integer values (bytes) for parameters that correspond to the records to delete data for each data type in the Operational database. The following are examples of how to modify retention settings using PowerShell:

```
#set the number of days before grooming resolved alerts to 5 days
Set-SCOMDatabaseGroomingSetting -AlertDaysToKeep 5

#set the number of days before grooming availability history to 10
days
Set-SCOMDatabaseGroomingSetting –AvailabilityHistoryDaysToKeep 10

# set the number of days before grooming state change data to 4 days
Set-SCOMDatabaseGroomingSetting -StateChangeEventDaysToKeep 4

# set the number of days before grooming maintenance mode history to 5
days
Set-SCOMDatabaseGroomingSetting -MaintenanceModeHistoryDaysToKeep 5

# set the number of days before grooming event data to 8 days
Set-SCOMDatabaseGroomingSetting -EventDaysToKeep 8

# set the number of days before grooming monitoring job data to 6 days
Set-SCOMDatabaseGroomingSetting -MonitoringJobDaysToKeep 6

# set the number of days before grooming task history to 5 days
Set-SCOMDatabaseGroomingSetting -JobStatusDaysToKeep 5

# set the number of days before grooming performance data to 5 days
Set-SCOMDatabaseGroomingSetting -PerformanceDataDaysToKeep 5
```

## Grooming and retention in the SCOM data warehouse

You can view the grooming settings for your reporting data warehouse in SQL Server Management Studio.

To view grooming settings for your reporting data warehouse datasets:

1. Open **Microsoft SQL Server Management Studio** for the supported version of SQL.

2. In the **Connect to Server** dialog box, from the **Server Type** list, select **Database Engine**. Then, from the **Server Name** list, select the server and instance for your data warehouse (that is, Computer\INSTANCE NAME). From the **Authentication** list, select **Windows Authentication** and click on **Connect**.

3. In the **Object Explorer** pane, expand **Databases**, select and right-click your reporting data warehouse database (default name is **OperationsManagerDW**)| select **New Query**, and run the following query:

```
SELECT DataSetDefaultName,
AggregationTypeId,
MaxDataAgeDays,
GroomingIntervalMinutes
FROM StandardDatasetAggregation sda
INNER JOIN dataset ds on ds.datasetid = sda.datasetid
ORDER BY DataSetDefaultName
```

| | DataSetDefaultName | AggregationTypeId | MaxDataAgeDays | GroomingIntervalMinutes |
|---|---|---|---|---|
| 1 | Alert data set | 0 | 400 | 240 |
| 2 | Client Monitoring data set | 0 | 30 | 240 |
| 3 | Client Monitoring data set | 30 | 400 | 240 |
| 4 | DPM event dataset | 0 | 400 | 240 |
| 5 | Event data set | 0 | 100 | 240 |
| 6 | Performance data set | 0 | 10 | 240 |
| 7 | Performance data set | 20 | 400 | 240 |
| 8 | Performance data set | 30 | 400 | 240 |
| 9 | State data set | 0 | 180 | 60 |
| 10 | State data set | 20 | 400 | 60 |
| 11 | State data set | 30 | 400 | 60 |

Your output should look like the preceding figure, and will give you some insight into the dataset retention values in your data warehouse's **StandardDatasetAggregation** table.

To modify data retention for the SCOM data warehouse database, make use of the `dwdatatarp.exe` command-line tool.

## Using DWDATARP.EXE

DWDATARP is a tool that enables you to view and configure the data warehouse retention policies configured within the Operations Manager DW database.

## To view current data retention settings

1.  Open a command prompt with elevated privileges.

2.  Run the following:

```
C:\dwdatarp> dwdatarp.exe -s "data warehouse servername" -d
"data warehouse databasename"
```

## To set data retention for a specific dataset

1.  Open a command prompt with elevated privileges.

2.  Run the following:

```
C:\dwdatarp> dwdatarp.exe -s "data warehouse servername"
-d "data warehouse databasename" -ds "dataset name" -a
"aggregation name" -m "days"
```

## How it works...

Out of the box, SCOM 2012 R2 includes rules that execute tasks and jobs that groom and optimize the SCOM operational database and the reporting data warehouse to keep them consistent.

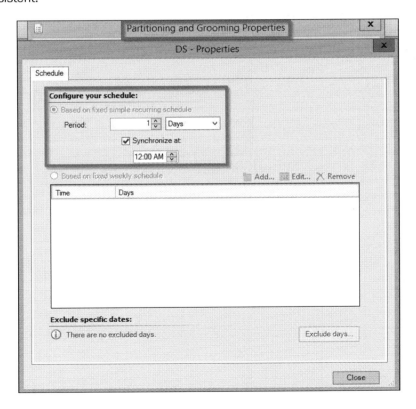

The **Partitioning and Grooming** rule runs a workflow to partition and groom the operational database. This rule executes once a day at **12** am, and it calls the p_ PartitioningAndGrooming stored procedure, which has a schema-bound dependency on the p_Partitioning and the p_Grooming stored procedures.

The **Optimize Indexes** rule calls a stored procedure that reindexes some operational database tables by default.

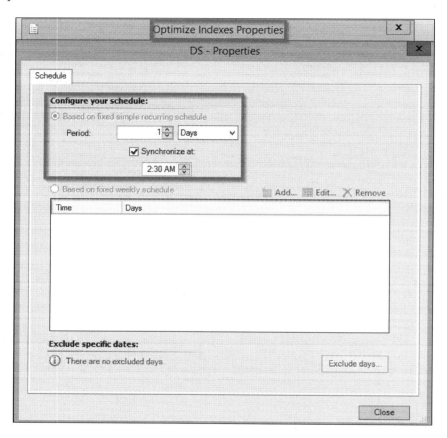

This rule runs daily at **2:30** am and calls the p_OptimizeIndexes stored procedure, which in turn calls the DomainTableIndexOptimize and p_ IncrementalPopulateDomainTable stored procedures which handle index operations. These sprocs affect the DomainTableIndexOptimizationHistory table and call the DomainTableRegisterIndexOPtimization stored procedure respectively.

The **Standard Data Warehouse Data Set maintenance rule properties** runs every 60 seconds by default. This rule calls the StandardDatasetOptimize stored procedure which in turn calls various other sprocs that perform indexing and optimization operations against the reporting data warehouse database.

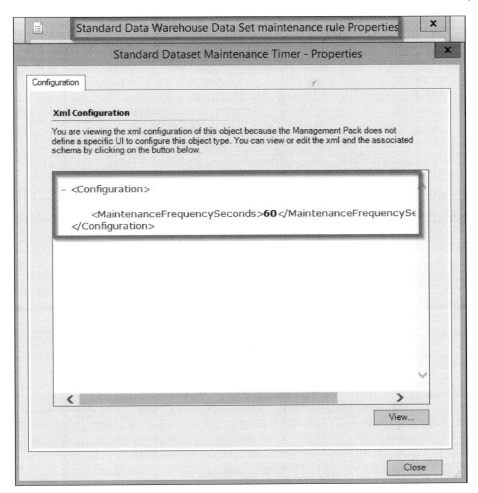

## There's more...

It's important to take note of the times during which the default grooming and maintenance jobs run against the SCOM operational database. Ensure that any other custom maintenance tasks are set to run outside these windows so that the jobs can run successfully on a daily basis to keep the databases consistent. While these rules can be overridden, refrain from making any changes to the default settings of the maintenance rules, as this could adversely affect the overall health and consistency of your databases. The rules will run at the specified times in your management group, based on your management servers' times.

While the default settings for the rules are ideal, the default data warehouse retention settings might not necessarily be relevant for your environment and should therefore be reviewed and modified if necessary. Review the default retention settings for your reporting data warehouse datasets with management and determine if the defaults should be changed to get the most out of your storage. Such a review will result in significant cost savings and more efficient utilization of the data warehouse, which can grow to become very large overtime. Use the `dwdatarp.exe` command-line tool to make any modifications to your dataset's retention settings. Refer to the *How to do it...* section of this recipe.

## See also

The following are useful links to information related to maintaining System Center 2012 R2 Operations Manager:

- ▸ Microsoft TechNet—How to Configure Grooming Settings for Operations Manager: `http://technet.microsoft.com/en-us/library/hh230753.aspx`
- ▸ Microsoft TechNet—Data Warehouse Data Retention Policy (`dwdatarp.exe`) tool: `http://blogs.technet.com/b/momteam/archive/2008/05/14/data-warehouse-data-retention-policy-dwdatarp-exe.aspx`

# Recovering Operations Manager

In the event of a failure or disaster that affects SCOM, you need to have a plan in place to recover SCOM and to minimize data loss due to the disaster. This requires you to have a well-documented **Disaster Recovery (DR)** plan. Because your backup strategy is an integral part of any DR plan, thoroughly review the recipe in this chapter on *Running daily, weekly, and monthly recommended tasks*. Although you may never have to recover from a complete loss of SCOM, your DR plan must have contingencies in place for any failure scenarios including but not limited to a complete loss of SCOM in your infrastructure.

## Getting ready

Review the recipe in this chapter on *Running daily, weekly, and monthly recommended tasks*, and ensure that you have a well-documented backup plan for protecting critical SCOM features. While possible failure scenarios are too many to cover in this recipe, we will review best-practice recommendations for recovering SCOM in the event of a total loss.

For the purpose of illustration, assume the following simplified scenario, and that you experience a total loss of SCOM:

▶ There are two management servers (**Server1** and **Server2**) and a gateway server in the management group

▶ The SCOM SQL instance is not clustered

▶ The operational database is installed on Server1

▶ SCOM web console is installed

▶ SCOM reporting is installed

▶ ACS is not installed

## How to do it...

The high-level steps for recovering SCOM 2012 R2 include the following:

1. Rebuild your servers in the same domain using the same **NETBIOS** names and install SQL Server and SSRS.

2. Enable the Windows server **Internet Information Services** (**IIS**) feature for the SCOM console and APM websites.

3. Apply security patches and service packs to bring your new installation up to the same level of updates as your original installation.

4. Install SCOM 2012 R2 from the installation media on Server1, using the same management group name, and the same service accounts used in your original SCOM installation.

5. After the installation finishes, stop the SCOM services to prevent any writes to your SCOM databases. You will subsequently be restoring your databases from backup. In the listed order, the following services should be stopped:

| Display Name | Service Name |
|---|---|
| **System Center Management Configuration** | Cshost |
| **Microsoft Monitoring Agent** | HealthService |
| **System Center Data Access Service** | Omsdk |

6. Install any SCOM server update rollups you had in your original installation.

7. Delete the operational database and reporting data warehouse database that were created during the SCOM installation in the fourth step.

8. Restore the latest operational database and reporting data warehouse database you created from your backup.

9. Install and test the SCOM web console.

10. Install the SCOM reporting feature and confirm that reports populate in the reporting workspace in your SCOM console.

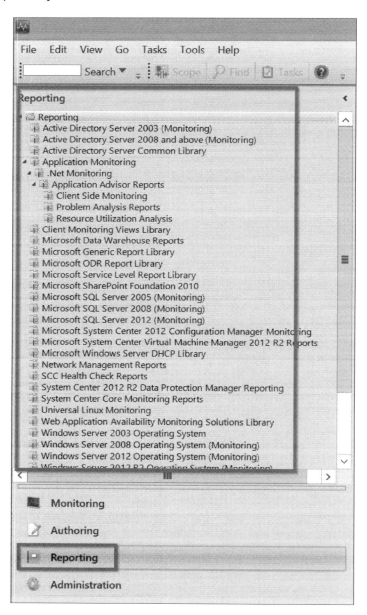

11. Restore the SSRS encryption keys using **SQL Server Reporting Services Configuration Manager**.

12. Restore the IIS metabase.

13. Import custom management packs from backup.

14. Import other management packs and files that changed after your last backup in your original SCOM environment.

15. Start the SCOM services on Server1 in the following order:

| Display Name | Service Name |
|---|---|
| **System Center Data Access Service** | Omsdk |
| **Microsoft Monitoring Agent** | HealthService |
| **System Center Management Configuration** | Cshost |

16. Install SCOM 2012 R2 from the installation media on Server2.

17. Install the gateway server feature from the installation media on your gateway server.

## To restore a database backup

The following steps apply to databases on SQL Server 2012, SQL Server 2012 SP1/2012 SP2, and SQL Server 2014:

1. Open **Microsoft SQL Server Management Studio** for the supported version of SQL.

2. In the **Connect to Server** dialog box, in the **Server Type** list, select **Database Engine**. Then, from the **Server Name** list, select the server and instance for your data warehouse (that is, Computer\INSTANCE NAME). From the **Authentication** list, select **Windows Authentication** and click on **Connect**.

3. In the **Object Explorer** pane, expand **Databases**, select and right-click your operational database (default name is **OperationsManager**) or your reporting data warehouse database (default name is **OperationsManagerDW**), and then point to **Tasks** and click **Restore**.

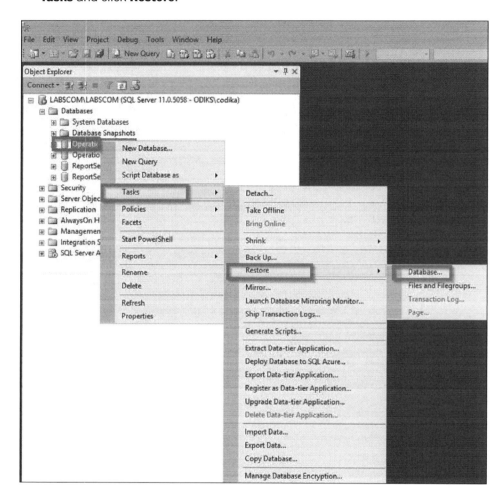

4. Select **Database** from the list of options to open the **Restore Database** dialog box.

5. On the **General** page, check a radio button under **Source** to select either a **Database** or **Device** source.

  ❑ **Database**: Verify the database or select a different database to restore from the drop-down list. The drop-down list will show only databases that have been backed up according to the msdb backup history.

❑ **Device**: Click the browse button to open the **Select backup devices** dialog box. In the **Backup media type** box, select a listed device type and click **Add** to select one or more devices for the **Backup media** box.

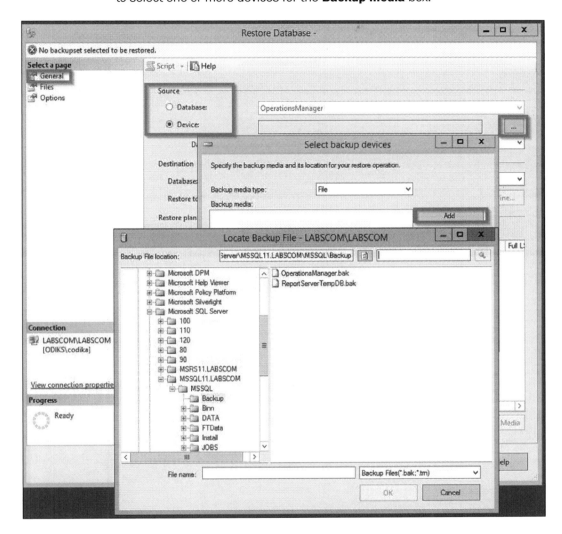

Click **OK** and return to the **General** page.

Select the name of the database which should be restored in the **Source** | **Device** | **Database** list box.

6. In the **Destination** section, the **Database** box is populated automatically with the name of the database to be restored. To change the database, select a different database from the **Destination** | **Database** | **Database** dropdown menu.

7.  In the **Restore to** box, leave the default as **the last backup taken <Date/ time>** or click on **Timeline** to access the **Backup Timeline** dialog box to manually select a different point in time to stop the recovery action.

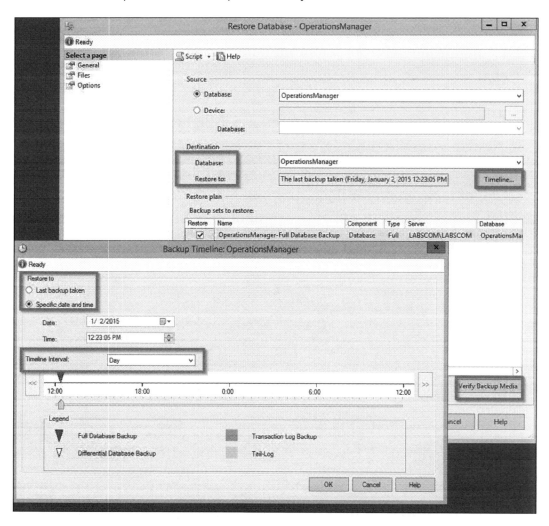

8.  In the grid for **Backup Sets to Restore**, review and leave the default suggested recovery plan, or select the backups to restore and click **OK**.

Assume in the previous management group scenario that Server1 is the first management server in the management group and, by default, the **Root Management Server** (**RMS**) Emulator. In the event that only Server1 fails, and assuming that the operational database is not on Server1, Server2 can be promoted to the RMS Emulator role using PowerShell, and the role can then be transferred back to Server1 after it gets rebuilt. To transfer the RMS Emulator role using PowerShell, use the `Set-SCOMRMSEmulator` cmdlet.

## To recover the RMS Emulator

1.  Open the **Operations Manager Shell** on Server2, or connect to Server2 remotely via PowerShell.

2.  Type the following:

    ```
    Get-SCOMManagementServer —Name "Server2.FQDN" | Set-
    SCOMRMSEmulator
    ```

3.  Confirm your settings by typing the following command:

    ```
    Get-SCOMRMSEmulator
    ```

4.  Build a new server and name it `Server1`.

5.  Install all features to ensure that it meets the minimum supported configurations for SCOM 2012 R2.

6.  Log on to Server1 with an account that has local administrative rights.

7.  Open the command prompt window in elevated mode (**Run as Administrator** option).

8.  Change the path to where the SCOM `setup.exe` file is located and run the following command to install an additional management server in your management group:

    ```
    setup.exe /silent /install /components:OMServer
    /SqlServerInstance: <server\instance>
    /DatabaseName: <OperationalDatabaseName>
    /ActionAccountUser: <domain\username>
    /ActionAccountPassword: <password>
    /DASAccountUser: <domain\username>
    /DASAccontpassword: <password>
    /DataReaderUser: <domain\username>
    /DataReaderPassword: <password>
    /DataWriterUser: <domain\username>
    /DataWriterPassword: <password>
    /EnableErrorReporting: [Never|Queued|Always]
    /SendCEIPReports: [0|1]
    /UseMicrosoftUpdate: [0|1]
    ```

9.  Optionally transfer the SCOM RMS Emulator role back to Server1 with the following command:

    ```
    Get-SCOMManagementServer —Name "Server1.FQDN" | Set-
    SCOMRMSEmulator
    ```

As per best-practice recommendations, the command in the eighth step stated previously specifies that we are using a domain account for the **Data Access service** account and the management server action account, as opposed to using the **Local System** account for these accounts.

### To recover a failed management server using the setup

1. Build a new server, and name it `Server1`.

2. Install all features to ensure that it meets the minimum supported configurations for SCOM 2012 R2.

3. Open a command prompt window in elevated mode (**Run as Administrator**) and run the following command to recover a failed management server in your management group:

```
Setup.exe /silent /AcceptEndUserLicenseAgreement
/recover
/EnableErrorReporting:[Never]
/SendCEIPReports: [0]
/UseMicrosoftUpdate: [1]
/DatabaseName:<OperationalDatabaseName>
/SqlServerInstance:<server\instance>
/DWDatabaseName:<DWDatabaseName>
/DWSqlServerInstance:<server\instance>
/DatareaderUser:<domain\username>
/DatareaderPassword:<password>
/DataWriterUser:<domain\username>
/DataWriterPassword:<password>
/ActionAccountUser:<domain\username>
/ActionAccountPassword:<password>
/DASAccountUser: <domain\username>
/DASAccountPassword: <password>
```

The setup will detect that Server1 was a management server in the management group, and it will recover the management server. The command stated previously assumes that we are specifying a **domain\user** and passwords for the **Data Access Service**, and the management server action account.

## How it works...

Continuing with the simplified failure scenario introduced previously, recovering SCOM in the event of a catastrophic failure or a total loss is fairly straightforward, but the ease of doing this will depend greatly on the quality of your backup sets. The better your backup strategy is, the easier it would be to recover SCOM with minimal data loss. At the risk of repeating this information, it is worth reiterating that backing up the SCOM databases and other important SCOM features will determine whether your recovery process will be relatively easy or unnecessarily arduous.

The SCOM databases, especially the operational database, are the most important SCOM features to back up because they contain all of the operational data, and most customizations collected for your management group. The data held in your databases is unique to your management group, and this is why during the recovery process you will need to use the same management group name so as to be able to make use of the existing data in your databases.

The newly built management servers are named with the same NETBIOS names as your original servers so that any agents that report to the management servers can reconnect to the management servers once you complete the recovery process.

## There's more...

You might want to consider implementing SQL High Availability so as to make your SCOM infrastructure more redundant. See the **Implementing SQL High Availability (HA)** recipe in *Chapter 2, Deploying System Center 2012 R2 Operations Manager*, of this book, for steps on how to configure SQL HA.

Thus far, we have looked at total-loss failure scenarios where your entire SCOM deployment had to be recovered. Other failure scenarios include the loss of a management sever or a gateway server for managing computers that reside outside of your management group's Kerberos realm.

## See also

The following are useful links to information related to recovering System Center 2012 R2 Operations Manager:

- ▶ Microsoft TechNet—Backup and Disaster Recovery in Operations Manager: `http://technet.microsoft.com/en-us/library/hh278864.aspx`
- ▶ Microsoft TechNet—Operations Manager Key Concepts: `http://technet.microsoft.com/en-us/library/hh230741.aspx`

# Updating System Center 2012 R2 Operations Manager

Microsoft periodically releases product updates that are meant to fix issues with the current supported iterations of applications in Microsoft's product ecosystems. The updates are released to address any known issues with the product, and/or improve the functionality of the product. Product updates can be obtained and installed automatically in a variety of ways, including but not limited to automatically through Windows updates, through a software update process using System Center Configuration Manager, manually by, say, downloading and installing the update packages.

This recipe will review product updates for System Center 2012 R2 Operations Manager, and provide best-practice recommendations on how to apply product updates to an SCOM management group(s).

## Getting ready

Perform the following steps with an account that has local administrative privileges to each server in your management group. You must also have access to an account that holds the **System Administrator** (**SA**) role on any SQL instances that host the SCOM databases for your management group(s).

Review the knowledge base (kb) article for the specific update that you would like to apply to your management group(s). This will provide you with detailed information about the key issues that are fixed by the SCOM update.

If you have a tiered management group structure, update the top management group first, and work your way down the group.

In the recommended order, steps for deploying an update to an SCOM 2012 R2 management group are as follows:

1. Automatically or manually install the update rollup files to the following server infrastructure (starting at the top of a tiered management group structure):
   - Management servers
   - Gateway servers
   - Web console servers
   - Operations Console servers
2. Apply SQL Scripts (if any).
3. Manually import the management packs.
4. Update SCOM agents.
5. Update UNIX/ Linux management packs.
6. Update UNIX/ Linux agents.

## How to do it...

Follow these steps to update your SCOM environment.

1. On a management server, navigate to **Start | Control Panel** and click on **Windows Updates**.
2. On the **Windows Update** page, click on **Change Settings**.

3.  On the **Select your Windows Update Settings** page, click on **Microsoft update**, check the **Give me updates for other Microsoft products when I update Windows** checkbox, and then click **OK**.

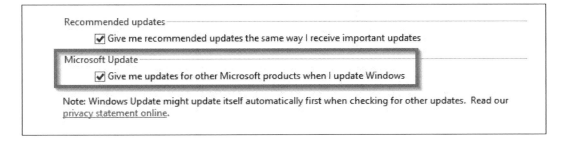

The server will now find and make available any applicable updates.

4.  Review the available updates for SCOM 2012 R2 updates and install them in the recommended order.

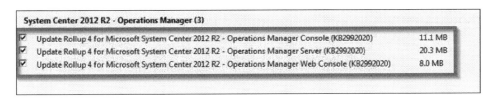

5.  Restart the management server after installing the SCOM 2012 R2 updates.

## Manually download and install SCOM update files

The following steps, apply to databases on SQL Server 2012, SQL Server 2012 SP1 and SQL Server 2012 SP2, and SQL Server 2014:

1.  Navigate to the Kb article page for the specific SCOM 2012 R2 update you would like to apply. At the time of writing this recipe, the Update Rollup 4 (UR4) is the latest update for SCOM 2012 R2. The kb page for this UR version is located at the following link: `https://support.microsoft.com/kb/2992020/en-us`.

2.  Download the update package from the **Microsoft Update Catalog**. The UR4 package for SCOM 2012 R2 is located at the following link: `http://catalog.update.microsoft.com/v7/site/Search.aspx?q=2992020`.

3.  Navigate to the download location for the SCOM updates, and for each of the updates select your server architecture (`amd64`, `i386`, and so on) language, if applicable, right-click and open the update folders, right-click and open the cabinet files, right-click the **Windows Installer patch**, and then select **Extract**.

4.  On the **Select a Destination** window, select a destination to save the **Windows Installer patch** (.msp) file.

5.  Open an elevated command prompt (**Run as Administrator**), then select and run the .msp file for the server, and any other role(s) that are installed on the management server. It's important to follow the recommended order for applying updates to SCOM roles so that the updates can get correctly applied.

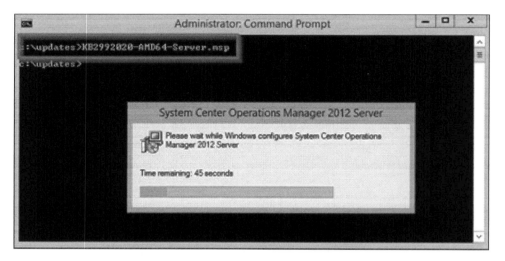

6.  Install the update for any gateway server(s) in your management group.

7.  Install the update for any web console role-holding servers in your management group.

8.  Install the update for any Operations Console role-holding servers in your management group.

9.  In **Windows Explorer,** navigate to %System Drive%:\Program Files\ Microsoft System Center 2012 R2\Operations Manager\Server\SQL Script for Update Rollups and review the Microsoft SQL Server Query files.

10. Select the **update_rollup_mom_db** query file, right-click the file, select **open with**, and then select **SQL Server Management Studio**.

11. In SQL Server Manager Studio, click on the **Available Databases** dropdown, select Operations Manager database (**OperationsManager** is the default name), and then execute the query.

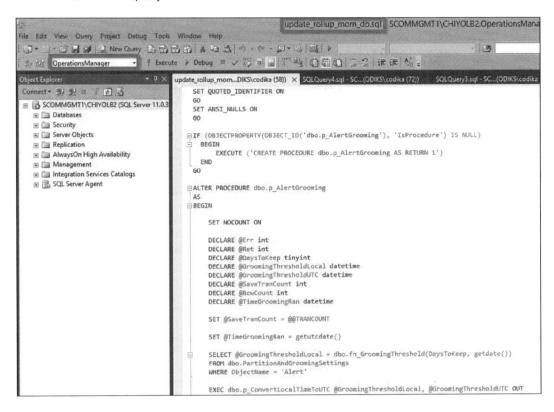

12. Confirm that the query executed successfully without any errors.

13. In Windows Explorer, navigate to `%System Drive%:\Program Files\Microsoft System Center 2012 R2\Operations Manager\Server\SQL Script for Update Rollups`, select the **UR_Datawarehouse** query file, right-click the file, select **open with**, and then select **SQL Server Management Studio**.

14. In SQL Server Manager Studio, click on the **Available Databases** dropdown, select data warehouse database (**OperationsManagerDW** is the default name), answer yes to the **Inconsistent line Endings** prompt, if you receive this, and then execute the query.

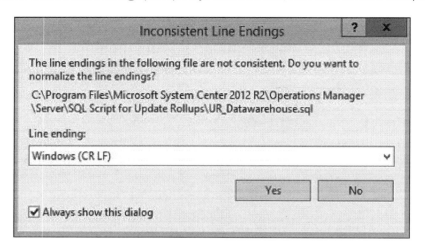

15. Confirm that the query executed successfully without any errors.

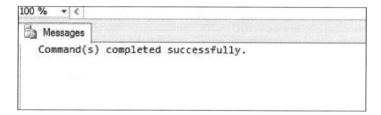

16. In **Windows Explorer**, navigate to `%System Drive%:\Program Files\Microsoft System Center 2012 R2\Operations Manager\Server\Management Packs for Update Rollups`, review the **update rollup management packs**, and then determine which management packs apply to your environment.

17. Log in to a computer that holds the Operations console, using an account that is a member of the Operations Manager Administrators role.

18. In the Operations Console, click **Administration**.

19. Right-click **Management Packs | select Import Management Packs**.

20. In the **Import Management Packs** wizard, click **Add**, click **Add from disk**, and then answer **Yes** in the **Online Catalog Connection** prompt.

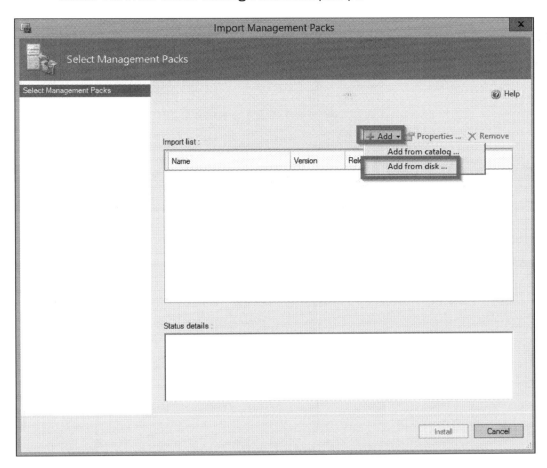

21. On the **Select Management Packs to Import** window, navigate to the location of your **Management Packs for Update Rollups**, select the management packs that update dashboards (Visualization) and optionally any other management packs for such features as Azure Operational Insights (**System Center Advisor**) and TFS, click **Open** to import the management pack(s) and return to the **Import Management Packs** window.

22. On the **Import Management Packs** window, click **Install** to finish importing the management packs.

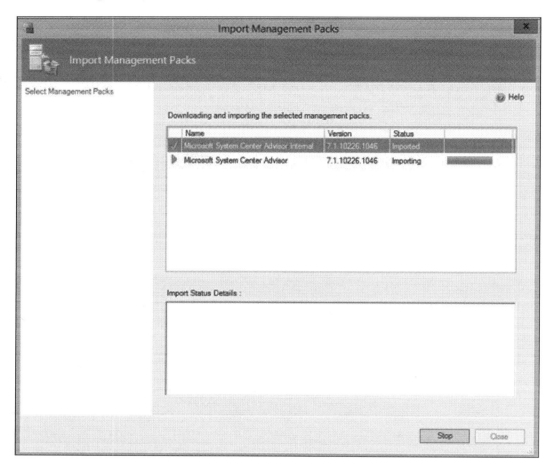

23. In the Operations console, click **Administration**, expand **Device Management**, and then click **Pending Management**.

24. In the **Pending Management** page, select all the agents under **Agents Require Update**, right-click your selection and click on **Approve** to update your agents.

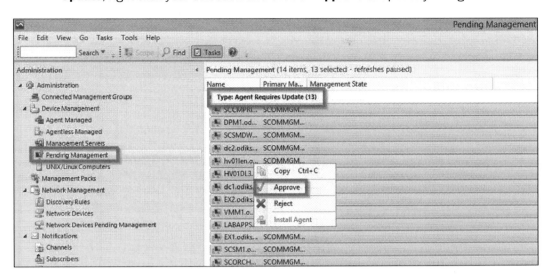

25. In the **Update Agents** dialog box, enter an account that is an administrator on the computers you want to update, then click **Update** to update your agents. This will open the **Agent Management Task Status** window.

26. Optionally, review the progress of your agent updates in the **Agent Management Task Status** window or click **Close** to exit this window.

## How it works...

If a connected management group or tiering is enabled in your SCOM environment, the updates should be applied to the top tier of the connected management group and/or tier and subsequently to the other management groups and/or tiers in your SCOM environment. Unlike in SCOM 2007 where updates had to be applied to servers, relative to the RMS role holding server, in SCOM 2012 R2, management server updates can be applied to management servers in any order and regardless of which server holds the Root Management Server Emulator (RMSE) role. This is because of the fundamentally different way in which SCOM 2012 and later iterations of the product differ from SCOM 2007 and/or 2007 R2. The introduction of the resource pooling concept in SCOM 2012 as a management group services' high-availability feature diminished the need for the RMS, with support for legacy products and SCOM features now assumed by the RMSE in SCOM 2012 and later versions of the product.

Running the update msp files will apply the updates for the specific SCOM role and automatically restart the SCOM services if this is necessary. The msp files will also generate the update management packs and the update rollup SQL scripts. The SQL scripts must be executed against the appropriate SCOM database. The scripts update the SCOM operational and reporting data warehouse databases, respectively. The management packs update existing management packs or enable additional SCOM functionality. Such functionality could include improved cross-platform monitoring, an added dashboard visualization feature, and so on. Review each update management pack to determine if you need it in your SCOM environment before importing it.

After the server updates are applied, SCOM will place the SCOM agents into a pending action state, indicating that they need to be updated to be made consistent with the new update in the SCOM management group. Agents that were manually installed will not be placed into a pending updates state, and will need to be manually updated. This should be done locally on the agent machine, using the specific windows installer patch file (.msp) for the SCOM agent.

## See also

The following are useful links to information related to Updating System Center 2012 R2 Operations Manager:

- Microsoft TechNet—Update Rollup 1 for System Center 2012 R2 Operations Manager: `http://support.microsoft.com/kb/2904678/en-us`

- Microsoft TechNet—Update Rollup 2 for System Center 2012 R2 Operations Manager: `http://support.microsoft.com/kb/2929891`

- Microsoft TechNet—Update Rollup 3 for System Center 2012 R2 Operations Manager: `http://support.microsoft.com/kb/2965445`

- Microsoft TechNet—Update Rollup 4 for System Center 2012 R2 Operations Manager: `https://support.microsoft.com/kb/2992020/en-us`

- Microsoft TechNet—Operations Manager Key Concepts: `http://technet.microsoft.com/en-us/library/hh230741.aspx`

# Optimizing for scale and performance

Out of the box, the default settings in SCOM 2012 R2 will work for most environments. In very large environments, however, certain optimization changes could be made to the SCOM configuration to augment any benefits that stem from a good, and "well-thought-out design." Review *Chapter 1, Architecting System Center 2012 R2 Operations Manager* of this title for best-practice guidelines on architecting and designing SCOM 2012 R2. Note the emphasis on good design. While the design of your SCOM environment is not the be-all and end-all of performance optimization, it is the foundation upon which you will build out your SCOM infrastructure, and as such, it must be formidable. In designing your SCOM infrastructure, make sure to incorporate best-practice recommendations for high availability and database hardware into your design. Poorly configured SCOM databases can hamper performance over time, and in larger environments, performance issues will become noticeable fairly quickly. The management group resource pooling concept introduced in SCOM 2012 provides many benefits that should be taken into account when designing any SCOM environment, regardless of the size. For instance, at a minimum, a management group should have at least two management servers to provide some level of redundancy. Also consider taking advantage of the HA features for Microsoft SQL Server. With these in mind, you can scale your SCOM infrastructure to monitor all environment types from small, single-site environments to environments that span multiple continents around the world, whether on premise, cloud-based, or hybrid.

## Getting ready

Review *Chapter 1, Architecting System Center 2012 R2 Operations Manager, Chapter 2, Deploying System Center 2012 R2 Operations Manager*, the *Configuring Resource Pools* recipe in *Chapter 3, Configuring System Center 2012 R2 Operations Manager*, and the *Implementing Tuning and Best Practice Recommendations* recipe in *Chapter 4, Operating System Center 2012 R2 Operations Manager*, of this book.

Some of the steps in this recipe will require you to be a local administrator on the management servers in your SCOM management group. You will need to log in to a computer that has the Operations Console, using an account that is a member of the Operations Manager Advanced Operator or the Operations Manager Administrators user role for your Operations Manager 2012 R2 management group.

## How to do it...

Consider the following to optimize SCOM for scale and performance:

 ▶ A great SCOM deployment starts with a great design. Design your SCOM environment according to best practices, and account for future growth to enable you to scale seamlessly if and when the need arises. Pay close attention to the supported configurations for SCOM 2012 R2 and the monitored item capacity when designing your environment.

▶ Use fast SQL disks for better database performance. Your SQL design is integral to performance optimization because all management group data stems from, and is written to, a SQL server and hence the operational database can hamper performance. The performance of your SCOM environment depends in large part on how much disk-level I/O your SQL server is capable of.

▶ Management servers that comprise a SCOM resource pool require very low latency for heartbeat detection. You must therefore endeavor to place your management servers on the same LAN segment, or as close as possible to the SCOM databases. This is a fundamentally important design principle in SCOM.

▶ Incorporate high availability into your design using the various options for SQL server, the SCOM consoles (web consoles and the Data Access Service), and resource pools.

▶ Use and configure resource pools strategically. Resource pools that are properly configured can have a significant impact on performance in your SCOM environment. Make good use of the resource pools by having at least two management servers, even in a small environment.

▶ Deploy gateway servers according to best practices, and only when they are needed. Gateways are not meant to be used in lieu of management servers.

▶ Frequently review the management group data volume generated by management packs and SCOM workflows.

▶ Update your environment, implement tuning best practices, and identify and remediate performance issues that could be caused by event collection, configuration churn, performance data collection, and alerts in SCOM.

▶ While SCOM's default settings are sufficient for most environments, you can score additional performance gains when monitoring "very large" environments, by changing certain registry settings on your management servers and rules in SCOM. While "large" can be a very relative term, it is used in this context to refer to a management group supporting any of the following:

  ❑ Over 1000 UNIX/ Linux computers

  ❑ Over 3000 Windows computers

  ❑ Over 8000 URLs

  ❑ Over 1500 network devices

The following settings should be applied in very large SCOM environments only.

## To add new optimization subkeys to the SCOM registry

1. Open a command prompt on a management server in elevated mode (**Run as Administrator**).

2. Run the following commands:

```
reg add "HKLM\SOFTWARE\Microsoft\Microsoft Operations Manager\3.0"
/v "GroupCalcPollingIntervalMilliseconds" /t REG_DWORD /d 600000
/f
```

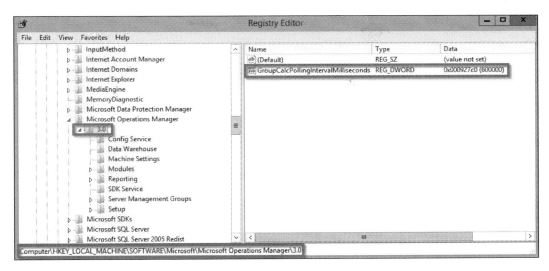

3. Also continue with:

```
reg add "HKLM\SOFTWARE\Microsoft\Microsoft Operations Manager\3.0\
Data Warehouse" /v "Command Timeout Seconds" /t REG_DWORD /d 1200
/f
```

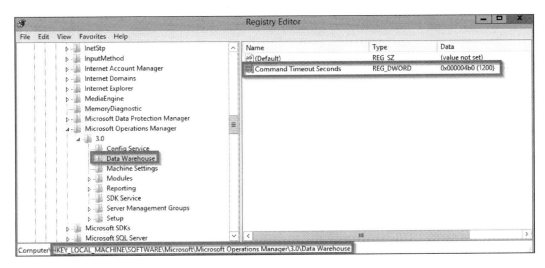

## To override data warehouse synchronization and deployment rules

1. Log in to the Operations console role computer, then click on **Authoring**.

2. In the **Authoring** workspace, expand **Management Pack Objects** and then click **Rules**.

3.  In the Rules pane, click on the **Find** icon in the Operations console toolbar. In the **Look for:** text box, type in the data warehouse monitor initial state synchronization rule, and then select the rule.

4.  On the Operations console toolbar, click **Overrides**, point to **Override the Rule | For all objects of class: Data Warehouse Synchronization Server**.

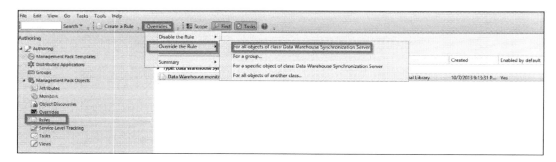

5.  Proceed to override the **Batch Generation Frequency Seconds** and **Batch Size** parameters from the default values of **30** and **100** to **300** and **1000**, respectively.

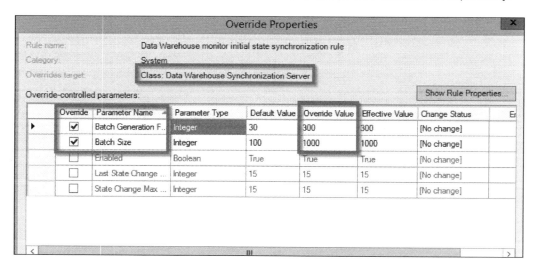

6. Repeat this procedure for the following synchronization and deployment rules, overriding the parameters listed in the following table from the default values to the listed override values:

| Rule name | Override parameter | Default value | Override value |
|---|---|---|---|
| Data Warehouse object synchronization rule | Batch Generation Frequency Seconds | 30 | 300 |
| Data Warehouse object synchronization rule | Batch Size | 100 | 1000 |
| Data Warehouse Relationship Synchronization Rule | Batch Generation Frequency Seconds | 30 | 300 |
| Data Warehouse Relationship Synchronization Rule | Batch Size | 100 | 1000 |
| Data Warehouse Managed object type synchronization rule | Batch Generation Frequency Seconds | 30 | 300 |
| Data Warehouse Managed object type synchronization rule | Batch Size | 100 | 1000 |

## How it works...

Properly sizing your SCOM environment, and taking future growth into account, will enable you to scale your environment seamlessly. Incorporating high availability into your design will provide you with such benefits as redundancy and separation of workloads using resource pools. Resource pools that are properly configured can have a significant impact on performance in your SCOM environment. When two or more management servers are added to an SCOM management group, the management servers form part of a resource pool and work is spread across the pool members. Hence, when a new management server is added to the resource pool, the management server will pick up some of the work from the existing management servers in the resource pool. When a pool member fails or becomes unavailable, the other pool members will pick up that member's workload. Now consider the implications of such a feature for a very large SCOM environment. You can use resource pools to demarcate specific workloads and assign workflows in a highly available manner in your SCOM environment.

Frequently reviewing the management group data volume generated by management packs and SCOM workflows will enable you to determine what management packs, workflows, and instances have the greatest impact against your operational database.

In very large environments, the default values for such settings as **GroupCalcPollingIntervalMilliseconds** and the **Command Timeout Seconds**, which respectively manage the frequency of group membership detection and the frequency of dataset maintenance can have an adverse impact on the SCOM database, and so the registry changes slow down the frequency to improve performance.

## See also

The following is a useful link related to information on optimizing System Center 2012 R2 Operations Manager for scale and performance:

> ▸ Microsoft TechNet—Preparing your environment for System Center 2012 R2 Operations Manager: `http://technet.microsoft.com/en-us/library/dn249696.aspx`.

# 6

# Monitoring Applications and IT Services with System Center 2012 R2 Operations Manager

In this chapter, we will be providing recipes for how to monitor applications across different platforms within your environment using System Center 2012 R2 Operations Manager. These recipes will cover topics such as:

- ▶ Creating a distributed application from a template
- ▶ Creating a custom distributed application
- ▶ Monitoring a .NET application
- ▶ Enabling Global Service Monitor

## Introduction

**System Center 2012 R2 Operations Manager** (**SCOM**) forms a foundation for monitoring within a standard Windows infrastructure. However, the flexibility of its extensible design allows you to do much more than basic infrastructure monitoring.

This chapter will delve deeper into the ways in which you can extend SCOM to obtain a deep insight into your locally developed applications and also a visual display of website performance from around the world.

# Creating a distributed application from a template

As you will have seen and understood from previous recipes, SCOM tracks the health and alerts of each agent on the agent itself. This allows for excellent scaling characteristics and enables one to really focus on each individual server and its health. However, in the modern IT landscape, the focus is on providing a service to the customer, and the health of a single server does not always adequately reflect the health of the overall service.

In order to achieve this, SCOM allows you to create a distributed application. A distributed application allows you to select and group components together to form a representation of the application, as illustrated by the following example from the Active Directory management pack.

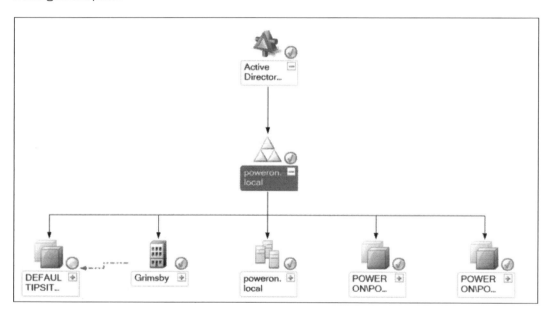

## Getting ready

One of the key first steps in getting ready to create a distributed application is to understand the application itself. You need to understand what it is that makes the application work and what components should impact the availability of the service. This can often be helped by an application diagram.

As an example of how to complete a distributed application, we will be building a representation of the SCOM website. This will use the website held on one of the management servers together with the operations database and the data warehouse database.

The SCOM agent has been installed on the server and all the components have been discovered. A management pack called SCOM Cookbook Management Pack has been created to store the distributed application as described in other recipes.

## How to do it...

To create the distributed application:

1. Open the SCOM console.

2. Navigate to **Authoring | Distributed Applications**.

3. Click on **Create a New Distributed Application** from the **Task** pane.

4. Enter the Name SCOM Website Demo Application and optionally a description. Choose the **Line of Business Web Application** template and the **SCOM Cookbook Management Pack**. Click **OK** to continue.

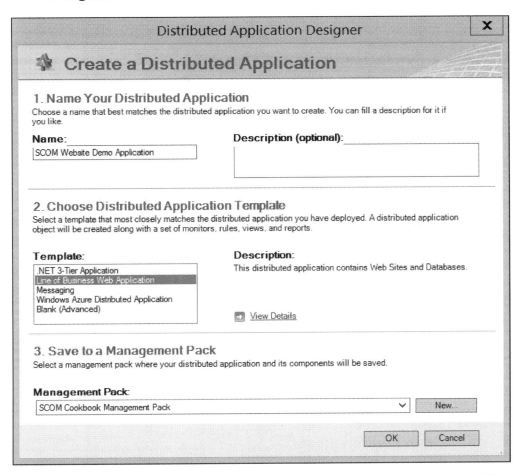

5. In the object types on the left-hand side, find the **Database** type and select it to display the list of databases. Choose the **OperationsManager** and the **OperationsManagerDW** databases and drag them to the Web Application Database component.

6. In the object types on the left hand side, find the Web Site type and select it to display the list of websites. Choose **Default Web Site** from the relevant management server and drag it to the Web Application Web Sites component.

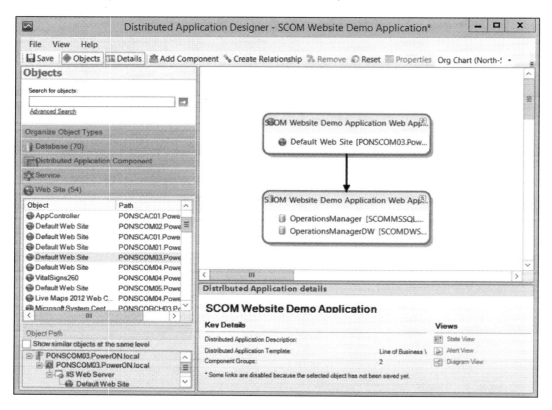

7. Click on **Save** and then close the editor.

8. Navigate to **Monitoring | Distributed Applications**.

9. Select the **SCOM Website Demo Application** distributed application and then choose **Diagram View** from the **Navigation** section of the **Task** pane. You should then see a diagram similar to the following one:

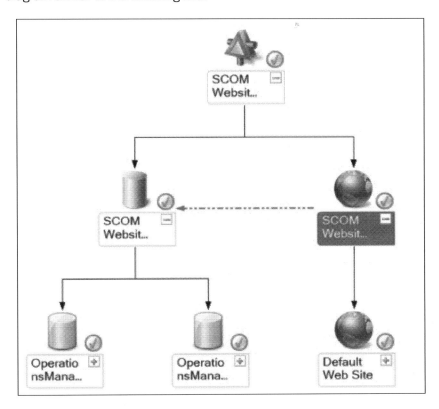

## How it works...

Working from a template can give you good results quickly, provided your application fits with one of the existing templates. From this demonstration, you can see that you can pick specific discovered items from within SCOM and then group them in a manner that works for your application and your service.

The next recipe shows creating a simple application containing computer objects.

## There's more...

By following a template, you can get the key components of your application down quickly, but there will often be additional items that you feel should be included in an application based on a template. You can add components to a diagram based on a built-in template or you can start again with a custom application from scratch.

# Creating a custom distributed application

From the previous recipe, you have seen how quickly and easily you can set up and create a diagram based on a template. When your application does not fit into one of the templates, though, you need to be able to create or add custom components to a diagram to ensure your application is represented properly.

## Getting ready

As with the previous recipe, the fundamental preparation is to understand the application itself. You need to understand what it is that makes the application work and what components should impact the availability of the service.

In this demo application, we will be using our SCOM management group again but, this time, we will be using three management servers and the database server. Because of our resilience, a problem on one of the management servers does not impact the availability of the service overall while a problem with the database server does. This recipe uses generic names for this application to show that it does not just have to be SCOM objects that you include here.

We will be using the SCOM Cookbook Management Pack to store this distributed application; so, if you did not create it for the last recipe, you should do that now.

## How to do it...

To create the distributed application:

1. Open the SCOM console.
2. Navigate to **Authoring | Distributed Applications**.
3. Click on **Create a New Distributed Application** from the **Task** pane.

4.  Enter the Name `Custom Application` and optionally a description. Choose the **Blank (Advanced)** template and the **SCOM Cookbook Management Pack**. Click on **OK** to continue.

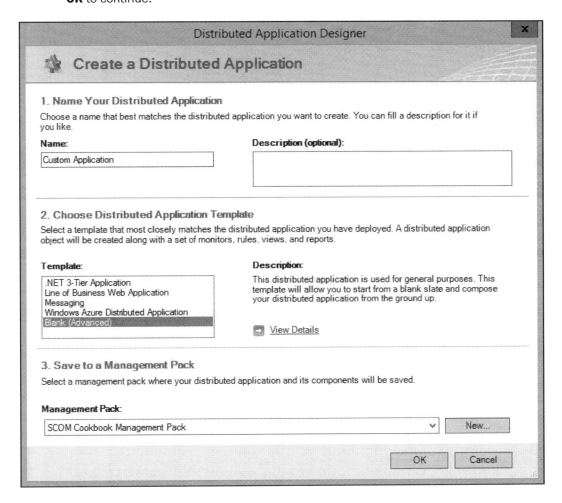

5.  Notice how there are no components created by default. Click on **Add Component**.

6. Enter the name **Application Servers**. Choose the **Objects of the following type(s)** radio button and then navigate to **Object** | **Configuration Item** | **Logical Entity** | **Device** | **Computer** | **Windows Computer** | **Windows Server**. Click on **OK** to continue.

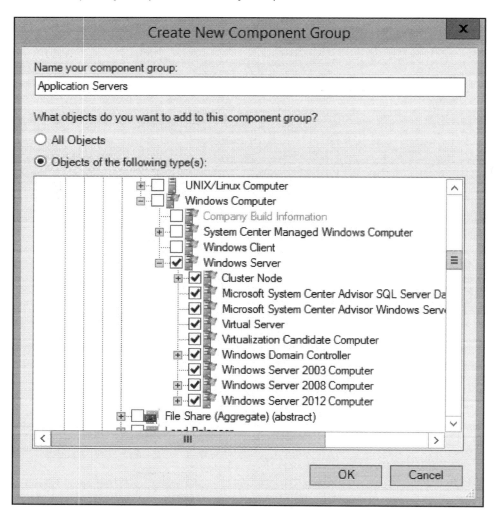

7. Create another group called **Database Server**.

8.   Click on the **Create Relationship** button, click on **Application Servers**, and then click **Database Server**.

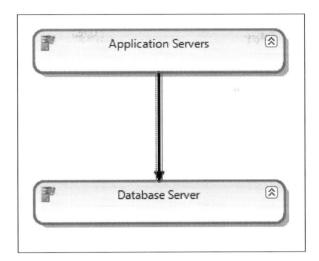

9.   Find three servers to add to **Application Servers** and one server to add to **Database Server**. Drag the servers to the relevant component.

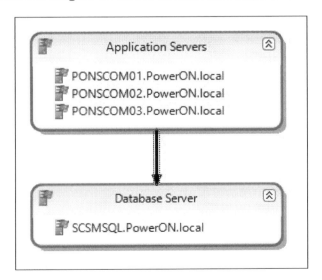

10. Click on **Save**. Once the distributed application has saved, click on **Application Servers** and then click on **Configure Health Rollup - Availability**.

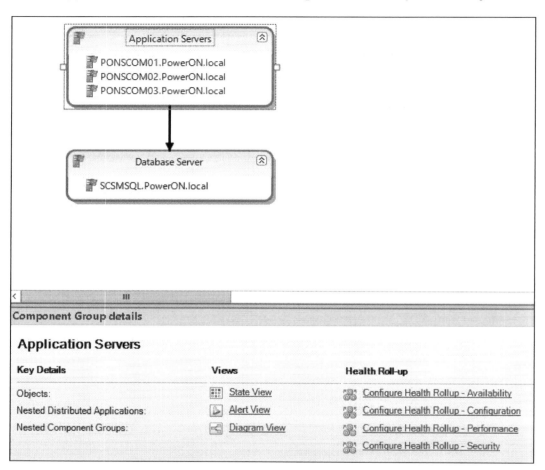

11. On the **Override Properties** window, click on **Rollup Algorithm** and change the override value to `Worst state of a percentage of members in good health state`. Additionally, click on **Percentage** and change the override value to `66`. Click on **OK**. The application may take some time to respond again.

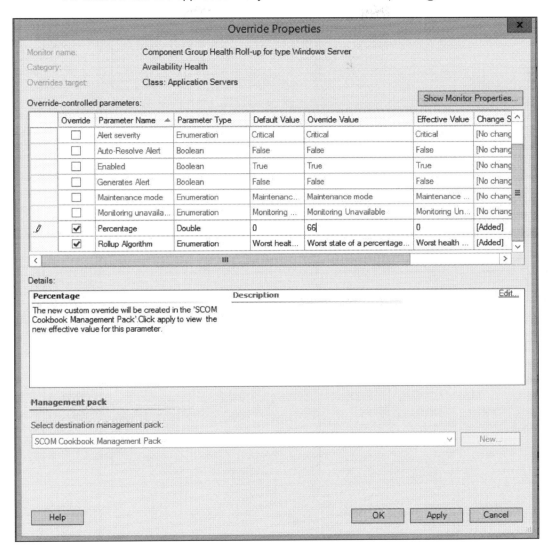

12. Click on **Save** and then exit the editor.

13. Navigate to **Monitoring | Distributed Applications**.

14. Select the **Custom Application** distributed application and then choose **Diagram View** from the **Navigation** section of the **Task** pane. You should then see a diagram similar to the following one:

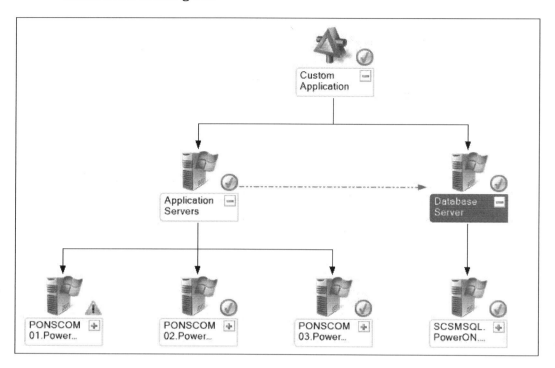

Notice that one of the application servers is showing as unhealthy, but the service overall is still healthy.

## How it works...

In this example, we have an application where we have three application servers of which two need to be healthy in order for the application to work. This was the point of the override we setup where we said we would look at the health of the best 66 percent (in this case the healthy two servers) and return the worst health of these servers, which is green.

If you think back to where we were selecting the components' object types, you will soon realize that we could have chosen any object type defined by SCOM. This makes the custom application extremely powerful, but at the same time quite complex to set up. In most cases, picking up the computer object will give you most of what you need.

## There's more...

It is possible to have large numbers of component groups, but the diagrams that can be generated in the console have all the component groups at the same logical level directly underneath the custom application. This is because the reference we created does not create a hierarchy as it may appear in the distributed application editor. You will notice that some of the distributed applications do have a hierarchy when you view the diagram, but this cannot be implemented in the current version of the console editor.

# Monitoring a .NET application

While some enterprises provide a service directly to consumers using internally developed software, almost all enterprises have some form of internally developed line of business applications. These are often based around the Microsoft .NET framework, but unfortunately monitoring the applications is often not considered during the development cycle.

Fortunately, Microsoft has developed an **Application Performance Monitoring** (**APM**) module within SCOM that allows for deep monitoring of a .NET application without the need for any change to the developed code. The following recipe shows how to enable this monitoring and to start receiving alerts.

## Getting ready

Before you can use the APM module, you will need to install the relevant APM management packs. These can be found on the installation DVD in the `Management Packs` folder. It is particularly important to install the APM Web management pack for your version of IIS.

You will also need to start talking to your internal developers about their application and the monitoring you will be enabling. While the defaults give a reasonable level of alerting without too much noise, this can be further tuned down to individual .NET method calls.

To view all the details of the alerts that are generated, the web console must also be installed as this will enable the viewing of more detailed alert information from the APM module.

As we are running through an example, we will be using the SCOM Cookbook Management Pack as used in previous recipes. If you have not created this already, please do so or substitute your own management pack name.

## How to do it...

First, you need to create a group containing the servers you want to monitor, in the following manner:

1. Open the SCOM console.

2. Navigate to **Authoring | Groups**.

3. Click on **Create a New Group** from the **Task** pane.

4. Enter the name SCOM Cookbook Production Web Servers and a description if desired. Choose the **SCOM Cookbook Management Pack** and click on **Next** to continue.

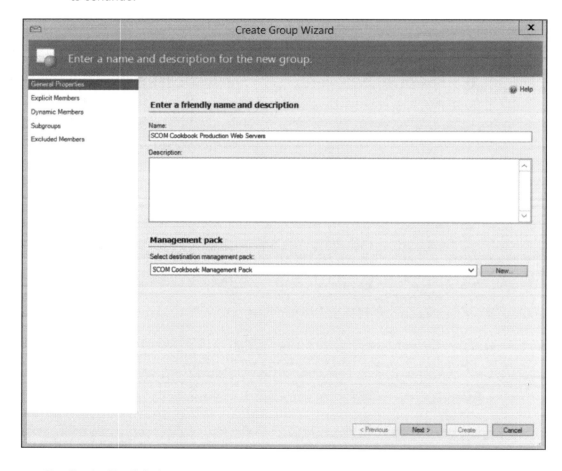

5. On the **Explicit Group Members** page, choose your server(s) and click on **Next** to continue.

6. On the **Dynamic Members** page, click on **Next** to continue.

7. On the **Subgroups** page, click on **Next** to continue.

8. On the **Excluded Members** page, click on **Create** to complete the wizard.

Next, we need to configure the APM itself as follows:

1. Open the SCOM console.

2. Navigate to **Authoring | Management Pack Templates**.

3. Click on **Add Monitoring Wizard** from the **Task** pane.

4. Select **.NET Application Performance Monitoring** from the list and click on **Next** to continue.

5. Enter the name **SCOM Cookbook Web Application** and a description if desired. Choose the **SCOM Cookbook Management Pack** and click on **Next** to continue.

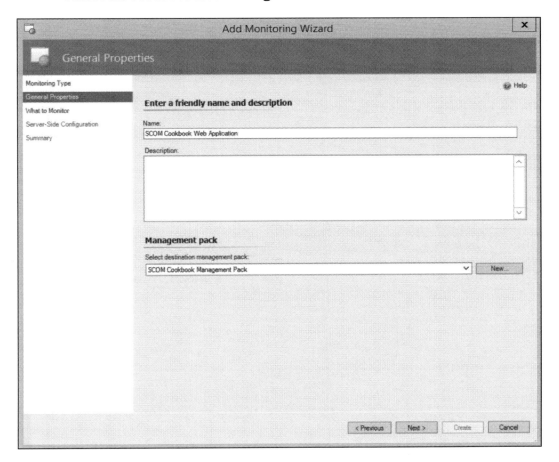

6. On the **Add application components to monitor** page, click on **Add**. On the **Object Search** screen, enter cookbook in the filter and then click on **Search**. Select the application you plan to monitor and click on **Add** and then **OK**. In our example, the application is the **SCOMCookBook** application hosted under the **Default Web Site**, as you can see in the following screenshot:

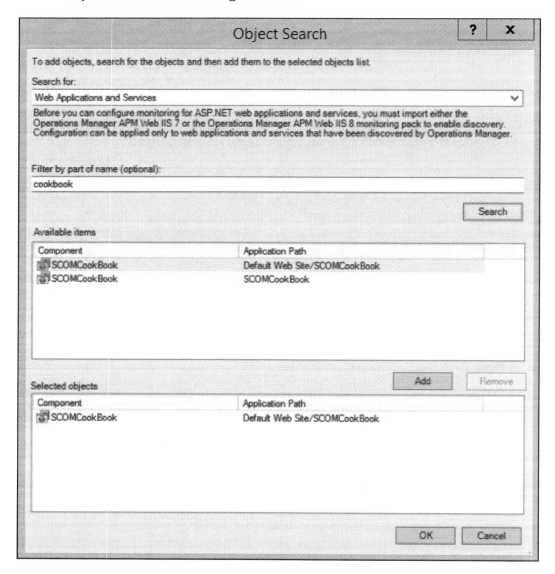

7. Back on the **Add application components to monitor** page, choose the **Production** environment and then choose the **SCOM Cookbook Production Web Servers** group for the **Targeted group**. Click on **Next** to continue.

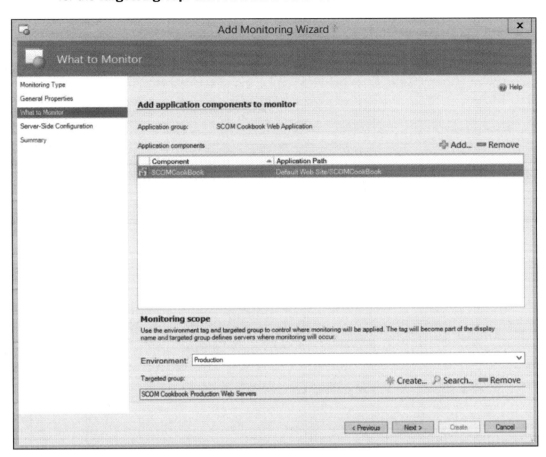

8. On the **Configure the default monitoring settings** page, check the box to **Enable additional configuration options for server-side and client-side monitoring** and then click on **Next** to continue.

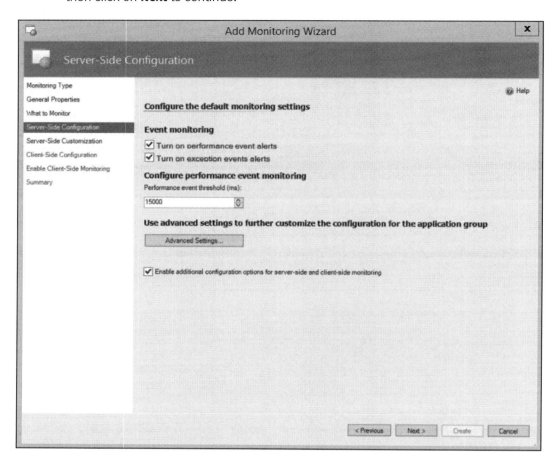

9. On the **Customize monitoring for individual application components** page, click on **Next** to continue.

10. On the **Configure client-side monitoring** page, remove the client IP address filter and then click on **Next** to continue.

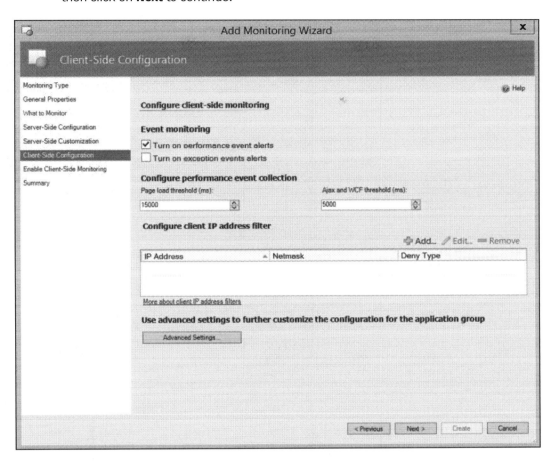

11. On the **Enable client-side monitoring for web applications** page, check the enabled box and then choose the **SCOM Cookbook Production Web Servers** group for the **Targeted group**. Click on **Next** to continue.

12. On the **Summary** page, note the warnings about restarts being needed and then click on **Create**.

13. The monitoring has now been created but it can take some time for the discovery to run. This discovery will then run some monitors that will tell you whether or not IIS needs to be restarted. These appear as warning alerts and have a helpful task associated with them to initiate this restart.

| Ic... | Path | Source | Name | Resolution ... |
|---|---|---|---|---|
| ▲ **Severity: Warning (2)** | | | | |
| ⚠ | SCOMCBSVR02.PowerO... | SCOMCBSVR02.Powe... | IIS Application Pools recycle is required | New |
| ⚠ | SCOMCBSVR02.PowerO... | SCOMCBSVR02.Powe... | IIS Restart is required | New |

Once restarted, your application will be monitored by APM.

## How it works...

APM works on the server side by registering itself at the .NET layer and capturing performance information and exception information as the calls are processed through the stack. This allows it to report on performance and exception data without the developers needing to make any change to the code.

On the client side, it injects JavaScript into the web page at runtime so that the browser returns additional data calls to the website to allow it to report on page load times. Because of this additional web load, it is recommended that, for production monitoring, you customize the settings so only a small percentage of the customers have JavaScript enabled.

## There's more...

The numbers and types of errors will depend very much on the settings you choose and the code behind them. The code will report on the stack involved in the errors and will report down to the line of code that is executed. As the application I am using for this recipe is a test application, it has no database back end but if your application does, it will report down to the level of detail relating to the SQL call and the parameters that are passed to it.

The application that I have used here generates an error that can be displayed if you choose to report on application errors in the Customize Server Side section. This error is caused when you put in a number bigger than can be represented by an integer. This gives the following SCOM alert.

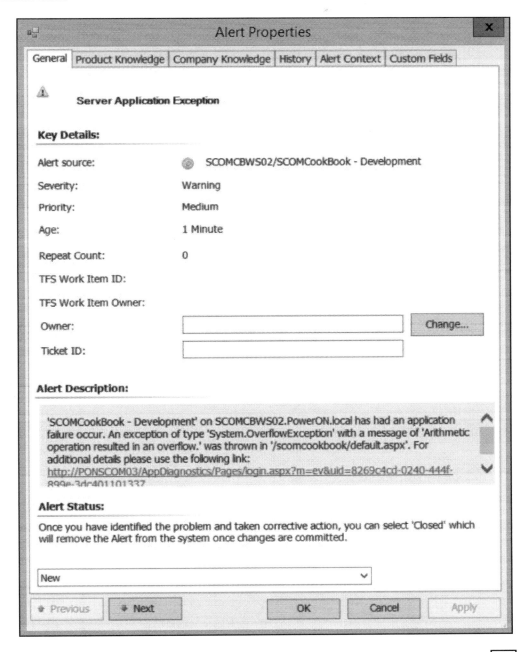

This SCOM alert gives you a link to the APM website where more details are shown. I have expanded the stack section and shown the member variables so a developer can easily see that the numbers are too big to be represented as integers and can redevelop his or her code to put some validation in place.

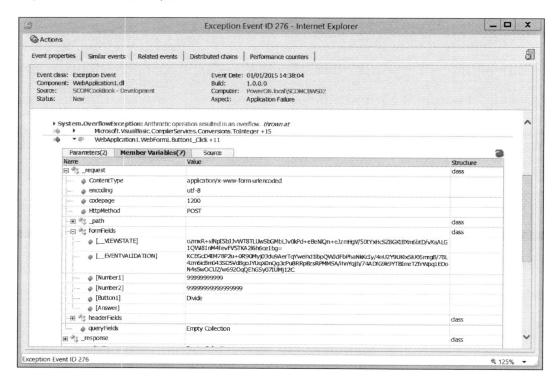

If you notice the other tabs, you will also see that recent performance data is captured so that the developer can see if there is a performance problem in the box that might be causing any issues.

APM also generates reports that can provide useful statistics to the lead developers to help them direct their teams to the problems that are causing the most issues in production.

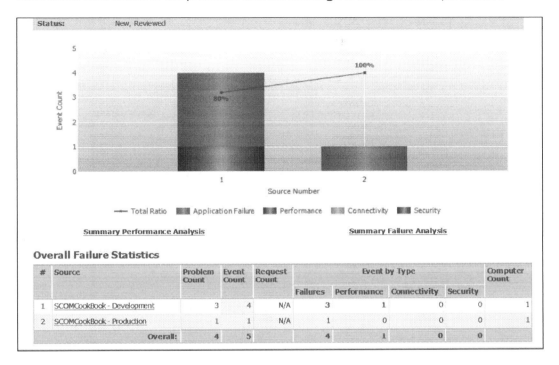

### Overall Failure Statistics

| # | Source | Problem Count | Event Count | Request Count | Event by Type | | | | Computer Count |
|---|--------|---------------|-------------|---------------|---------------|---|---|---|----------------|
| | | | | | Failures | Performance | Connectivity | Security | |
| 1 | SCOMCookBook - Development | 3 | 4 | N/A | 3 | 1 | 0 | 0 | 1 |
| 2 | SCOMCookBook - Production | 1 | 1 | N/A | 1 | 0 | 0 | 0 | 1 |
| | **Overall:** | **4** | **5** | | **4** | **1** | **0** | **0** | |

While this recipe is a basic example, it starts to show the potential of APM to help you get useful information on issues with your internally developed .NET applications. For further reading, look at *Monitoring .NET Applications* on TechNet at `http://technet.microsoft.com/en-us/library/hh212856.aspx`, and for details on the *.NET Application Performance Monitoring Template*, refer to `http://technet.microsoft.com/en-us/library/hh457578.aspx`.

# Enabling Global Service Monitor

**Global Service Monitor** (**GSM**) is a cloud-based service that allows SCOM to monitor your externally facing websites from various locations around the world. SCOM uploads the configuration of the tests to the GSM service and then polls for availability and performance information. This allows SCOM to get an overall view of the availability and performance of a website from various geographies and allows SCOM to highlight external network problems that would not otherwise be apparent.

## Getting ready

There are various steps that need to be carried out before enabling GSM. The first of these is to install the additional prerequisites for GSM. These are on TechNet at `http://technet.microsoft.com/en-us/library/jj860373.aspx` but can be summarized as follows:

 ▶ Ensure the management servers for communication with GSM have internet access

 ▶ Ensure that Windows Identity Foundation is installed on the management servers

Once the prerequisites are installed, you need to follow the sign-up process, again documented on the same page. This can be summarized as follows:

 1. Sign up to GSM through the commerce portal.
 2. Download and install GSM management packs.

Once this is done, you are ready to enable GSM from within SCOM and then to start using it.

As in previous recipes, we are using the SCOM Cookbook Management Pack. Please create this if it does not exist already or use your own management pack if you prefer. For demonstration purposes, we will be using a PowerOn website; you should substitute your own names as appropriate.

## How to do it...

Let's now look at ways to enable GSM and then move on to configuring web application availability tests.

### Enabling GSM

To configure the management server pool to be used for GSM:

 1. Open the SCOM console.
 2. Navigate to **Administration | Resource Pools**.
 3. Click on **Create Resource Pool** from the **Task** pane.

4. Enter the name `Global Service Monitor Pool` and a description if desired. Click on **Next** to continue.

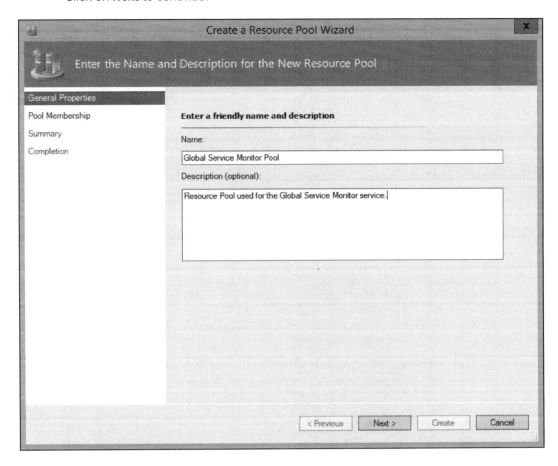

5. Add the management server to the list of **Resource Pool Members** and click on **Next** to continue.

6. On the summary page, click on **Create** and, once completed, click on **Close**.

To enable the GSM subscription in SCOM:

1. Open the SCOM console.

2. Navigate to **Administration | Global Service Monitor**.

3. Click on the **Start Subscription** link in the middle of the screen. If there are multiple links, including a **Stop Subscription** link, then the subscription has already been enabled.

4.  On the **Enter Subscription Credentials** screen, enter the username and password of an administrator to your organizational account and then click on **Sign In**.

> When configuring the subscription within SCOM, the instructions tell you to use the same account you used to activate the subscription on the commerce portal. Practice has shown that this does not need to be the same account, but rather any account with administrative permissions.

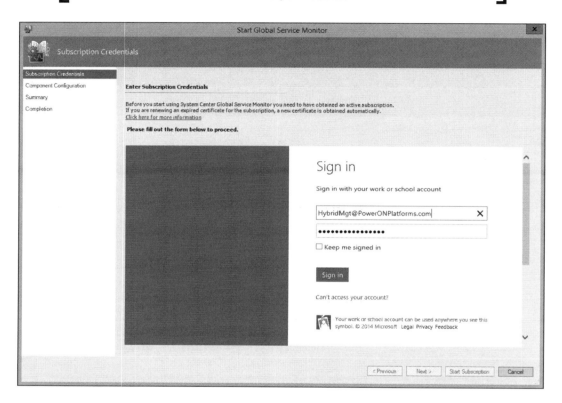

5.  Now you will see a window similar to the following one. Click on **Next** to continue.

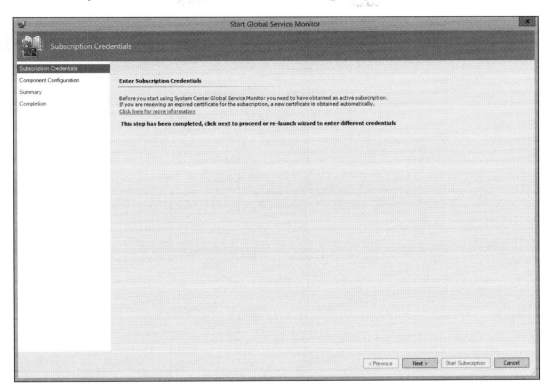

6. Choose the **Global Service Monitor Pool** resource pool and click on **Next** to continue.

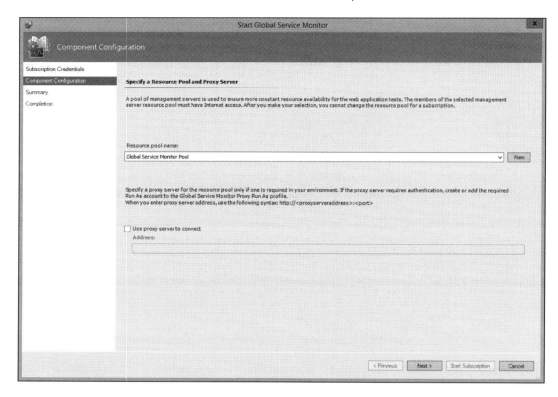

7. On the **Confirm the settings** screen, click on **Start Subscription**. Once the wizard has completed successfully (this can take some time), click on **Finish** to exit the wizard.

8. The links will now show the option to configure the tests and to stop the subscription.

## Configuring web application availability tests

To configure a web application availability test:

1. Open the SCOM console.

2. Navigate to **Authoring | Management Pack Templates**.

3. Click on **Add Monitoring Wizard** from the **Task** pane.

4. Choose **Web Application Availability Monitoring** for the monitoring type and click on **Next** to continue.

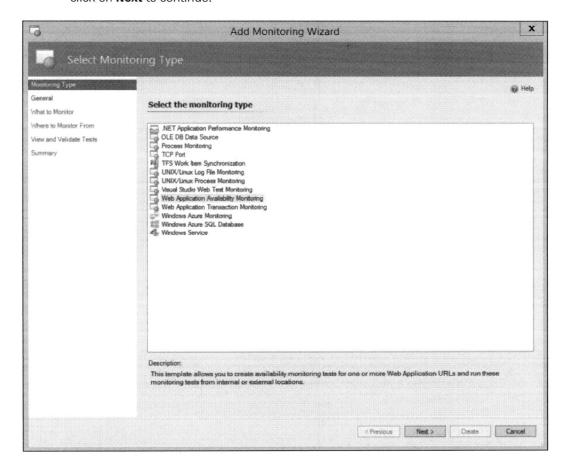

5.  Enter the name `PowerOn Platforms RDS Website`, choose the **SCOM Cookbook Management Pack**, and then click on **Next** to continue.

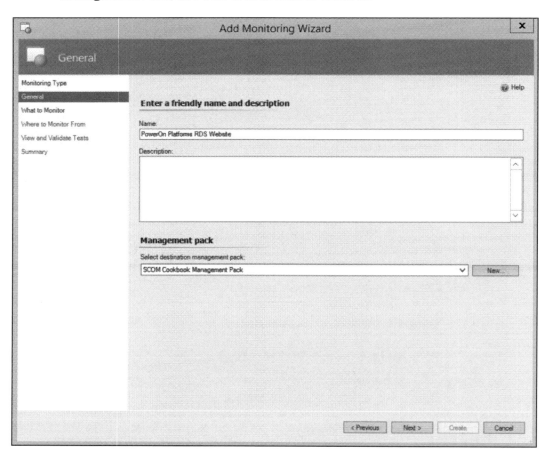

6.  Enter the name **PowerOn Platforms RDS website** and the URL of the website. Click on **Next** to continue.

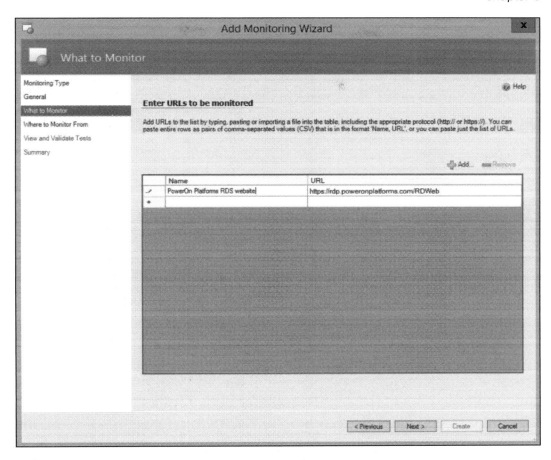

7. On the **External locations** screen, click on **Add**.

8. On the **Select external locations** screen, click on **Search**. The list of locations can vary, but select some locations, click on **Add**, and then click on **OK**.

9. On the **Internal locations** screen, click on **Add**.

10. On the **Select internal location** screen, click on **Search**. Choose a relevant internal server, click on **Add**, and then click on **OK**.

11. Back on the **Add Monitoring Wizard** screen, click on **Next** to continue.

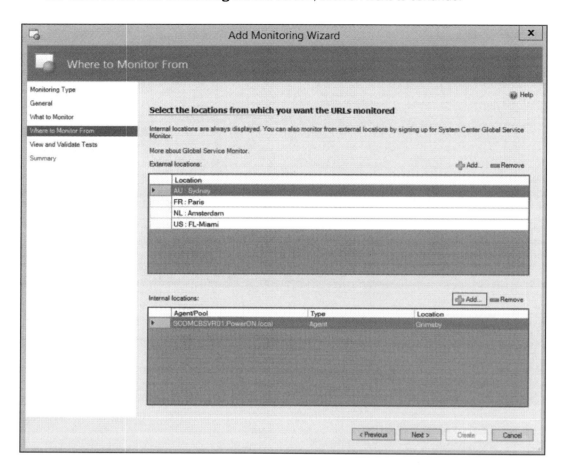

12. On the **Test list** screen, review the settings and click on **Next** to continue.

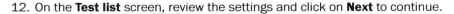
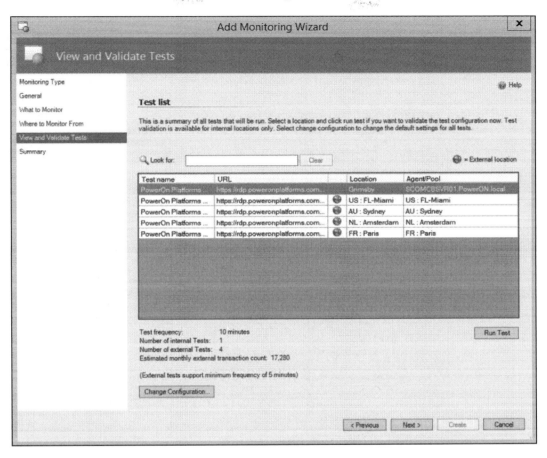

13. On the **Summary** screen, click on **Create** to complete the wizard.

14. To view the data, navigate to **Monitoring | Application Monitoring | Web Application Availability Monitoring | Web Application Status**.

15. Select the web application and then click on **Summary Dashboard - Map** to show a map of the health of all the checks.

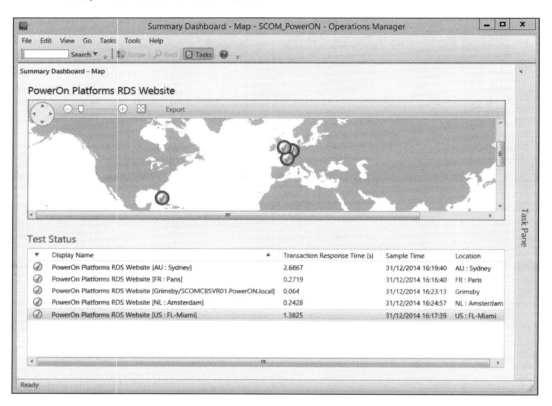

16. Alternatively, click on **Details Dashboard – List** to display a dashboard containing more performance information about the results of the tests.

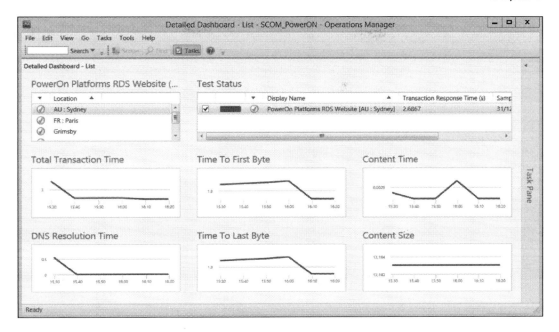

# How it works...

The GSM web service has been well designed with no need to open any firewalls to allow incoming traffic. This means that the data about the external tests needs to be collected by the management servers regularly; otherwise, data can be lost. This should be borne in mind when considering the management servers to include in the resource pool.

You will have noticed that, when configuring a web test, there is a reference to the estimated monthly external transaction count. When the GSM service was being developed, there was some uncertainty about the way it would be charged. The decision has since been made to make the service free to users with Software Assurance but to limit the number of tests that can be run. You should also note that, in line with the terms and conditions, you are only allowed to run these tests against websites under your control.

## There's more...

As well as being able to configure simple URL web availability tests as in the preceding recipe, it is possible to configure Visual Studio Web Tests to be run externally. This uses an XML-formatted document to define a series of URLs that can be run and the various rules to either check the results or to extract data to be fed into the next URL to check. This is very powerful and is used by many companies during development to ensure that the websites are performing as expected during their development testing. These same web tests can then be executed against the website in production to ensure that any problems are discovered immediately.

Unfortunately, the only version of Visual Studio that supports the recording and manipulation of these tests is the Ultimate edition, which can be expensive. An alternative is to use the Fiddler2 software to record your transaction and this can then be exported in the appropriate format.

## See also

The following are useful links to information related GSM:

> ► The article of Microsoft TechNet, *Global Service Monitor*: http://technet.microsoft.com/en-us/library/jj860368.aspx
> ► Fiddler2: http://www.fiddler2.com

# 7
# Authoring Custom Monitoring Solutions with System Center 2012 R2 Operations Manager

In this chapter, we will be providing recipes for how to start creating your own advanced customizations to System Center 2012 R2 Operations Manager and which tools and design methodologies may be best suited to your needs. These recipes will cover topics such as:

- ▶ Storing customizations in management packs
- ▶ Editing a management pack in Notepad
- ▶ Creating a new attribute for all computers
- ▶ Creating a custom view
- ▶ Discovering a new application in MP Author
- ▶ Creating a custom view in MP Author
- ▶ Deploying a management pack from MP Author
- ▶ Creating service monitors in MP Author
- ▶ Monitoring and capturing performance in MP Author

# Introduction

**System Center 2012 R2 Operations Manager** (**SCOM**) is a powerful tool for monitoring and alerting against any IT environment. So far, we have looked at how to tune existing monitoring to the appropriate levels for your environment. However, there may be other information that you wish to gather or additional items of interest that you wish to monitor and alert, that are specific to your environment.

This chapter will delve deeper into the ways in which you can produce customized discoveries and monitors that will allow you to fully implement the appropriate monitoring for your environment. The recipes will also show some of the advantages and disadvantages of the different authoring tools to help you decide on the best tool for you.

No book can realistically expect to be able to cover all individual monitoring needs, but following these recipes to begin with and then adapting them to your requirements should give you the monitoring you require and also the skills to create other customizations for further monitoring.

We will cover writing customizations in the console and MP Author by Silect. Both of these use wizards to help, which eases the learning curve, but lack the flexibility to create some of the more complex solutions. We will also cover the use of Visual Studio to create some monitoring in a later chapter as the learning curve for this product is much steeper owing to the very limited scope of the wizards.

# Storing customizations in management packs

Almost all configuration and customization in SCOM is stored in management packs. This recipe shows you how to create a management pack to store the customizations you need for your environment.

## Getting ready

Once you have an SCOM installation and access to the SCOM console, you have everything you need to start creating management packs.

## How to do it...

1. Open the SCOM console.
2. Navigate to **Administration | Management Packs**.
3. In the **Task** pane, click on **Create Management Pack**.

4. In the **Name** field, enter the name of your management pack. In this case, we are using Windows Server 2012 Customisation. Note how the ID field is set to the **Name** field entry but without spaces or numbers in the following screenshot:

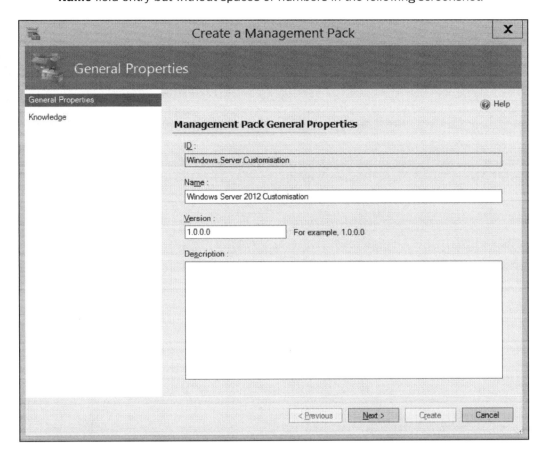

5. Enter a description if desired and then click on **Next**.
6. Click on **Create** to create the designed management pack.

## How it works...

Management packs are simply formatted XML describing configurations that SCOM will apply. This formatted XML will then be distributed to all computers that require any of the configurations specified within that pack. In theory, you can store all of the custom configuration in the same management pack, but best practice would be to divide out the customization in a similar way to what you do for overrides. This separation reduces the size of each pack and allows you to remove or upgrade each set of custom monitoring separately.

## There's more...

While creating a management pack is deceptively simple, there are some factors that you should bear in mind when you are starting to create your packs to ensure that you do not hit problems later on.

First, it is important to remember the automatic population of the ID field when you enter the name of the pack. While it makes sense to begin with `Windows Server 2008 Customisation`, because the ID removes the numbers the pack will have the ID **Windows.Server.Customisation**. When you then come to create `Windows Server 2012 Customisation`, the ID will become **Windows.Server.Customisation0**.

> This can be prevented by creating the management pack in one of the other authoring tools such as MP Author or Visual Studio. Even if you create the pack in the monitoring console, you can still fix the ID in Notepad using the next recipe.

# Editing a management pack in Notepad

As the previous recipe showed, there are times when you need to export a management pack from the Operations console and edit the management pack manually. Common reasons for doing this are to fix typographical errors or other misspellings that the console will not let you change. This recipe will show you how to export a management pack, edit some information, and reimport the pack.

For this recipe, we will be using the example of changing the ID of the management pack for our Windows Server 2012 Customisation management pack.

## Getting ready

Before this recipe, you should have an unsealed management pack that you wish to edit. While in this example we will be changing the ID of the management pack, an almost identical procedure will apply to editing any management pack created and maintained in the Operations console.

## How to do it...

1. Open the SCOM console.

2. Navigate to **Administration | Management Packs**.

3. In the list of management packs, find the pack you wish to edit. You may find it by using the **Look for** option at the top of the list (click on the **Find Now** button if it is not there).

4. Click on the management pack and select **Export Management Pack** from the task list. Export it to a suitable folder.

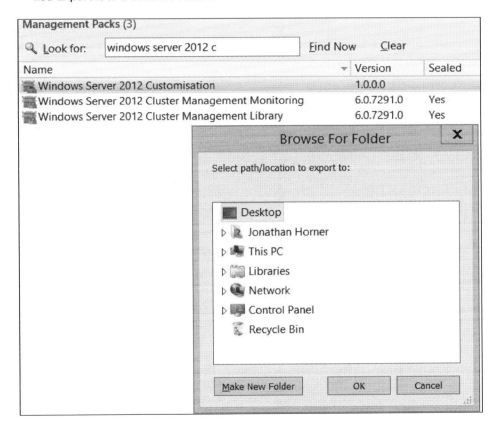

5. As we are changing the ID of the management pack, there are a couple of additional steps that do not need to be carried out for most examples:

   1. We need to remove the old management pack, so click on **Delete** from the task menu. This is only needed because we are changing the ID.

   2. We need to rename the XML file produced and save in the relevant folder. Change the filename from `Windows.Server.Customisation.Xml` to `Windows.Server.2012.Customisation.Xml`.

6. Open the management pack in Notepad. This will look something like the following:

```
Windows.Server.2012.Customisation.xml - Notepad          —  □  ×
File  Edit  Format  View  Help
<?xml version="1.0" encoding="utf-8"?><ManagementPack ContentReadable="tru
  <Manifest>
    <Identity>
      <ID>Windows.Server.Customisation</ID>
      <Version>1.0.0.0</Version>
    </Identity>
    <Name>Windows Server 2012 Customisation</Name>
    <References>
      <Reference Alias="SystemCenter">
        <ID>Microsoft.SystemCenter.Library</ID>
        <Version>7.0.8433.0</Version>
        <PublicKeyToken>31bf3856ad364e35</PublicKeyToken>
      </Reference>
    </References>
  </Manifest>
  <Presentation>
    <Folders>
```

7. Go to the `<ID>` line and change `Windows.Server.Customisation` to `Windows.Server.2012.Cusomisation`. Change the `<Version>` from `1.0.0.0` to `1.0.0.1` and save and close Notepad.

8. Back in the Operations console, click on **Import Management Packs** and select **Add | From Disk**. Decline the option to search the online catalog and then select the appropriate management pack.

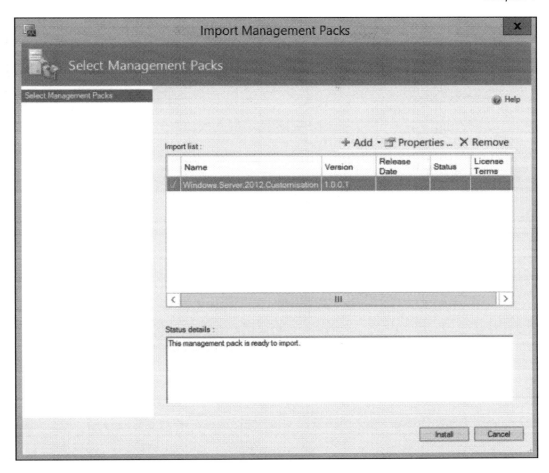

9. Click on **Install** and, once installed, we are done.

## How it works...

What we are showing here is that the configuration stored within the management is simply XML and can be edited with something as simple as Notepad. While this recipe shows a simple change, the technique can be used at any later point to change settings that are otherwise blocked.

 If we are changing the ID of the management pack, we have to edit the filename of the XML document to match. This is a requirement to allow you to import the management pack.

We also increased the version number of the management pack. It is best practice to always update this version number when making any change. This has a number of benefits including always being sure that the latest version has been imported as well as being able to check that the management pack has been downloaded to any clients correctly.

## There's more...

While we have shown how to import the management pack through the console, it is possible to import and export management packs using PowerShell. The following command will export a management pack:

```
Get-SCOMManagementPack -Name Windows.Server.Customisation | Export-
SCOMManagementPack -Path C:\temp
```

The following command will import the new management pack:

```
Import-SCOMManagementPack
c:\temp\Windows.Server.2012.Customisation.Xml
```

It is worthwhile looking at the XML of a management pack as you create it and add information to it. This can be very helpful in assisting you to gain an understanding of the management pack structure and how everything holds together. If you look at a management pack created in the Operations console, you will start to spot the potential for complication even with an empty management pack. If you look a few lines down from the top, you will find the <Presentation> section that contains the folder that is automatically generated when you create a management pack in the Operations console:

```
<Presentation>
  <Folders>
    <Folder ID="Folder_f56f59d7f8824b93819ce9908e32a8a9"
    Accessibility="Public"
    ParentFolder="SystemCenter!Microsoft.SystemCenter.Monitoring
    .ViewFolder.Root" />
  </Folders>
</Presentation>
```

As you can see, the ID of the folder has been set to include a GUID. You can then see what the folder is called by moving down to the language packs section:

```
<DisplayString
  ElementID="Folder_f56f59d7f8824b93819ce9908e32a8a9">
  s<Name>Windows Server 2012 Customisation</Name>
</DisplayString>
```

While this is easy to do in a nearly empty management pack, when you have a large number of management pack items, all referenced only by GUIDs, this very quickly becomes difficult to maintain.

# Creating a new attribute for all computers

The Windows computer object within SCOM contains many bits of useful information such as the Active Directory OU and details of the number of processors. However, many organizations add information about their custom build into their registry and find that it would be useful to capture this information as well.

The following recipe will introduce you to the customizations needed to capture this kind of attribute.

## Getting ready

For this recipe, you will need to have an existing SCOM installation. This customization can then be carried out in the authoring section of the SCOM console.

In our example for the recipe, the custom build information is stored in the software section of the local machine hive as shown in the following screenshot. This recipe can easily be modified for any information stored in the registry.

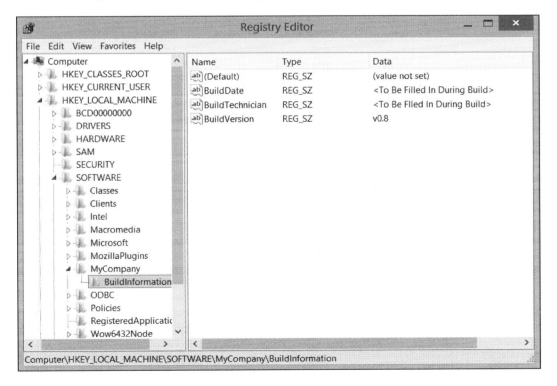

## How to do it...

1. Open the SCOM console.

2. Navigate to **Authoring** | **Management Pack Objects** | **Attributes**.

3. Click on **Create a New Attribute** from the **Task** pane.

4. Enter the **Name** as Build Version and a description if desired. Click on **Next** to continue.

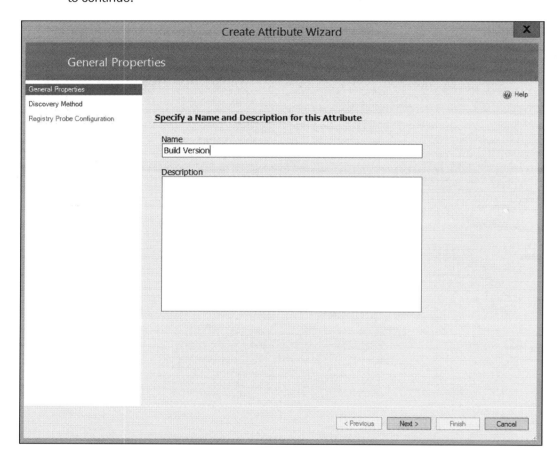

5. Leave the **Discovery Type** as **Registry**.

6. To choose the **Target**, click on **Browse** and then type Windows Computer in the **Look for** section at the top of the page.

7. Select the **Windows Computer** target and click on **OK**.

8. Note that the default name is **Windows Computer_Extended**. Change this to `Company Build Information`.

9. Either use the drop-down option under **Management Pack** to select an existing management pack or click on **New**. I have chosen to use a management pack called **Company Build Information**. Click on **Next** to continue.

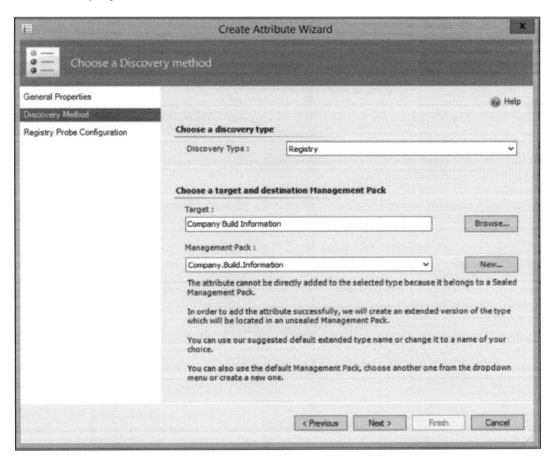

10. Choose the **Registry Value** option and enter the path `SOFTWARE\MyCompany\BuildInformation\BuildVersion` and change the **Attribute Type** to **String**. Change the **Frequency** to **43200** seconds and click on **Finish**.

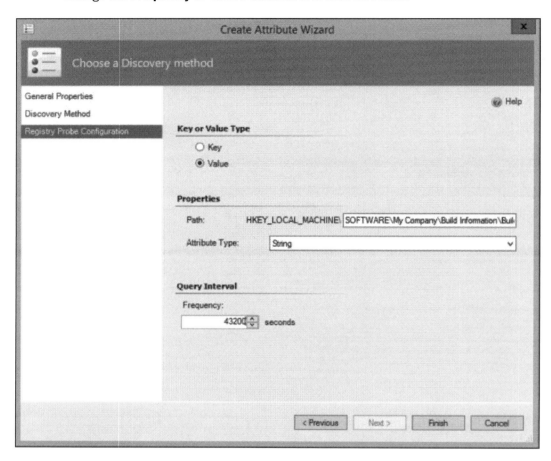

To see the resulting attribute, follow the next recipe *Creating a custom view*.

## How it works...

It can be instructive at this point to export your management pack and open it in Notepad as described in the previous recipe. This allows you to see several new sections that have appeared compared to an empty pack. These include the definition of a new class type. This uses the targeted class (Windows Computer) as its base class, which allows you to see all properties of that class as well as the new property we have defined. Note, however, that, as I described before, all the IDs are GUID-based, which makes it tricky to identify each one.

As well as the class type, there is also a discovery. This uses a built-in data source and passes it a path to a registry setting. This returns the setting and SCOM allocates the returned value to the attribute we have defined. This discovery will be run at the interval we specified. While this is a very lightweight query that will only require minimal resources, as the data is not expected to change regularly, the default of every hour is excessive. In the recipe, I chose every 12 hours as an acceptable compromise that would pick up any change if it was to happen without running the check too regularly.

## There's more...

It is perfectly possible to create multiple attributes by running the wizard multiple times. It is important to remember to use the new class (Company Build Information) as the target in the future to ensure that only a single extended class is created. If you do this, you will notice that the management pack is getting more and more complicated and you may also realize that each property is being captured with its own dedicated discovery.

In order to have more control over this and other aspects of a management pack, many people quickly start to move from the use of the Operations console to the use of a dedicated management pack editing tool. While the Operations console has a great advantage in speed and availability, the use of GUIDs for the objects and its general inflexibility push many people towards a more powerful tool once their requirements become a little more advanced.

# Creating a custom view

In order to display our newly discovered attribute, the easiest way is to create a custom state view. This will allow us to choose the information we wish to show and control how best to display it.

## Getting ready

As creating a management pack in the Operations console automatically creates a folder ready for custom views like this, we already have everything we need to get going.

## How to do it...

1. Open the SCOM console.
2. Navigate to **Monitoring** | **Monitoring** | **My Company Build Information**.
3. Right-click on the folder and select **New** | **State View**.
4. Enter `Build Information` in the **Name** field.

5. Click on the ellipses next to the object in the **Show data related to:** field and choose the **Company Build Information** class. Click on **OK** and then **Yes** in the confirmation box.

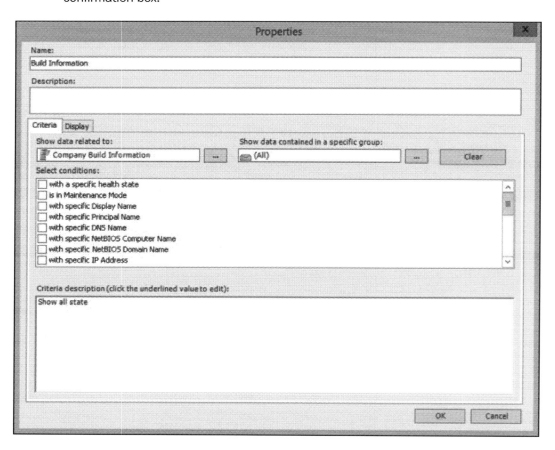

6. Click on the **Display** tab and choose the attributes to display. I have chosen **IP Address** from the Windows Computer class and **Build Version** from our new class.

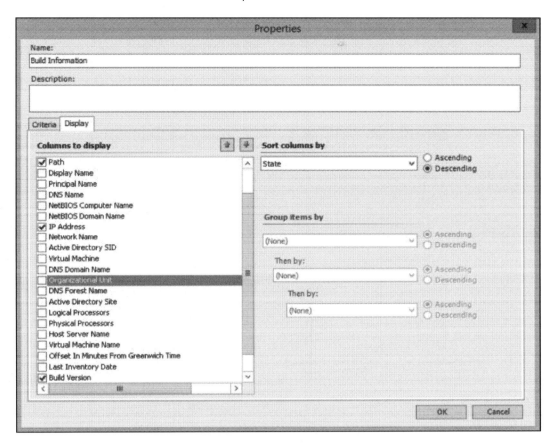

7. Click on **OK** to create the view and wait a few moments for that view to populate into the console. Once visible, it will look something like the following:

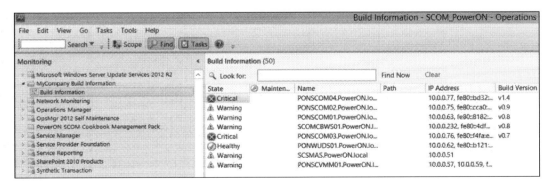

## How it works...

Custom views are a very simple way to display the health of an object or even just to display certain attributes as we have done in this example. While all users can build their own views in the My Workspace section, creating a custom view in the Monitoring section allows it to be made visible to all SCOM users.

Note that, because we are creating an attribute targeted at Windows Computers, this shows the attribute value for all Windows Computers, not just the ones where the registry has been set.

## There's more...

If we take another export of the management pack and have a look at it, you will see that the management pack is expanding and now takes up several screen pages, even though it is still a relatively simple pack. This expansion, and the related difficulty in finding the right place in the management pack, is one of the reasons why many people can be put off editing packs in Notepad and why people start using other authoring tools to help them.

On the subject of the custom view itself, this is stored in the Presentation section within the management pack.

```
Company.Build.Information - Notepad
File  Edit  Format  View  Help
<Presentation>
  <Views>
    <View ID="View_3a3fd9766c4b48f0993781b9fed81deb" Accessibility="Public" Enabled="
      <Category>Operations</Category>
      <Criteria>
        <InMaintenanceMode>false</InMaintenanceMode>
      </Criteria>
      <Presentation>
        <ColumnInfo Index="0" SortIndex="0" Width="100" Grouped="false" Sorted="true"
          <Name>State</Name>
          <Id>Type7b047b7eff514b3e8bb9b63efeb842da-*-289e80e5-56ed-8e16-6f47-09461d37
        </ColumnInfo>
        <ColumnInfo Index="1" SortIndex="-1" Width="100" Grouped="false" Sorted="fals
          <Name>Maintenance Mode</Name>
          <Id>InMaintenanceMode</Id>
        </ColumnInfo>
        <ColumnInfo Index="2" SortIndex="-1" Width="100" Grouped="false" Sorted="fals
```

Note that all the possible columns are now listed in the XML, but most of them have the visible flag set to false. Please remember that, if you change the settings here, you are changing the default settings for the view, and anyone who has customized their view will still see the settings they have chosen. It is possible for a user to reset his or her settings using the **Reset to Default** option on the **Personalize View** screen, but it is not possible for an administrator to force that to happen for other people.

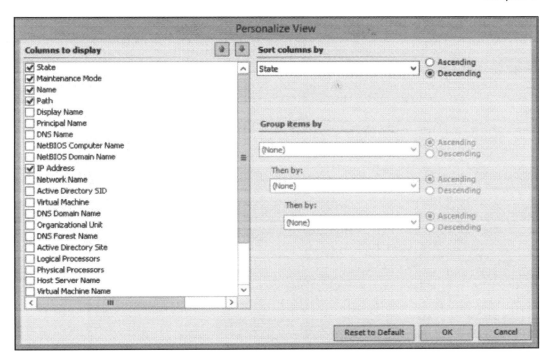

If you look again at the contents of the view, you will notice that, even though we only have the registry key defined on a couple of the servers, all servers are listed in the view. This is because the Authoring console is aimed at extending existing classes such as Windows Computer or SQL 2012 DB Engine. This is fine for attributes such as build information that should probably apply to all computers. However, most companies need to use monitoring for specific services or counters that form part of a custom application and these should only be targeted at specific computers. In order to do this, you need to start creating a custom class and discovery; to do this, you really need to use a different authoring tool. How to do this will be the subject of the next recipe.

# Discovering a new application in MP Author

The ability to provide custom monitoring to different servers is key to the success of SCOM. We are all familiar with the monitoring that is targeted at SQL Servers or IIS Servers, but SCOM is highly extensible and can be configured to discover custom applications and target specific monitoring for them as well.

The key task when developing custom monitoring is to work out the service model that represents your application. A service model is broadly speaking a description of the classes and their relationships. Once you have this, you can work out how you will identify the servers hosting this application as being different from a server that does not host the application. For example, a SQL Server is identified by the existence of a registry key `HKLM\SOFTWARE\Microsoft\Microsoft SQL Server\110\Machines`. Later scripts can be used to identify the specific components of SQL that are installed. The registry is used because this is the most efficient way of checking every server rather than having all servers check individually for each separate component.

In our example, we will start with a simple application that is identified by the existence of a registry key `HKLM\SOFTWARE\MyCompany\MyApplication`. Within this key are a couple of settings with information about the application, as follows:

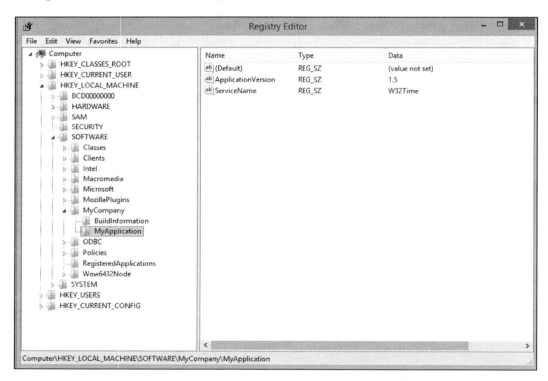

## Getting ready

MP Author for Operations Manager is a free tool from Silect Software, which has been developing an easy-to-use wizard-based tool for management pack authoring. This tool provides much more flexibility for creating management packs without fully understanding the underlying MP structure. This application can be obtained for free by simply registering your information on the Silect website, at which point you will be given a download link. Once you have downloaded the software and installed it on a suitable machine, you will be ready to start this recipe.

## How to do it...

To discover a new application in MP Author follow the steps:

1. Open MP Author.
2. Click on **File | New** to start the **Management Pack Creation Wizard**.
3. On the **Introduction** page, click on **Next**.
4. Enter `MyCompany.MyApplication.Monitoring` as the ID of the management pack and then click on **Next**.

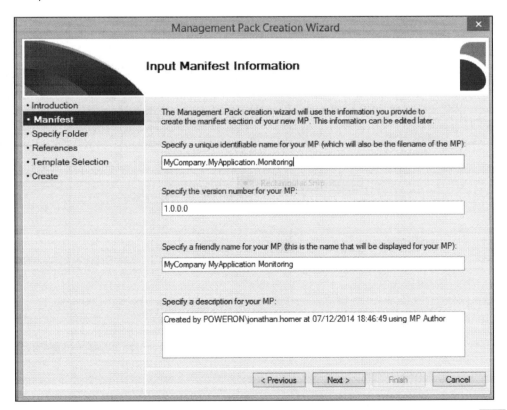

5. Choose an appropriate place to save the management pack and click on **Next**.

6. We will not be adding any additional references at this stage, so click on **Next**.

7. On the **Template Selection** page, select **Empty Management Pack** and click on **Next**.

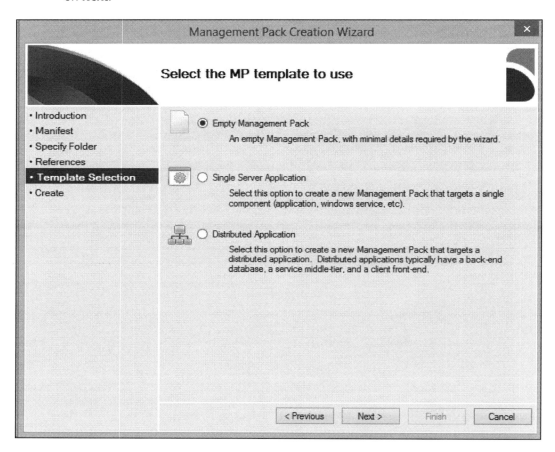

8. Click on **Finish** to create the management pack.

9. When the management pack becomes accessible, click on **MP Component | Targets** (targets are equivalent to classes in traditional SCOM terminology).

10. Navigate to **New | Create New Registry Target**.

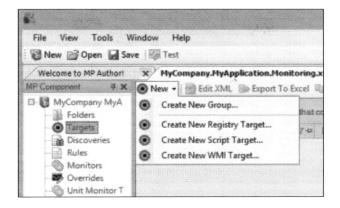

11. In order to help read the registry, MP Author allows you to connect to a machine to read the registry configuration directly. Enter the name of a computer that hosts the appropriate registry keys and click on **Next**.

12. In the **Discovery** section, click on **Browse** to open the **Select Registry Keys** window. Drill through to find the **HKEY_LOCAL_MACHINE\SOFTWARE\MyCompany\MyApplication\ApplicationVersion** key and then click on **Add** and **OK**.

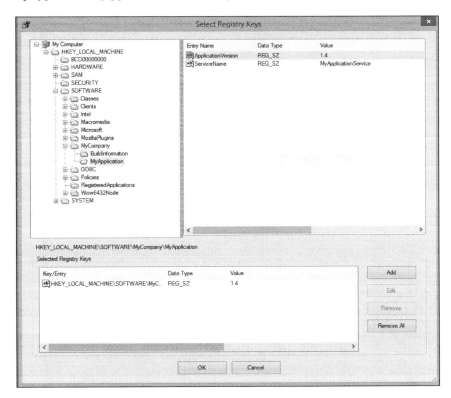

13. Repeat this process for the **Properties** but add the **ApplicationVersion** and **ServiceName** registry keys to create two properties. Click on **Next** when complete.

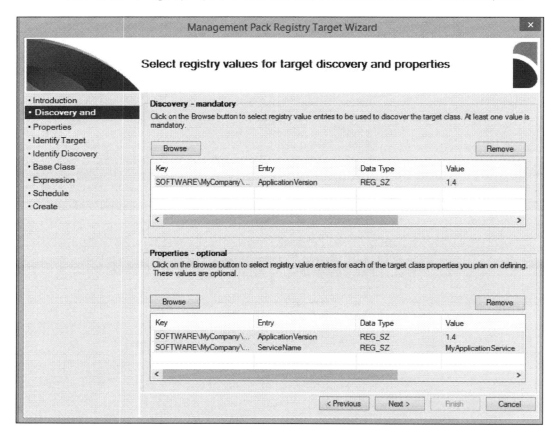

14. Uncheck the **Key** property box and click on **Next**.

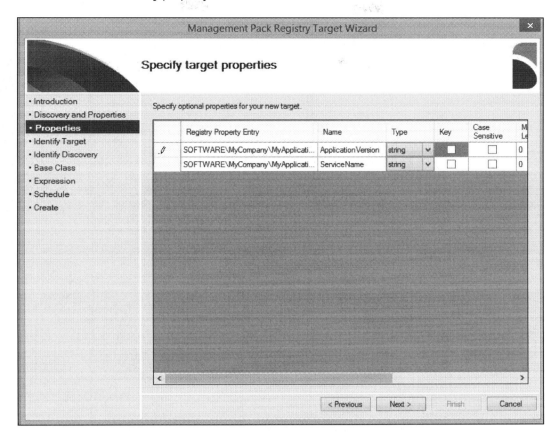

15. On the **Identify registry target** page, change the **Name** field to `MyCompany.`
    `MyApplication.Monitoring.MyApplication.Class`, and change the
    **Display Name** to `MyCompany MyApplication Class`.

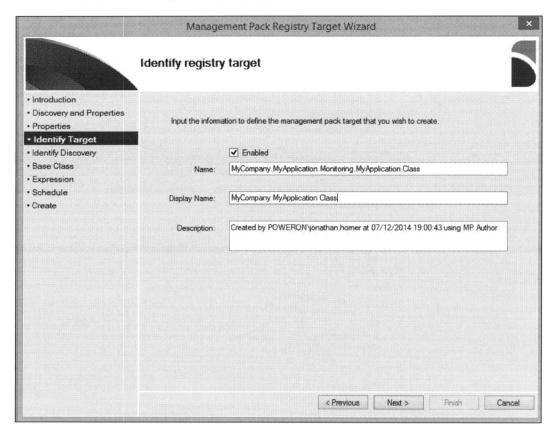

16. Leave the **Discovery** names as the default and click on **Next**.

17. Change the expression type to **Check for existence of registry values** and click on **Next**.

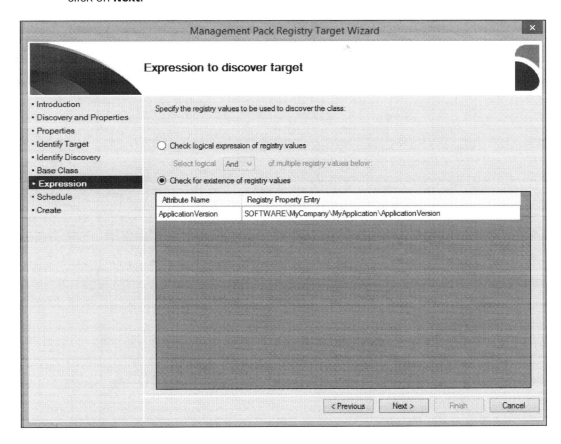

18. Leave the schedule at the reasonable default of 1 day and click on **Next**. Click on **Finish** to create the discovery.

As before, we will create a view to show the results of the discovery in the next recipe.

## How it works...

One point immediately to note on creating the management pack is how MP Author asks you for the ID of the management pack, suggests a friendly name for the pack, but allows you to change both as required. This is in clear contrast to the Operations console, which does not allow you to alter the suggested ID of the management pack.

In the fourteenth step, we uncheck the key property box. This is worthy of a little explanation. When creating an application in this way, it is most likely that we will only ever have one application of this class on any server. A key property is designed so that, if we need more than one example of a class on a server, we can distinguish between the two by having different values in this key property. Also in this step, there is the ability to make the contents of the field case sensitive and to supply minimum and maximum lengths for the parameters.

In the fifteenth step, we look at the name of the class we are creating. This needs to be unique within the SCOM management group. Thus, the Operations console will generate a GUID for this name so that it is guaranteed to be unique. With MP Author, they use the ID of the management pack and some additional text to help guarantee uniqueness. While there is nothing to stop you from using any ID that you wish, care should be taken to ensure that you make the ID unique.

## There's more...

Service model design is a large topic within the breadth of things that could be talked about with respect to management pack authoring. Microsoft is continuing to develop more and more content to help you with this and there is now an online course hosted at the Microsoft Virtual Academy.

## See also

The following links will be helpful as you are looking deeper into creating your own custom management packs:

- Silect Software MP Author: `http://www.silect.com/mp-author`.
- The Microsoft Virtual Academy course on management pack authoring: `http://www.microsoftvirtualacademy.com/training-courses/system-center-2012-r2-operations-manager-management-pack`. Note that this course focuses on authoring in Visual Studio, which is described in a later chapter.

# Creating a custom view in MP Author

In the Operations console, creating a management pack automatically creates a folder to put custom views in. With MP Author (and most authoring tools), there is no folder created automatically and so we will have to create this in the recipe as well.

## Getting ready

For this recipe, we will be building on the management pack we created in the previous example. This gives us the application definition and discovery already set up. In this recipe, we will look at building the view with MP Author.

# How to do it...

To create a custom view in MP Author follow the steps:

1. Open MP Author and the previous management pack if they are not already open.

2. Click on the **Folders** section. Select **New | Create New Folder**.

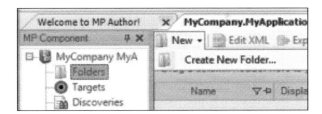

3. From the drop-down option, select **Microsoft.SystemCenter.Monitoring.ViewFolder. Root** and then click on **Next**.

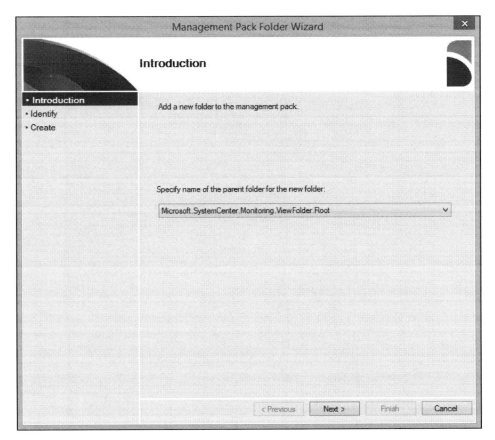

4.  Change the **Name** field to MyCompany.MyApplication.Monitoring. CustomViews.Folder.

5.  Change the **Display Name** field to Application Views and then click on **Next**.

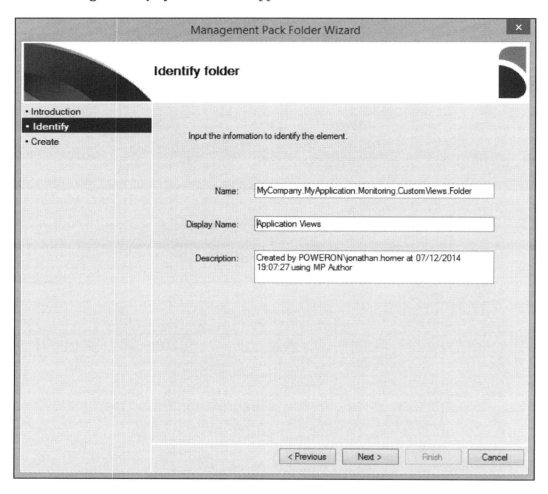

6.  Click on **Finish** to create the folder.

7. Click on the **Views** section and then navigate to **New | Create New State View**.

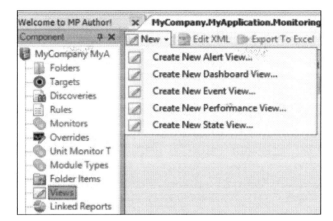

8. On the **Introduction** page, select the **MyCompany.MyApplication.Monitoring. CustomViews.Folder** defined in the fourth step and then click on **Next**.

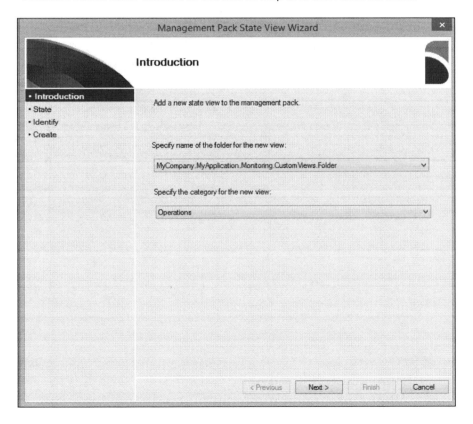

9. Change the **Target** field for the view to **MyCompany MyApplication Class** defined in the previous recipe. Check all the options in the **Severity** section and then click on **Next**.

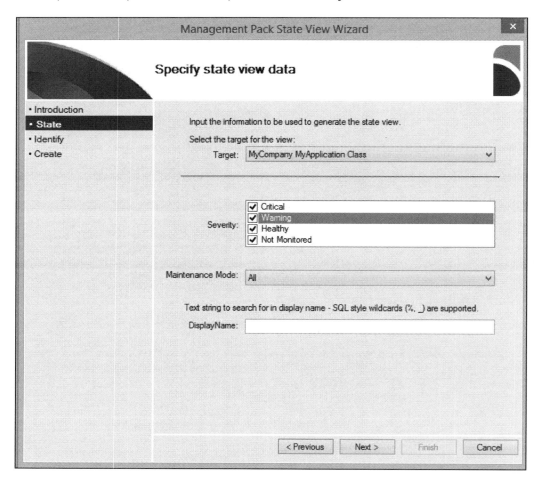

10. Change the **Name** field of the view to `MyCompany.MyApplication.Monitoring.MyApplication.StateView`. Change the **Display Name** field to `State View`. Click on **Next**.

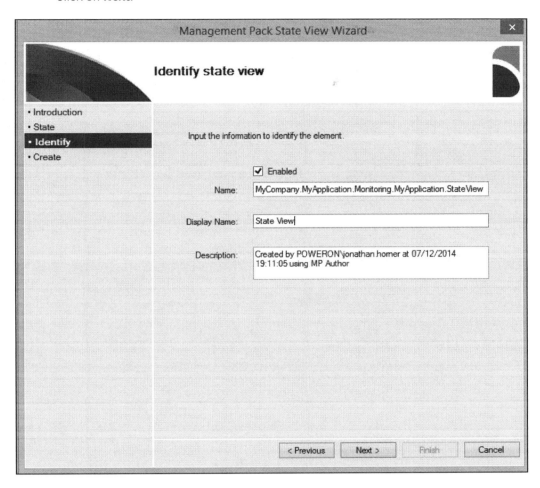

11. Click on **Finish**.

12. Save the management pack and then import it in the normal way. Once the discovery has run, the view will be populated in a manner similar to the following:

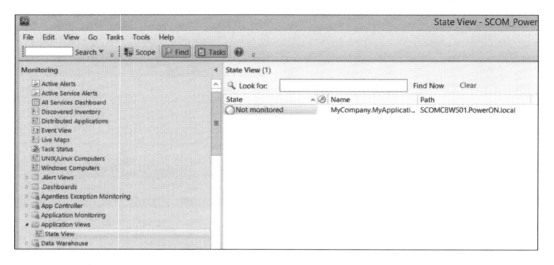

## How it works...

When you compare this with creating a view in the console, you will notice that we have not been given a choice of fields as we created the view. This means that the view will display certain fields by default, and the user can then select the other ones he chooses. While this keeps the management pack smaller, and you can certainly edit the XML to include the relevant columns if you wish, this is an example of one of the compromises that an authoring tool needs to make when considering what functionality to include in the tool.

You will also notice another difference between discovering an application and a new attribute. While the new attribute is for all computers, the application is only on servers that match the registry criteria and so only a subset of servers are discovered. This has the advantage that any monitors or rules targeted at the application only execute on the relevant servers and do not waste computing cycles on other machines.

There is a small issue with the view that can happen from time to time. When looking in the **Views** section, select the **State View** and click on **Edit XML**. Examine the XML for the severity list that is generated. If it looks like the following:

```
<SeverityList>
  <Severity>Red</Severity>
  <Severity>Yellow</Severity>
  <Severity>Unknown</Severity>
  <Severity>Unknown</Severity>
</SeverityList>
```

Please change the third option to the following:

```
<SeverityList>
  <Severity>Red</Severity>
  <Severity>Yellow</Severity>
  <Severity>Green</Severity>
  <Severity>Unknown</Severity>
</SeverityList>
```

This will ensure that your green agents display properly once the view has been deployed.

## There's more...

You will notice that, at the moment, the state view shows an empty circle indicating that the application is not monitored. While strictly true, the reason for this is that we have not created any monitoring yet. This will be the subject of one of the next recipes.

You can also create Alert Views and Performance Views targeted at our new application class. This will then show any alerts generated by the monitors or the performance data gathered by rules in subsequent recipes. This can be created in MP Author by following a very similar wizard.

Instead of having to import the management pack manually into your environment, you can use MP author to deploy the management pack directly. This will be the subject of the next recipe.

# Deploying a management pack from MP Author

Many authoring tools have the facility to deploy the management packs directly to your SCOM management group from the editor without having to manually import the pack from the Operations console. This can be a time-saver and reduces the possibility of picking up the wrong version of the management pack.

## Getting ready

Make sure that you have followed the previous recipes or their equivalent. This means you will have a SCOM environment and MP Author already installed and available for use.

## How to do it...

To deploy a management pack from MP Author, perform the following steps:

1. Open MP Author and the previous management pack if they are not already open.

2. Click on the **Management Pack** section. Navigate to **New** | **Deploy Management Pack...**.

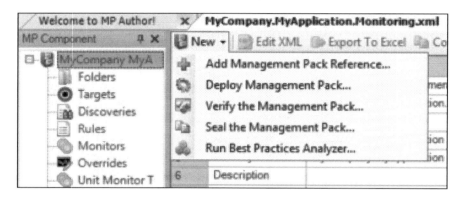

3. Enter the name of a management server and the appropriate credentials and click on **Add**.

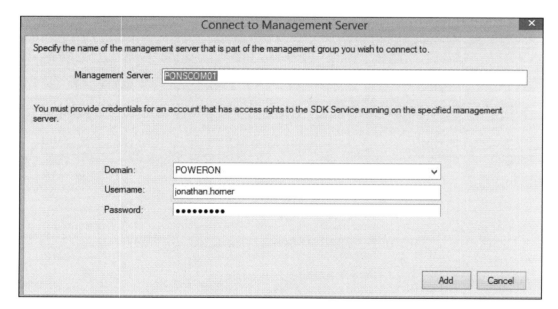

4.  Review the management pack to be deployed and any messages and then click on **Deploy**.

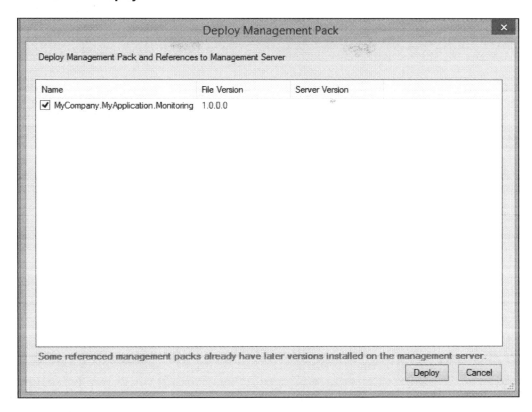

There is a progress bar in the bottom left that will show you that the management pack is deploying. Once complete, the following window will be displayed and the management pack deployed.

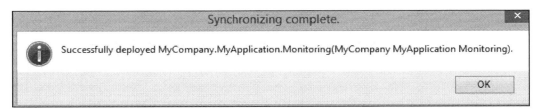

# Creating service monitors in MP Author

Monitors are used by SCOM to affect the health of a particular object. Often a custom application will have a custom service to monitor, but for the purposes of making this recipe generic, we will choose to monitor the Print Spooler service. This is to allow you to stop and start this service on your test machine to observe the results without causing too many problems. This recipe builds on the management pack developed in the previous recipe to build a more featured management pack.

## Getting ready

Make sure that you have followed the previous recipes or their equivalent. This means you will have a SCOM environment and MP Author already installed and available for use.

## How to do it...

To create service monitors in MP Author, perform the following steps:

1. Open MP Author and the previous management pack if they are not already open.

2. Because we are making a change, we should increase the management pack version number. To do this, click on the **Management Pack** section, click on **Version**, and increment the version number of the management pack by 1 to 1.0.0.1.

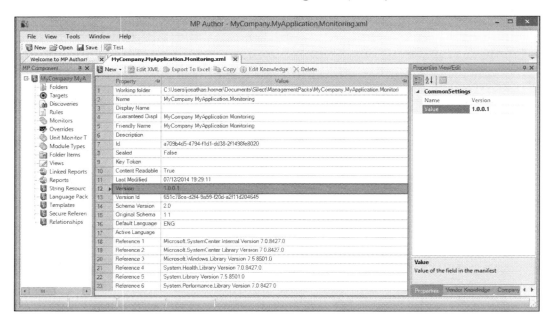

3. Click on the **Monitors** section. Select **New | Create New Service Monitor....**

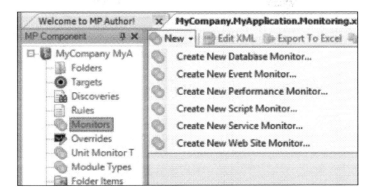

4. On the **Introduction** screen, select the name of the computer hosting the application and click on **Next**.

5. Change the drop-down option for the **Target** field to match your application. In our example, this is **MyCompany MyApplication Class**.

6. Scroll down the list of services, choose **Print Spooler** from the list, and click on **Next**.

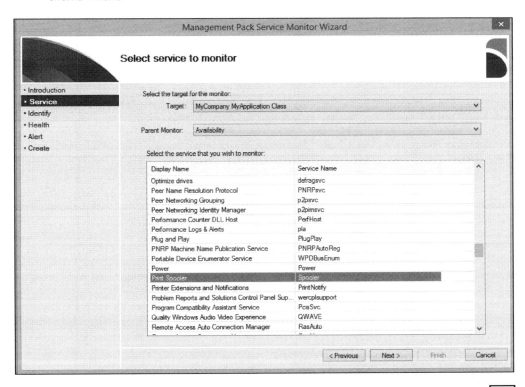

7. Change the **Name** field to `MyCompany.MyApplication.Monitoring.`
   `ServiceMonitoring.Print Spooler`. Change the **Display Name** field to `Print`
   `Spooler Service Monitor` and then click on **Next**.

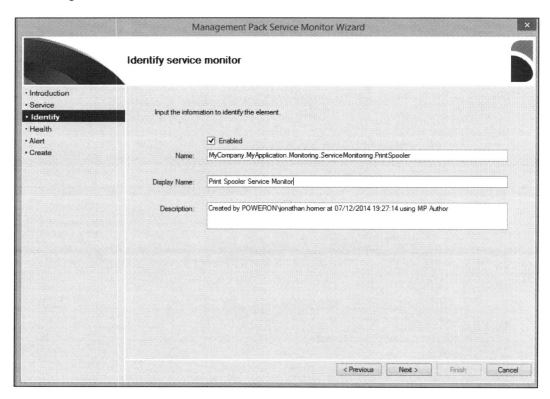

8. Change the **Service is not running** state to **Critical** and click on **Next**.

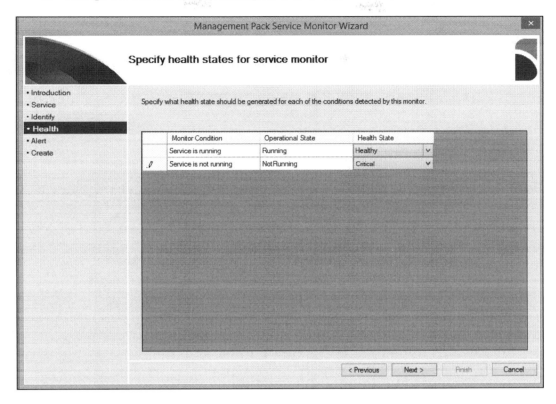

9. Check the box to create alerts for the monitor.

10. Change the **Generate an alert when the health state changes to** drop-down option to **Error**. Change the **Severity** drop-down option to **Error**. Click on **Next** to continue.

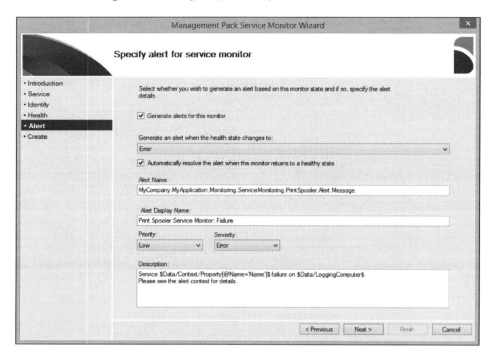

11. Click on **Finish** to complete the wizard.
12. Save the management pack and deploy the pack into SCOM. Notice that the health will now be set to green once the monitor has initialized.

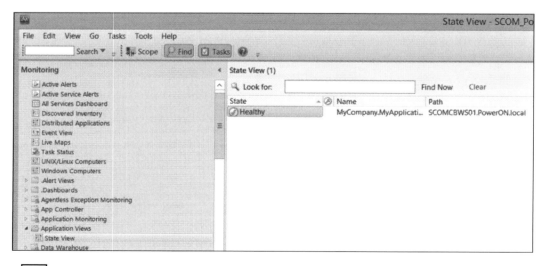

## How it works...

This recipe uses a built-in module within SCOM to check the state of the service monitor. This reacts quickly to any changes in the running state of the service, changes the health, and raises an alert if that is appropriate.

We target this monitor at our discovered class to ensure that this service is monitored on just the servers that are relevant. The health of the application can then be viewed to see the health of this monitor in the state view we have created in earlier recipes. Experiment with stopping and starting the service and view the health changing and the alerts that are generated. If you have created an alert view for this application, then this alert will appear there as well.

If you try this with different services, you will soon realize that this monitor will only work for services that are set to start automatically. In order to monitor for a service that is set to start automatically, edit the XML and change `<CheckStartupType />` to `<CheckStartupType>false</CheckStartupType>`.

Alternatively, you can create this as an override as described in other recipes.

## There's more...

If you are finding that the service is taking a while to be picked up by the state change, then please be aware that this is not normal. An issue was detected and a fix included in SCOM 2012 R2 UR4.

## See also

For more details about SCOM 2012 R2 UR4, visit `https://support.microsoft.com/en-us/kb/2992020`.

# Monitoring and capturing performance in MP Author

Another common need for a custom application is recording a performance counter for later viewing and monitoring the value of a counter. As an example in this recipe, we will be using the System Up Time counter, but please be aware that this is already captured in a standard pack. This recipe again builds on previous recipes, so please follow those first to acquire an understanding of how we got to this point.

## Getting ready

Make sure that you have followed the previous recipes or their equivalent. This will provide you with a SCOM environment and MP Author already installed and available for use. We are building on the previous recipes for this example, but you should be able to follow this recipe for any future requirements.

## How to do it...

To monitor and capture performance in MP Author, follow these steps:

1. Open MP Author and the previous management pack if they are not already open.

2. Because we are making a change, we should increase the management pack version number. Do this as specified in the previous recipe.

3. To create the performance capture rule, click on the **Rules** section. Navigate to **New | Create New Performance Rule...**.

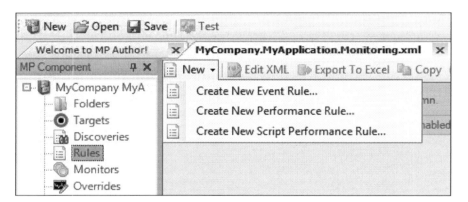

4. Select the name of the computer hosting the relevant performance counter and click on **Next**.

5.  Change the **Object** drop-down option to **System**. Change the **Counter** field to **System Up Time**. Leave the **Num Samples** and **Sampling Rate** fields at the defaults and set the **Target** field to **MyCompany MyApplication Class**. Click on **Next** to continue.

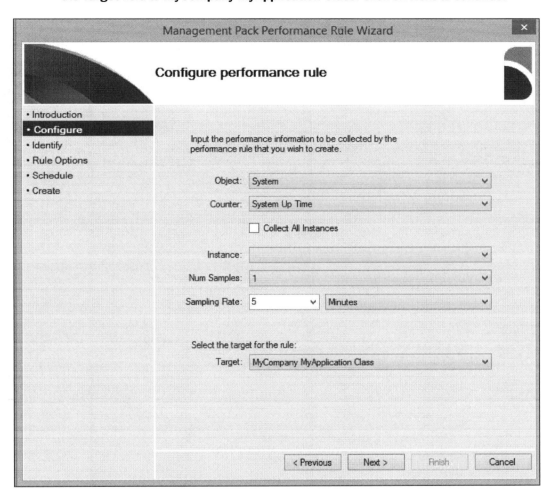

6. Change the **Name** field to `MyCompany.MyApplication.Monitoring.CollectSystemUpTime`. Change the **Display Name** field to `Collect System Up Time Counter`. Click on **Next** to continue.

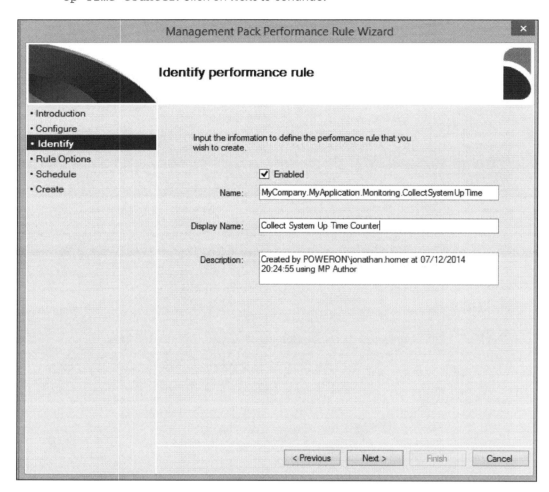

7. Check **Save to Data Warehouse**. Click on **Next** to continue.

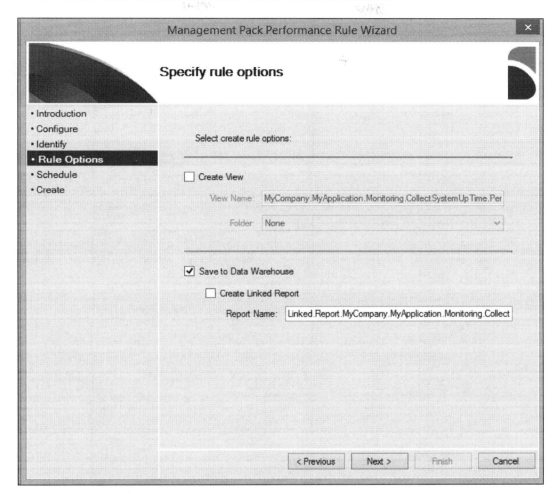

8. On the **Specify Schedule** screen, leave the settings as the default and click on **Next** to continue.

9. Click on **Finish** to create the performance-capturing rule.

10. Click on the **Monitors** section. Navigate to **New** | **Create New Performance Monitor....**

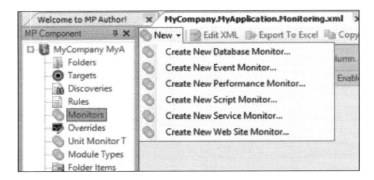

11. On the **Introduction** screen, select the name of the computer hosting the performance counter and click on **Next**.

12. Change the **Object** drop-down option to **System**. Change the **Counter** field to **System Up Time**. Leave the **Num Samples** and **Sampling Rate** fields at the defaults and set the **Target** field to **MyCompany MyApplication Class**. Click on **Next** to continue.

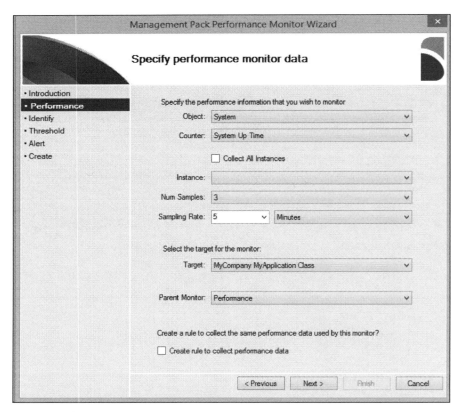

13. Change the **Name** field to `MyCompany.MyApplication.Monitoring.`
    `MonitorSystemUpTime` and **Display Name** field to `Monitor System Up Time`
    `Counter`.

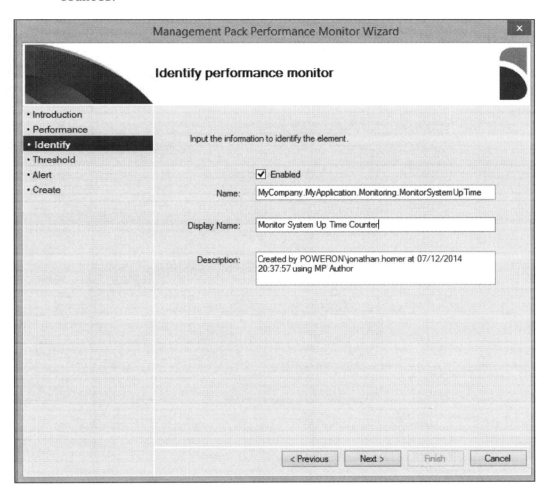

14. Change the **Type** field to **Consecutive** and the **Threshold** field to **greater than** and enter `1728000` (this equates to 20 days). Click on **Next** to continue.

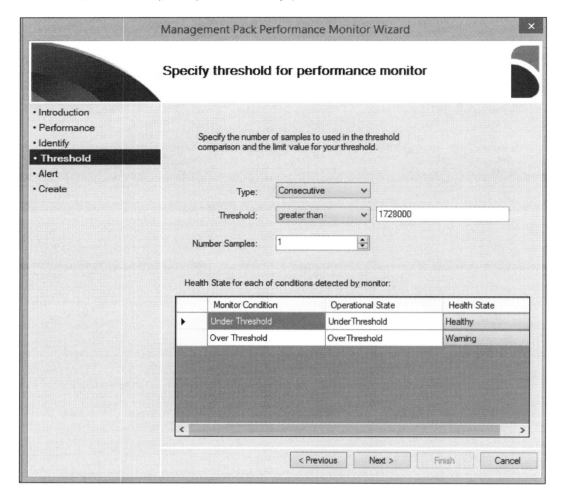

15. Check the **Generate alerts for this monitor** box and change the **Severity** field to **Warning**. Click on **Next** to continue.

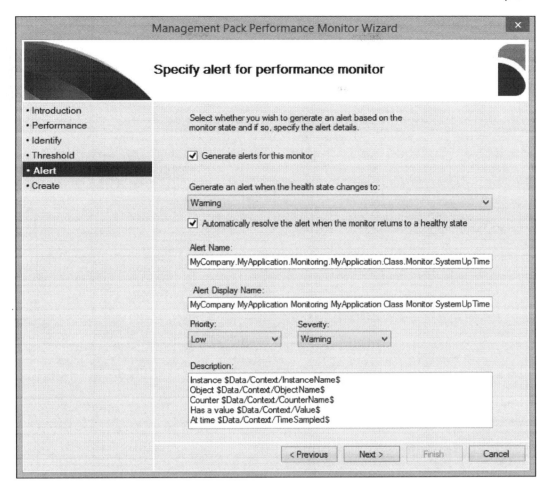

16. Click on **Finish** to complete the wizard.

17. Save and deploy the management pack.

## How it works...

One of the key things to realize about performance counters is that the monitor to check the value is completely different from the rule that will collect the value. For example, you may want to check the value to see whether it is over the threshold every 5 minutes, but you may be happy just recording the value every 10 minutes. This lets you keep the granularity you need for your monitoring without filling the database with data. You will have noticed that, in the monitor creation wizard, there is a checkbox to automatically create a rule to capture the counter at the same time with the same settings, but I wanted to show you that you can create them separately to illustrate this point.

When thinking about capturing performance data to the database, there is an often misunderstood setting about optimization of the data. The following three settings that control this optimization can be found when you edit the rule XML:

```
<Tolerance>1</Tolerance>
<ToleranceType>Absolute</ToleranceType>
<MaximumSampleSeparation>12</MaximumSampleSeparation>
```

These settings can really help you keep the amount of data you store in the database to a minimum, but are often ignored because people think they will affect their monitoring. As I have already mentioned, these are handled separately and so you can use these settings with no risk to the monitoring of the application.

Optimization works in such a way that a data point is only written to the database if either of the following conditions are true:

- The value of the performance counter has changed by more than the tolerance (the type chosen means that this can be an absolute value change or a percentage value change)
- It has been more than the maximum number of samples since the last data point was written to the database

These two combined means that, for the counter defined in the recipe, it will record a data point every 5 minutes if the value changes each time but, if it remains the same, it will only write a data point every hour. In many cases, you can change the tolerance to reduce the number of data points even further.

## There's more...

You will have noticed that, in the rule wizard, there were checkboxes to automatically create a view and a report for a performance counter. These are interesting options to select and experiment with to see if they provide information that can be useful. A later chapter on creating reports will go deeper into the kinds of things you can do with reports.

## See also

While we have created several management pack items using MP Author, Visual Studio allows you to customize these items to a much greater extent. We will be covering this in more depth in the next chapter.

# 8

# Authoring Management Packs in Visual Studio

In this chapter, we will be delving deeper into using Visual Studio to author your custom monitoring solutions. This tool is a complex one if you have not used it before and is often used for more complex custom monitoring solutions. This can result in people being put off by the interface. So, in this chapter, we will use the following recipes to start you off with using Visual Studio:

- ▶ Discovering a new application in Visual Studio
- ▶ Creating a custom view in Visual Studio
- ▶ Deploying a management pack from Visual Studio
- ▶ Creating and extending service monitors in Visual Studio
- ▶ Monitoring and capturing performance in Visual Studio

## Introduction

In the last chapter, we looked at authoring custom solutions using the console and the MP Author tool from Silect. These tools use wizards to simplify the authoring process and to shield the author from the complexities of the XML underneath. Visual Studio takes a different approach, providing minimal wizards and often requiring you to modify the XML directly.

This has the advantage of enabling you to use the full power and depth of the features available to you rather than relying on wizards created by people to cater to the majority of requirements. Unfortunately, it also has the effect of making even the simplest customization more complex because of the need to learn a complicated tool, such as Visual Studio, to edit XML that you may be unfamiliar with.

In this chapter, we will take an example from our previous chapter but author it in Visual Studio. We will make a couple of enhancements that are not currently possible using wizard-driven interfaces. Visual Studio stores each element of a management pack in a separate XML based document called a fragment. These fragments are combined to generate the management pack. At each recipe, we will go through the XML to explain what we are doing so that you can apply this to your own custom monitoring. This should help you get a grip of the basics of using Visual Studio, which will provide a firm and solid foundation for you when you come to design and author your own custom monitoring solutions in the future.

# Discovering a new application in Visual Studio

There are times when we need to step away from the wizard-driven interfaces of the console and tools like MP Author. These times come when we are moving away from the common scenarios that can be catered for with a general tool. Fortunately, Microsoft has provided a better tool than editing the XML directly in a text editor like Notepad.

The scenario we will be working towards is one where, instead of having to monitor the Print Spooler service, we wish to monitor the service specified in the **ServiceName** registry key that was discovered right back at the beginning.

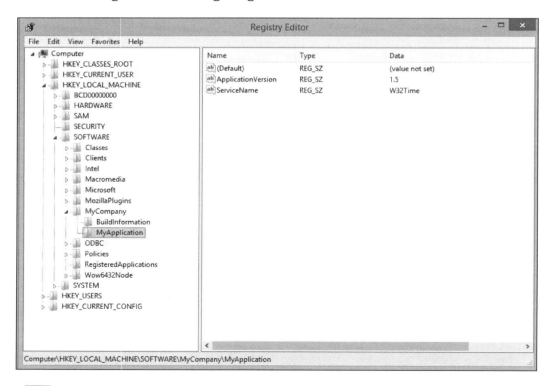

The tool that Microsoft has provided is a plugin for Visual Studio called System Center 2012 **Visual Studio Authoring Extensions** (**VSAE**). The link to download this plugin has been provided under the *See also* section of this recipe. While some editions of Visual Studio can be expensive, Microsoft has recently released a Community Edition of Visual Studio for free. This removes the price barrier when starting to use this product for editing management packs.

It should also be noted that you can register for a free source control system based in the cloud called Visual Studio Online. This allows you to manage versions of your code, including management packs, online. This greatly simplifies the problems of trying to find a specific version of a management pack at a later date. From here, you can even get a version of Visual Studio paid for by the month if you do not qualify for the Community Edition but do not want to pay for a full license.

## Getting ready

As discussed earlier, download Visual Studio and the VSAE plugin. Once you have downloaded the software and installed it on a suitable machine, you will be ready to start this recipe.

## How to do it...

1. Open Visual Studio.

2. Go to **File | New | Project** to start the **New Project** dialog box.

3. In the **New Project** dialog box, choose **Templates | Management Pack | Operations Manager** and then select **Operations Manager 2012 R2 Management Pack**.

 Later versions of SCOM can import management packs designed for earlier versions of SCOM (from 2007 R2 onwards), but the reverse is not true. You should make sure that you choose the appropriate version for your environment; but choosing too old a version will prevent you from using newer features such as the new visualizations in SCOM 2012.

4. Enter `MyCompany.MyApplication.Monitoring` in the **Name** field and enter `MyCompany.MyApplication.Solution` in the **Solution name** field. Click on **OK** to start creating the management pack.

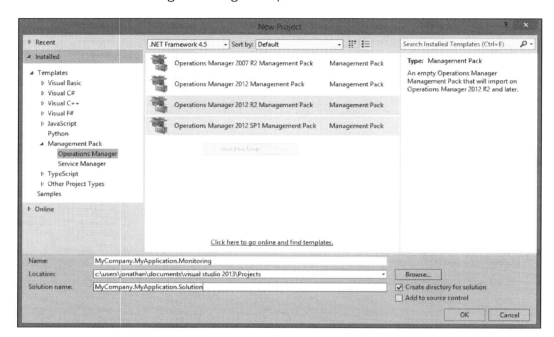

 You can create multiple projects within one solution, including report projects as well as multiple management pack projects. This allows you to group all the source code for your application in one place.

5. In a default installation, the **Solution Explorer** pane will now be open on the right-hand side with the project name highlighted. Right-click on the project and choose **Add | New Folder**. Name the folder `Classes and Discoveries`. Repeat this to create folders called `Monitors and Rules` and `Presentation`. The view should now look similar to the following screenshot:

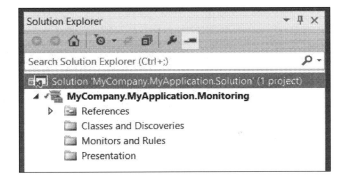

 As you develop your management packs, you will also develop your own preferred style to organize the different fragments. The structure of the code in Visual Studio will not affect the format of the final management pack.

6. Right-click on the `Classes and Discoveries` folder and click on **Add | New Item** to bring up the **Add New Item** dialog. Click on the **Class** item and enter `MyApplication Class` in the **Name** field. Click on **Add**.

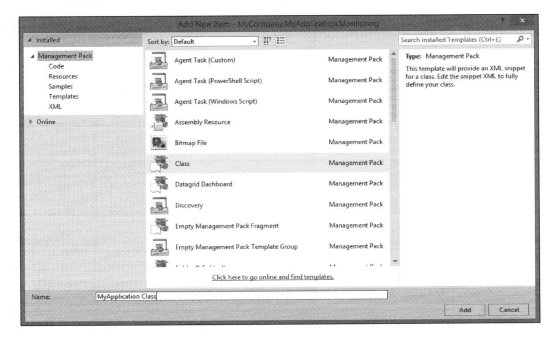

7. Review the XML that has been created and read some of the comments. Consider the following content in the XML file:

```
<ClassType ID="MyCompany.MyApplication.Monitoring.MyApplication_
Class"
Base="Windows!Microsoft.Windows.ApplicationComponent"
Accessibility="Internal" Abstract="false" Hosted="false"
Singleton="false">

<!-- Inside this section, you can add and remove properties
as needed.
 More information can be found in the Management Pack
Development Kit:
 http://msdn.microsoft.com/en-us/library/ee533714.aspx -->
<!--
<Property ID="Property1" Key="false" Type="string" />
-->
</ClassType>
```

Replace it with the following code:

```
<ClassType ID="MyCompany.MyApplication.Monitoring.MyApplication_
Class"
Base="Windows!Microsoft.Windows.LocalApplication"
Accessibility="Internal" Abstract="false" Hosted="true"
Singleton="false">

<Property ID="ApplicationVersion" Key="false" Type="string"
/>
<Property ID="ServiceName" Key="false" Type="string" />

</ClassType>
```

8. Now, consider the following code:

```
<!--
<DisplayString ElementID="MyCompany.MyApplication.Monitoring.
MyApplication_Class" SubElementID="Property1">
  <Name>Property1 Property</Name>
  <Description></Description>
</DisplayString>
-->
```

Replace it with the following:

```
<DisplayString ElementID="MyCompany.MyApplication.Monitoring.
MyApplication_Class" SubElementID="ApplicationVersion">
<Name>Application Version</Name>
<Description></Description>
```

```
</DisplayString>

<DisplayString ElementID="MyCompany.MyApplication.Monitoring.
MyApplication_Class" SubElementID="ServiceName">
<Name>Service Name</Name>
<Description></Description>
</DisplayString>
```

9. Save the management pack fragment and then close it.

> As you can see, without any wizards, we go straight into editing the XML, which can seem very daunting. However, all we have done here is told the class that it will be hosted on a Windows computer and then created a couple of properties: `Application Version` and `Service Name`.

10. Right-click on `Classes and Discoveries` and select **Add | New Item**. Choose **Discovery** from the list and enter `Discoveries` in the **Name** field. Then click on **Add**.

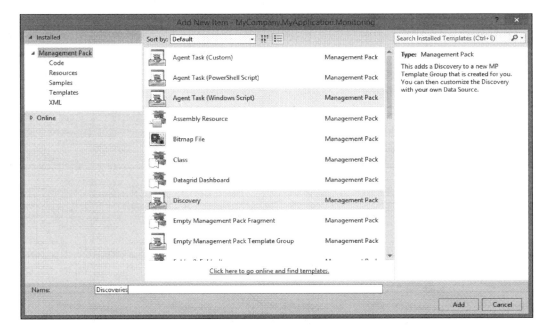

> This opens a completely different style of fragment. This style uses the **Properties** window to capture bits of information and then builds the XML we saw in the last fragment behind the scenes. The use of these two different styles is one of the reasons Visual Studio appears more complicated than other tools.

11. Click on the first line in the window that has opened and observe the **Properties** window. By default, this is in the bottom right-hand corner of the screen. We will change multiple properties to get a result that looks like the following screenshot:

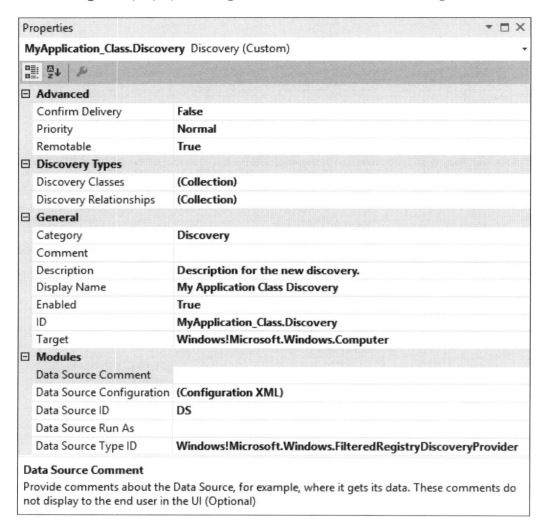

12. Locate the **ID** property in the **General** section. Change the value to `MyApplication_Class.Discovery`.

By default, the properties are ordered into sections. However, the icon at the top of the **Properties** window can be switched to order the list of properties alphabetically.

13. Locate the **Display Name** property in the **General** section. Change the value to My Application Class Discovery.

14. Locate the **Target** property in the **General** section. Change the value to Microsoft. Windows.Computer.

15. Locate the **Data Source Type ID** property in the **Modules** section. Click on the ellipsis and choose **Microsoft.Windows.FilteredRegistryDiscoveryProvider**.

16. Locate the **Data Source Configuration** property in the **Modules** section. Click on the ellipsis and insert the following XML before the </Configuration> tag:

```
<ComputerName>$Target/Property[Type="Windows!Microsoft.Wind
ows.Computer"]/NetworkName$</ComputerName>
<RegistryAttributeDefinitions>
<RegistryAttributeDefinition>
<AttributeName>MyApplicationExists</AttributeName>
<Path>SOFTWARE\MyCompany\MyApplication</Path>
<PathType>0</PathType>
<AttributeType>0</AttributeType>
</RegistryAttributeDefinition>
<RegistryAttributeDefinition>
<AttributeName>ApplicationVersion</AttributeName>
<Path>SOFTWARE\MyCompany\MyApplication\ApplicationVersion</
Path>
<PathType>1</PathType>
<AttributeType>1</AttributeType>
</RegistryAttributeDefinition>
<RegistryAttributeDefinition>
<AttributeName>ServiceName</AttributeName>
<Path>SOFTWARE\MyCompany\MyApplication\ServiceName</Path>
<PathType>1</PathType>
<AttributeType>1</AttributeType>
</RegistryAttributeDefinition>
</RegistryAttributeDefinitions>
<Frequency>28800</Frequency>
<ClassId>$MPElement[Name="MyCompany.MyApplication.Monitorin
g.MyApplication_Class"]$</ClassId>
<InstanceSettings>
<Settings>
<Setting>
```

```
<Name>$MPElement[Name="Windows!Microsoft.Windows.Computer"]/
PrincipalName$</Name>
<Value>$Target/Property[Type="Windows!Microsoft.Windows.Com
puter"]/PrincipalName$</Value>
</Setting>
<Setting>
<Name>$MPElement[Name="System!System.Entity"]/DisplayName$</Name>
<Value>$Target/Property[Type="System!System.Entity"]/Displa
yName$</Value>
</Setting>
<Setting>
<Name>$MPElement[Name="MyCompany.MyApplication.Monitoring.M
yApplication_Class"]/ApplicationVersion$</Name>
<Value>$Data/Values/ApplicationVersion$</Value>
</Setting>
<Setting>
<Name>$MPElement[Name="MyCompany.MyApplication.Monitoring.M
yApplication_Class"]/ServiceName$</Name>
<Value>$Data/Values/ServiceName$</Value>
</Setting>
</Settings>
</InstanceSettings>
<Expression>
<SimpleExpression>
<ValueExpression>
<XPathQuery
Type="String">Values/MyApplicationExists</XPathQuery>
</ValueExpression>
<Operator>Equal</Operator>
<ValueExpression>
<Value Type="String">True</Value>
</ValueExpression>
</SimpleExpression>
</Expression>
```

> Don't worry if this looks complicated. We will go through it in the next *How it works...* section.

17. Locate the **Discovery Classes** property in the **Discovery Types** section. Click on the ellipsis to display the **Discovery Classes Collection Editor**. Click on **Add**. A **Discovery Types** section will now appear; locate the **Class** property and click on the ellipsis to display the **Choose a Class** dialog. Choose **MyCompany.MyApplication.Monitoring. MyApplication_Class** and click on **OK**. Click on the ellipsis next to **Class Properties** to display the **Choose a Property** dialog. Check the boxes next to **ApplicationVersion**, **DisplayName**, and **ServiceName** and then click on **OK**. When back at the **Discovery Classes Collection Editor**, click on **OK** one last time to complete this property.

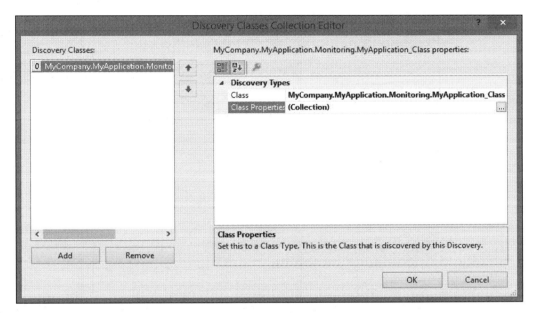

 The management pack will work without the **Discovery Classes** property being set as it does not change the functionality of the pack. However, it does allow the console to know where it can display the discovery in the authoring pane, and so without it being set, you cannot later find the discovery to override any settings.

18. Locate the **Discovery Relationships** property in the **Discovery Types** section. Click on the ellipsis to display the **Discovery Relationships Collection Editor** screen. Click on **Add**. A **Discovery Types** section will now appear; locate the **Relationship** property and click on the ellipsis to display the **Choose a Relationship** dialog. Choose **Microsoft. Windows.ComputerHostsLocalApplication** and click on **OK**. Click on **OK** one last time to complete this property.

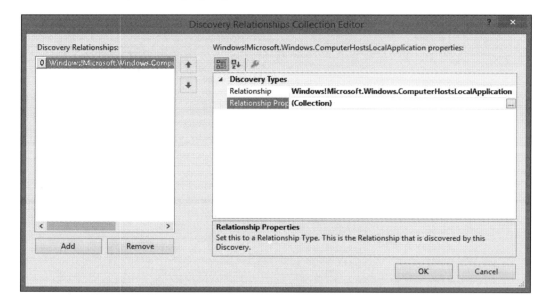

19. With the properties all set, save and close the discoveries fragment.

20. Right-click on the project name and select **Build**. If you have set everything correctly, the management pack will build and verify. There will be a warning about unsealed management packs, but this can be ignored at the moment.

## How it works...

As you can see from this recipe, there is a lot going on in this tool with very little assistance to make the learning curve a little less daunting. If you have used Visual Studio before, then you will be familiar with the approach of editing code at times and properties at others, but this is likely to be new for most people. Hopefully, as we go through what we have done, things will become a little clearer.

The first thing to note is that each of the fragments created in Visual Studio is merged together during compilation into the final management pack. Each fragment can therefore contain all the information needed to make that part of the management pack work. This is a big improvement over editing with Notepad, where you have to remember to make changes in multiple sections of the XML.

Let's go through what we did in the first fragment, `MyApplication` class, step by step.

The first line simply says that we are starting a new fragment, and the next three simply define that we are starting to create a new class type:

```
<ManagementPackFragment SchemaVersion="2.0"
xmlns:xsd="http://www.w3.org/2001/XMLSchema">
<TypeDefinitions>
<EntityTypes>
<ClassTypes>
```

The following section is a comment that is giving you more information on where you can go to find more details on management pack authoring:

```
<!-- In this section, modify the attributes based on your needs.
Ensure the Base attribute matches the application you are
modeling. More information can be found in the Management Pack
Development Kit: http://msdn.microsoft.com/en-
us/library/ee533867.aspx -->
```

The next section defines our class. There are two areas that we change from the default: the `Base` class and the `Hosted` property. The `Hosted` property is relatively simple to explain—it means that the class is *owned* by its parent (which is the local computer in our example). The computer is then responsible for all the monitoring for this class, and any performance counters or event logs we look at will be local to the computer. If it was not hosted, then the management servers in the management group would be responsible for the monitoring of the class and the counters or logs would be of the management server instead:

```
<ClassType ID="MyCompany.MyApplication.Monitoring.MyApplication_Class"
|Base="Windows!Microsoft.Windows.LocalApplication"
Accessibility="Internal" Abstract="false" Hosted="true"
Singleton="false">
```

The base class will be familiar to you if you do any programming, but if not, then you can think of it as a template. In MS Word, when you create your document from a template, it will often have pictures and text ready for you to use. A base class can have properties and relationships with other classes; all new classes that use this template automatically get these properties and relationships as well. In this code, we have used the base class of `Microsoft.Windows.LocalApplication`. This is a commonly used class when defining an application, as it has a built-in relationship with the computer object, which establishes the hosting relationship automatically. A similar base class would be `Microsoft.Windows.ComputerRole`, which apart from having a hosting relationship defined, will automatically rollup the health of this class to affect the health of the overall computer. We are not doing this in our example, so the `Microsoft.Windows.LocalApplication` base class is ideal.

You can define your own base classes by setting the **Abstract** property to true in the class definition. They then cannot be used for discovering objects directly but can be used as base classes.

After we have told SCOM which base class we are using as our template, we then define a couple of additional properties that will only exist in our version of the class. Think of this as when you add some text to the Word document you created when you used the template. The document is then your customized version. In this case, we are adding the new properties we need to record, namely `ApplicationVersion` and `ServiceName`:

```
<Property ID="ApplicationVersion" Key="false" Type="string" />
<Property ID="ServiceName" Key="false" Type="string" />
```

The final lines simply indicate that you have finished the changes to the class definition:

```
</ClassType>
</ClassTypes>
</EntityTypes>
</TypeDefinitions>
```

The final section is the **Language Packs** section, which simply sets the descriptive text that you will see in the console. When a SCOM console is installed on a server that is built with the French Language, it will look in this section to see whether the management pack author has created a French Language version of the descriptive text. If not, it will use the default language pack. You can define as many language packs as you like in this section.

The second fragment is the discovery fragment. Here, we define the code that will be run and the configuration that it needs to find in order to create an instance of the class. Again, we will step through the changes we made one by one.

Firstly, we set the properties in the **General** category. Most of these are straightforward, such as **ID** and **Display Name**, but **Target** may require some explanation. All discoveries need to run somewhere, and this discovery wants to run on every computer in the environment to check the registry on each. For this reason, we target the **Microsoft.Windows.Computer** class so that all computers will be checked. Only those computers that match the criteria we set will have one of our class instances created.

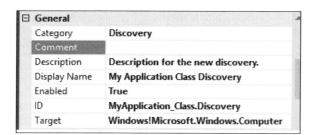

Next, we set the properties in the **Modules** category. This is where a discovery is most complicated as it chooses the underlying code that will be run and the parameters that will be given to that code to change its behavior. The code chosen is specified in the **Data Source Type ID** property, and we use **Microsoft.Windows.FilteredRegistryDiscoveryProvider**. This provider checks the registry to see whether the information specified in the parameters is present. If so, the parameters will create an instance of the class specified in other parameters.

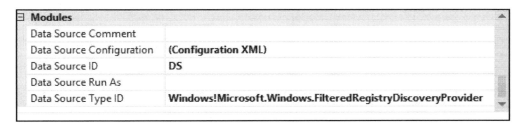

| Modules | |
|---|---|
| Data Source Comment | |
| Data Source Configuration | (Configuration XML) |
| Data Source ID | DS |
| Data Source Run As | |
| Data Source Type ID | Windows!Microsoft.Windows.FilteredRegistryDiscoveryProvider |

You can check out the **Filtered Registry Discovery Provider** in great detail on MSDN (the link is in the *See also* section). If you do, you will notice that there are layers upon layers of different data sources and other modules that make up this provider.

The parameters could do with some explanation, and while they look complicated, they are actually fairly straightforward. The first parameter is the `ComputerName` parameter. This simply specifies the name of the computer that we want to read the registry from. Because we are targeting the computer class, we can read the `NetworkName` property that SCOM has captured for the computer we are targeting. The $ symbol tells SCOM that what is coming is a property that can be substituted at runtime:

```
<ComputerName>$Target/Property[Type="Windows!Microsoft.Windows.Com
puter"]/NetworkName$</ComputerName>
```

The next parameter is the `RegistryAttributeDefinitions` parameter:

```
<RegistryAttributeDefinitions>
```

This contains a list of registry settings (or attributes) that the code should bring back and pass to the discovery module. The first of these is a check that the `MyApplication` key even exists on the computer. The path type `0` indicates that it is looking for the existence of a key and the attribute type `0` tells it to return **true/false**:

```
<RegistryAttributeDefinition>
<AttributeName>MyApplicationExists</AttributeName>
<Path>SOFTWARE\MyCompany\MyApplication</Path>
<PathType>0</PathType>
<AttributeType>0</AttributeType>
</RegistryAttributeDefinition>
```

The second attribute is to read the `ApplicationVersion` value from the registry. This uses a path type of `1` to say that it is looking for the value held within a registry key and the attribute type of `1` indicates that it should expect to read a string value:

```
<RegistryAttributeDefinition>
<AttributeName>ApplicationVersion</AttributeName>
<Path>SOFTWARE\MyCompany\MyApplication\ApplicationVersion</Path>
<PathType>1</PathType>
<AttributeType>1</AttributeType>
</RegistryAttributeDefinition>
```

The third attribute is to read the `ServiceName` value in the same way the `ApplicationVersion` value was read:

```
<RegistryAttributeDefinition>
<AttributeName>ServiceName</AttributeName>
<Path>SOFTWARE\MyCompany\MyApplication\ServiceName</Path>
<PathType>1</PathType>
<AttributeType>1</AttributeType>
</RegistryAttributeDefinition>
```

Finally, we just say that we have finished our list of attributes and end this parameter:

```
</RegistryAttributeDefinitions>
```

> The possible settings for the `Registry Attribute Definitions` parameter can be found on MSDN, the link to which is in the *See also* section of this recipe.

The next parameter is the frequency with which we will repeat the check on the registry. This is specified in seconds and the value shown here means it will check every 8 hours:

```
<Frequency>28800</Frequency>
```

The `ClassID` parameter indicates which class will be discovered if the registry check is successful. We tell it that we will be using the class named `MyCompany.MyApplication.Monitoring.MyApplication_Class`, as this is what we are trying to find:

```
<ClassId>$MPElement[Name="MyCompany.MyApplication.Monitoring.
MyApplication_Class"]$</ClassId>
```

The next parameter is the `InstanceSettings` parameter:

```
<InstanceSettings>
<Settings>
```

This contains the information needed to set all the properties of the class we have defined. Firstly, because we are hosting our class on a Windows computer, we need to tell it which Windows computer will be doing that job. We do this by specifying the `Key` property of the Windows computer. Again, because we have targeted the Windows computer, we can just read the correct value from the SCOM properties already captured:

```
<Setting>
<Name>$MPElement[Name="Windows!Microsoft.Windows.Computer"]/
PrincipalName$</Name>
<Value>$Target/Property[Type="Windows!Microsoft.Windows.Computer"]
/PrincipalName$</Value>
</Setting>
```

The next setting we define is the display name. Again, we will just read this from the SCOM properties already captured for the Windows computer:

```
<Setting>
<Name>$MPElement[Name="System!System.Entity"]/DisplayName$</Name>
<Value>$Target/Property[Type="System!System.Entity"]/DisplayName$<
/Value>
</Setting>
```

The next two settings are the properties we want SCOM to store for our class. Here, we simply set the SCOM class property to the `ApplicationVersion` registry attribute we defined earlier, which will be returned from the registry checking part of the code into the `Data` dataset. The correct format for reading this is as follows:

```
<Setting>
<Name>$MPElement[Name="MyCompany.MyApplication.Monitoring.MyApplic
ation_Class"]/ApplicationVersion$</Name>
<Value>$Data/Values/ApplicationVersion$</Value>
</Setting>
<Setting>
<Name>$MPElement[Name="MyCompany.MyApplication.Monitoring.MyApplic
ation_Class"]/ServiceName$</Name>
<Value>$Data/Values/ServiceName$</Value>
</Setting>
```

Finally, we close the `InstanceSettings` parameter to show we have finished:

```
</Settings>
</InstanceSettings>
```

The final parameter is the `Expression` parameter, which simply defines the condition that needs to be met before the class instance is created. In this case, we use the true/false returned from the first registry attribute to tell us whether the `MyApplication` key has been created:

```
<Expression>
<SimpleExpression>
<ValueExpression>
<XPathQuery Type="String">Values/MyApplicationExists</XPathQuery>
</ValueExpression>
<Operator>Equal</Operator>
<ValueExpression>
<Value Type="String">True</Value>
</ValueExpression>
</SimpleExpression>
</Expression>
```

 If we wanted to also check for a specific version of the application, we could do so by adding additional checks to this expression section. The syntax of the `Expression` type is on MSDN and the link is in the *See also* section of this recipe.

The properties in the **Discovery Types** section are there mainly for information, but it is best practice to complete them so that you can find the discovery in the console once the management pack is imported.

As you can see, while the code that you need to write for Visual Studio can seem daunting, when you break it down, it is fairly straightforward. I would recommend spending time with the Microsoft Virtual Academy course on management pack authoring as this goes into much more detail on the properties and parameters than I can provide here. As before, this management pack will be built on during the next few recipes.

## See also

- System Center 2012 Visual Studio Authoring Extensions, which can be downloaded from http://www.microsoft.com/en-us/download/details.aspx?id=30169

- Visual Studio Community Edition, found at http://www.visualstudio.com/products/visual-studio-community-vs

- Details on Visual Studio Online, found at http://www.visualstudio.com/en-us/products/what-is-visual-studio-online-vs.aspx

> ▸ Information on the Filtered Registry Discovery Provider at `https://msdn.microsoft.com/en-us/library/jj129810.aspx`

> ▸ Information on the Registry Attribute Data Type at `https://msdn.microsoft.com/en-us/library/jj130492.aspx`

> ▸ Information on the Expression Data Type at `https://msdn.microsoft.com/en-us/library/jj130463.aspx`

> ▸ Microsoft Virtual Academy course on management pack authoring with Visual Studio at `http://www.microsoftvirtualacademy.com/training-courses/system-center-2012-r2-operations-manager-management-pack`

# Creating a custom view in Visual Studio

In this recipe, we will create a custom folder with an alert view and a state view contained within it. These views are relatively simple to define in the console, but creating them in Visual Studio allows them to be stored in the same management pack, and therefore, to be kept in the same source control we configured in the previous recipe. These views will reference the class created and discovered in the previous recipe, so you should complete the previous recipe first.

## Getting ready

To prepare for this recipe, you need to have Visual Studio installed with the Authoring Extensions configured. In order to follow the instructions fully, you should have created the class and discovery from the previous pack.

## How to do it...

1. Open Visual Studio and the solution containing the management pack from the previous recipe.

2. Find the **Solution Explorer**. Right-click on the **Presentation** folder and select **Add | New Item** to bring up the **Add New Item** dialog. Click on **Folder & Folder Item** and enter `MyApplication Folder` in the **Name** field. Click on **Add**.

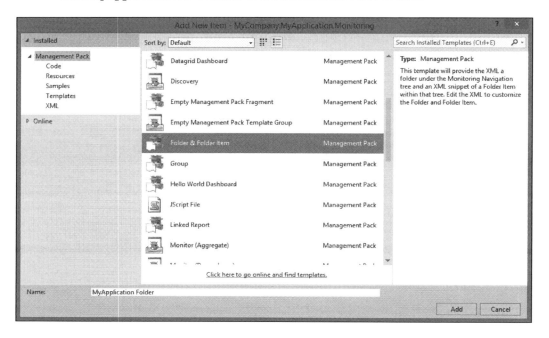

3. Review the XML of the management pack fragment that opens and read the comments. Scroll down to find `DisplayString` and find the following code:

   `<Name>MyApplication_Folder Folder</Name>`

   Replace it with the following code:

   `<Name>MyApplication Views</Name>`

4. Save and close this management pack fragment.

5. Right-click again on the **Presentation** folder and select **Add | New Item** to bring up the **Add New Item** dialog. Click on the **View (Custom)** item and enter `MyApplication Views` in the **Name** field. Click on **Add**.

6.  Click on the first line in the window that has opened and observe the **Properties** window. By default, this is in the bottom right-hand corner of the screen. We will change multiple properties to get a result that looks like the following screenshot:

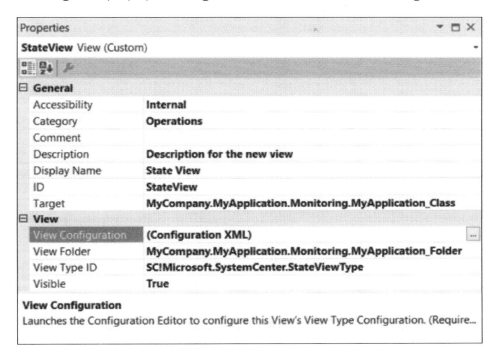

7.  Locate the **ID** property in the **General** section. Change the value to StateView.

8.  Locate the **Display Name** property in the **General** section. Change the value to State View.

9.  Locate the **Target** property in the **General** section. Click on the ellipsis and select the **MyCompany.MyApplication.Monitoring.MyApplication_Class** class.

10. Locate the **View Type ID** property in the **View** section. Click on the ellipsis and select the **Microsoft.SystemCenter.StateViewType** type.

11. Locate the **View Folder** property in the **View** section. Click on the ellipsis and select the **MyCompany.MyApplication.Monitoring.MyApplication_Folder** folder.

12. Locate the **View Configuration** property in the **View** section. Click on the ellipsis and insert the following XML before the `</Configuration>` tag:

```
<Presentation>
<ColumnInfo Index="0" SortIndex="0" Width="100"
Grouped="false" Sorted="true" IsSortable="true"
Visible="true" SortOrder="Descending">
<Name>State</Name>
<Id>MyCompany.MyApplication.Monitoring.MyApplication_Class<
/Id>
</ColumnInfo>
<ColumnInfo Index="1" SortIndex="-1" Width="25"
Grouped="false" Sorted="false" IsSortable="true"
Visible="true" SortOrder="Ascending">
<Name>In Maintenance Mode</Name>
<Id>InMaintenanceMode</Id>
</ColumnInfo>
<ColumnInfo Index="2" SortIndex="-1" Width="200"
Grouped="false" Sorted="false" IsSortable="true"
Visible="true" SortOrder="Ascending">
<Name>Name</Name>
<Id>Name</Id>
</ColumnInfo>
<ColumnInfo Index="3" SortIndex="-1" Width="100"
Grouped="false" Sorted="false" IsSortable="true"
Visible="false" SortOrder="Ascending">
<Name>Path</Name>
<Id>Path</Id>
</ColumnInfo>
<ColumnInfo Index="4" SortIndex="-1" Width="100"
Grouped="false" Sorted="false" IsSortable="true"
Visible="true" SortOrder="Ascending">
<Name>Application Version</Name>
<Id>MyCompany.MyApplication.Monitoring.MyApplication_Class/
ApplicationVersion</Id>
</ColumnInfo>
<ColumnInfo Index="5" SortIndex="-1" Width="100"
Grouped="false" Sorted="false" IsSortable="true"
Visible="true" SortOrder="Ascending">
<Name>Service Name</Name>
<Id>MyCompany.MyApplication.Monitoring.MyApplication_Class/
ServiceName</Id>
</ColumnInfo>
</Presentation>
```

Again, don't worry if this looks complicated. We will go through it in the *How it works...* section of this recipe.

13. Click on **OK** to close the configuration box.

14. Right-click on the **MyApplication Views** window and select **Add Template**. In the dialog box, select **View (Custom)** and click on **OK**.

15. Click on the **NewView** line that has been created. We will change multiple properties to get a result that looks like the following screenshot:

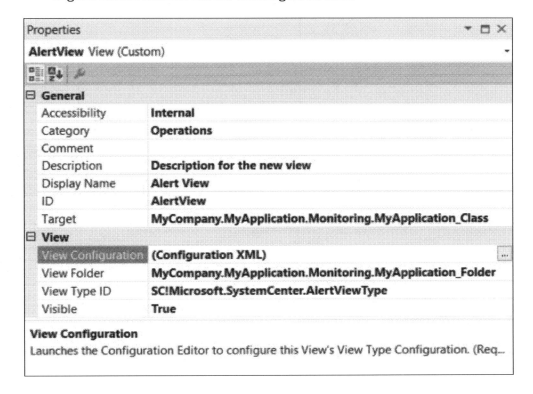

16. Locate the **ID** property in the **General** section. Change the value to `AlertView`.

17. Locate the **Display Name** property in the **General** section. Change the value to `Alert View`.

18. Locate the **Target** property in the **General** section. Click on the ellipsis and select the **MyCompany.MyApplication.Monitoring.MyApplication_Class** class.

19. Locate the **View Type ID** property in the **View** section. Click on the ellipsis and select the **Microsoft.SystemCenter.AlertViewType** type.

20. Locate the **View Folder** property in the **View** section. Click on the ellipsis and select the **MyCompany.MyApplication.Monitoring.MyApplication_Folder** folder.

21. Locate the **View Configuration** property in the **View** section. Click on the ellipsis and insert the following XML before the `</Configuration>` tag:

```
<Criteria>
<ResolutionState>
<StateRange Operator="NotEquals">255</StateRange>
</ResolutionState>
</Criteria>
```

22. Click on **OK** to close the configuration box.

23. Save and close the **MyApplication Views** fragment.

24. Right-click on the project name and select **Build**. If you have set everything correctly, the management pack will build and verify. There will be a warning about unsealed management packs, but this can be ignored at the moment.

We will talk about deploying the management pack in the next recipe, but once deployed, the view will look similar to the following screenshot:

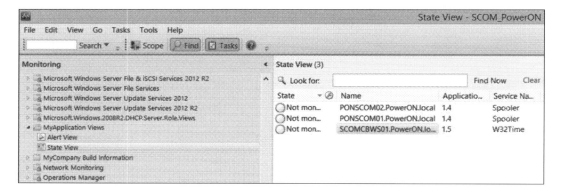

## How it works...

In the previous recipe, we discussed how Visual Studio has two fragment types. This recipe again uses the same two types, so you can see that you quickly get used to the interface and switching between the two styles.

Let's go through the **View** folder fragment. The first line simply says that we are starting a new fragment, and the next lines define that we are starting to create a new folder:

```
<ManagementPackFragment SchemaVersion="2.0" xmlns:xsd="http://www.
w3.org/2001/XMLSchema">
<Presentation>
<Folders>
```

The next section is simply a comment that is giving you more information on where you can go to find more details on management pack authoring:

```
<!-- In this section, you can create more folders. Edit the
DisplayString for this folder to change the name the user sees in
the console. More information can be found in the Management Pack
Development Kit: http://msdn.microsoft.com/en-us/library/ee533810.aspx
-->
```

 Comment sections start with `<!--` and end with `-->` Any text between these markers will be ignored and it is good practice to comment your code wherever possible.

The next section defines our folder. The main point to note here is the `ParentFolder` property, which shows where this folder will appear in the SCOM console. The folder listed here is the `Monitoring` folder you see at the top of the console view. If you want to nest multiple subfolders, you can create a large tree:

```
<Folder ID="MyCompany.MyApplication.Monitoring.MyApplication_Folder"
Accessibility="Internal"
ParentFolder="SC!Microsoft.SystemCenter.Monitoring.ViewFolder.Root
" />
```

The next section closes the `Folders` section of the XML and looks at the `FolderItems` section. We do not need to put anything in here as the second fragment creates these `FolderItems` for our views automatically:

```
</Folders>
<FolderItems>
<!-- In this section, uncomment and edit the ElementID to
reference a View or Folder you've created to place that item into
the Folder referenced by the Folder attribute. FolderItems do not
need display strings; The referenced ElementID's DisplayString is
used and shown to the user. More information can be found in the
Management  Pack Development Kit: http://msdn.microsoft.com/en-
us/library/ee533579.aspx -->
<!--
<FolderItem ID="MyCompany.MyApplication.Monitoring.FolderItem1"
ElementID=""
Folder="MyCompany.MyApplication.Monitoring.MyApplication_Folder"
/>
-->
</FolderItems>
</Presentation>
```

The final section again is the **Language Packs** section, which simply sets the descriptive text that you will see in the console.

The second fragment is the `Views` fragment. Here, we have defined multiple views that will all be generated at build time. In both cases, most of the properties are self-explanatory. The Target property is set at the new class we have created so that it will show health states and alerts just for our new classes, and not the whole Windows computer. The configuration sections may need a little explanation.

The `State View` configuration lists the columns that will be displayed. Many examples on the Internet will leave this blank, but it can be helpful to specify the columns to create a consistent starting view for all users. The first of these is the state column. The ID of this is the ID of the class, and this ensures that the health of the class object is displayed in the expected place:

```
<Presentation>
<ColumnInfo Index="0" SortIndex="0" Width="100" Grouped="false"
Sorted="true" IsSortable="true" Visible="true"
SortOrder="Descending">
<Name>State</Name>
<Id>MyCompany.MyApplication.Monitoring.MyApplication_Class</Id>
</ColumnInfo>
```

The next column is the maintenance mode column. Note that we have changed the width of this column to 25. If we do not specify any configuration, the view will show the maintenance mode but with a default width of 100:

```
<ColumnInfo Index="1" SortIndex="-1" Width="25" Grouped="false"
Sorted="false" IsSortable="true" Visible="true"
SortOrder="Ascending">
<Name>In Maintenance Mode</Name>
<Id>InMaintenanceMode</Id>
</ColumnInfo>
```

The next columns simply display further properties of the class. Note that some have been set to be not visible by default. You can change the parameters to alter the width of the view as well as to set whether or not they are sorted or grouped:

```
<ColumnInfo Index="2" SortIndex="-1" Width="200" Grouped="false"
Sorted="false" IsSortable="true" Visible="true"
SortOrder="Ascending">
<Name>Name</Name>
<Id>Name</Id>
</ColumnInfo>
<ColumnInfo Index="3" SortIndex="-1" Width="100" Grouped="false"
Sorted="false" IsSortable="true" Visible="false"
SortOrder="Ascending">
<Name>Path</Name>
<Id>Path</Id>
</ColumnInfo>
<ColumnInfo Index="4" SortIndex="-1" Width="100" Grouped="false"
Sorted="false" IsSortable="true" Visible="true"
SortOrder="Ascending">
```

```
<Name>Application Version</Name>
<Id>MyCompany.MyApplication.Monitoring.MyApplication_Class
/ApplicationVersion</Id>
</ColumnInfo>
<ColumnInfo Index="5" SortIndex="-1" Width="100" Grouped="false"
Sorted="false" IsSortable="true" Visible="true"
SortOrder="Ascending">
<Name>Service Name</Name>
<Id>MyCompany.MyApplication.Monitoring.MyApplication_Class
/ServiceName</Id>
</ColumnInfo>
</Presentation>
```

All of these settings define the default view seen when you first enter the console. The user can personalize their own view from the columns you have selected but cannot alter the columns you have made visible.

The Rule View configuration is much smaller as it is just there to ensure that closed alerts will not be displayed:

```
<Criteria>
<ResolutionState>
<StateRange Operator="NotEquals">255</StateRange>
</ResolutionState>
</Criteria>
```

## There's more...

It should be noted that you can put Criteria in a state view and Presentation in an alert view as well. These would allow you to show only critical servers in a state view or to control the default columns visible in an alert view.

# Deploying a management pack from Visual Studio

Visual Studio has a mechanism for deploying management packs directly to your SCOM management group. This can be helpful to ensure that the correct version of the management pack is selected for deployment.

## Getting ready

Make sure that you have followed the previous recipes or their equivalent. This means you will have a SCOM environment and Visual Studio already installed and available for use. The management pack should have some content to deploy in it. We will now go in and name the management pack properly and deploy it to the management group.

## How to do it...

To deploy a management pack from Visual Studio, perform the following steps:

1. Open Visual Studio and the solution containing the management pack from the previous recipes.

2. Right-click on the **MyCompany.MyApplication.Monitoring** project and select **Properties**.

3. On the **Properties** page, click on the **Find or Create the Management Pack Display Name and Description** link.

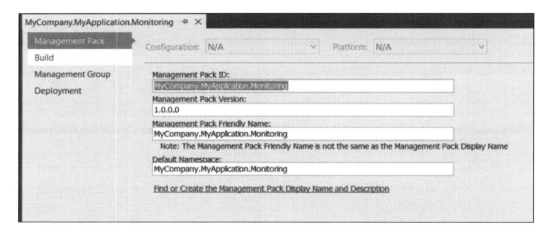

4. In the management pack fragment that opens, review the XML. By now, you will probably recognize that this is just a `LanguagePack` section that will control how the name of the management pack appears in the console. Find the `DisplayString` with the following code:

```
<Name>MyCompany.MyApplication.Monitoring</Name>
<Description>MyCompany.MyApplication.Monitoring
</Description>
```

Replace it with the following code:

```
<Name>MyCompany - MyApplication Monitoring Management
Pack</Name>
<Description>This management pack contains the monitoring
for MyApplication</Description>
```

5. Save and close this management pack fragment.

6. Back in the **Properties** window, click on the **Management Group** tab and then on the **Add** button.

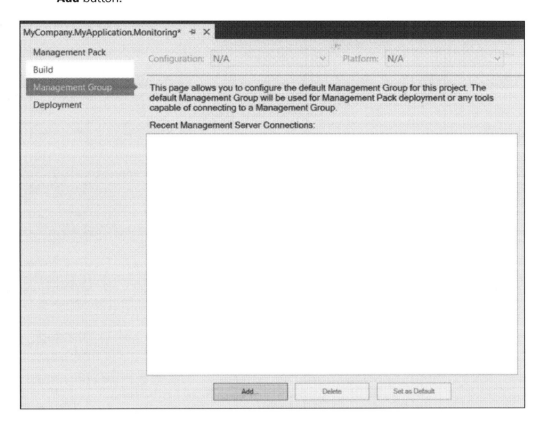

7. In the **Add Management Server** dialog box, enter the server name in the **Server Name** field of your management server and choose **Use my current Windows credentials**. Click on the **Add Server** button.

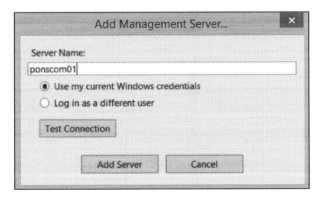

If you only have one management group, you may wish to choose the **Log in as a different user** option to provide you with a final check that allows you to abort the deployment to ensure you don't accidentally deploy a partly-developed management pack to production.

8.  In the **Deployment** tab, select the **Deploy projects to default management group only** radio button.

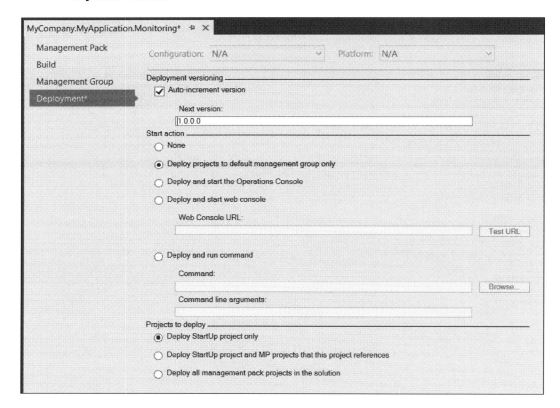

 Note the **Projects to deploy** section. If you have more than one management pack in a solution, you may wish to switch this button to allow all the updated management packs to deploy in a single action.

9.  Save the properties and close the window.

10. Click on the **Start** button in the task bar, or press *F5*. This will build the management pack and attempt to deploy it.

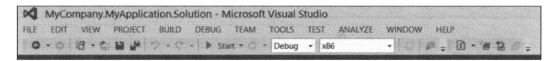

This will now connect and deploy the management pack.

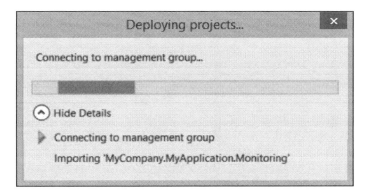

Once complete, the dialog box closes automatically and no final confirmation that it has deployed is given.

# Creating and extending service monitors in Visual Studio

In previous recipes, we have showed how to discover an application, create some custom views, and how to deploy this pack automatically. We have also seen in other sections how to create a monitor for a specific service with other authoring tools. However, if you look at the following screenshot, you will see that there are different options under **Service Name** to monitor different computers. This recipe will show you how to set up a single service monitor in Visual Studio that will check for the appropriate service on the appropriate computer.

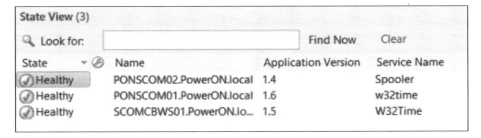

## Getting ready

As before, this recipe builds on the work done earlier in this chapter. So, you should have Visual Studio with the Authoring Extensions plugin installed and have the management pack we have been developing at hand.

## How to do it...

To create and extend service monitors in Visual Studio, follow these steps:

1. Open Visual Studio and the solution containing the management pack from the previous recipe.

2. Find the **Solution Explorer**. Right-click on the **Monitors and Rules** folder and select **Add | New Item** to bring up the **Add New Item** dialog. Click on the **Monitor (Unit)** item and enter `Unit Monitors` in the **Name** field. Click on **Add**.

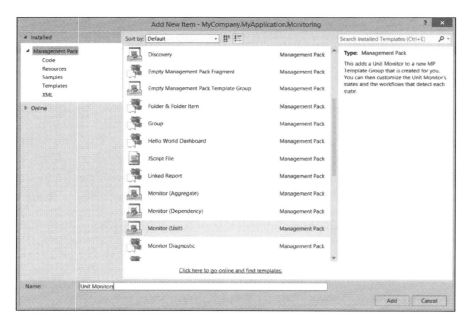

3. Click on the first line in the window that has opened and observe the **Properties** window. By default, this is in the bottom right-hand corner of the screen. We will change multiple properties to get a result that looks like the following screenshot:

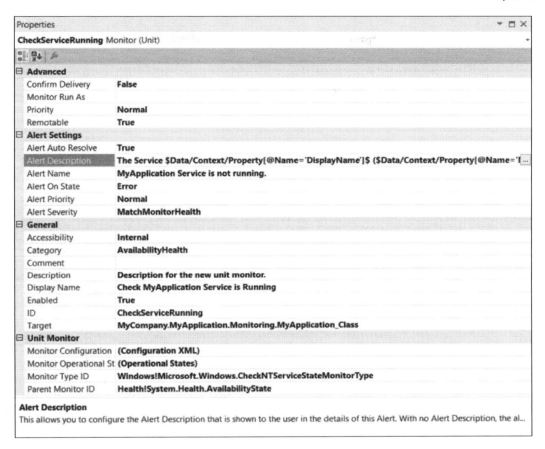

4. Locate the **ID** property in the **General** section. Change the value to
   `CheckServiceRunning`.

5. Locate the **Display Name** property in the **General** section. Change the value to `Check MyApplication Service is Running`.

6. Locate the **Target** property in the **General** section. Click on the ellipsis and select the **MyCompany.MyApplication.Monitoring.MyApplication_Class** class.

7. Locate the **Parent Monitor ID** property in the **Unit Monitor** section. Click on the ellipsis and select the **System.Health.AvailabilityState** parent monitor.

8. Locate the **Monitor Type ID** property in the **Unit Monitor** section. Click on the ellipsis and select the **Microsoft.Windows.CheckNTServiceStateMonitorType** monitor type.

There are many monitor types listed here, with very little description to help you. This illustrates both the power of Visual Studio, as you are not restricted to the types that have wizards, and the learning curve associated with this, because there is no help in the tool about when these should be used.

9. Locate the **Monitor Operational States** property in the **Unit Monitor** section. Click on the ellipsis and change the running state to be **Healthy**. Click on **OK** to close the window.

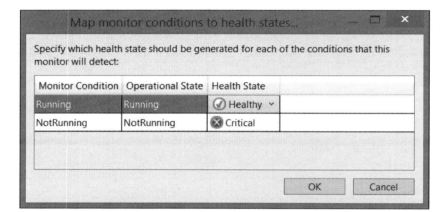

 If you want the health to only show a warning when the service is stopped rather than an error, then you can change the mapping here.

10. Locate the **Monitor Configuration** property in the **Unit Monitor** section. Click on the ellipsis and insert the following XML before the `</Configuration>` tag:

```
<ComputerName>$Target/Host/Property[Type="Windows!Microsoft
.Windows.Computer"]/NetworkName$</ComputerName>
<ServiceName>$Target/Property[Type="MyCompany.MyApplication
.Monitoring.MyApplication_Class"]/ServiceName$</ServiceName
>
<CheckStartupType>false</CheckStartupType>
```

 While this is not as long as some of the configurations we have carried out so far, there are some new things going on here, which I will explain in the *How it works...* section.

11. Click on **OK** to close the configuration box.

12. Locate the **Alert On State** property in the **Alert Settings** section. Change the value to **Error**.

 If you only have a warning state, you should change this value to warning to ensure the alert is raised. If you do not want any alert raised, leave this value at **None**.

13. Locate the **Alert Name** property in the **Alert Settings** section. Change the value to **MyApplication Service is not running**.

14. Locate the **Alert Description** property in the **Alert Settings** section. Change the value to `The Service $Data/Context/Property[@Name='DisplayName']$ ($Data/Context/Property[@Name='Name']$) is not running.`

15. Save and close the management pack fragment.

16. Build and deploy the management pack.

Once deployed, you can stop the services, which will give you alerts similar to those seen in the following screenshot. Note that the alerts are for different services on different servers and have different text displayed.

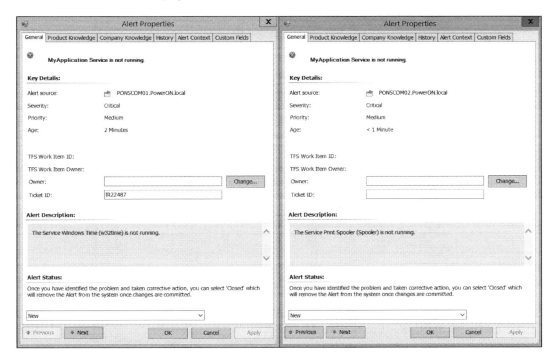

## How it works...

As we have discussed previously, the wizard approach works very well for cases where the wizard author has catered for the situation you need to monitor. But there will always be the need to move away from this approach when a more difficult requirement comes along. It is in these places where the flexibility of Visual Studio comes into play.

When looking at the **Unit Monitors** fragment, much of the configuration is carried out through straight property fields. The **General** properties such as **ID** and **Name** are self-explanatory, and we use the **Target** property to ensure that this monitor is only run on servers where our class has been discovered.

The **Unit Monitors** section of **Properties** has a few new properties. The first of these is **Parent Monitor ID**. This is purely there to locate this monitor in the **Health Explorer**. By setting the parent to be **System.Health.AvailabilityState**, it places the monitor in the availability part of the hierarchy.

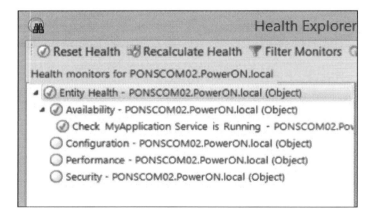

 You can create aggregate monitors of your own to act as additional levels in the hierarchy. This can be helpful when there are lots of monitors to create.

The next property is the **Monitor Type ID** property. This defines the actions that will be taken by the monitor. There are many default monitor types, and it can seem confusing to know which one to choose. But often, if you start stepping through the wizards in the SCOM console, it will start to become clear which type matches its wizard option. The Microsoft Virtual Academy course is again helpful here in being able to spend more time on this area.

The **Monitors Operational States** property is straightforward, but the Monitor Configuration needs a little explanation. This property contains the configuration that acts as a parameter to the chosen Monitor Type. In our example, this type is `Microsoft.Windows.CheckNTServiceStateMonitorType`, and it takes just three parameters. These are:

```
<ComputerName></ComputerName>
<ServiceName></ServiceName>
<CheckStartupType> </CheckStartupType>
```

The `ComputerName` parameter is simply the computer that we will be checking the service on. We have targeted our new class, and this is hosted by the Windows Computer object. We can therefore read the name of the Windows computer from SCOM by starting at the Target, moving up one level to the Host, and then picking the `NetworkName` property from this SCOM object. We put this in the following syntax surrounded by $ signs so that SCOM knows that this is something it should look up, and that it is not just a very weird computer name:

```
<ComputerName>$Target/Host/Property[Type="Windows!Microsoft
.Windows.Computer"]/NetworkName$</ComputerName>
```

The next parameter is `ServiceName`. We know that this needs to be set to one of the SCOM properties we extracted from the registry when discovering our new class. We therefore can read this property directly from `Target`:

```
<ServiceName>$Target/Property[Type="MyCompany.MyApplication
.Monitoring.MyApplication_Class"]/ServiceName$</ServiceName>
```

 If we want to monitor the same service at all times, then we can hardcode the service using `<ServiceName>spooler</ServiceName>`.

The final property in this section is the `CheckStartupType`. If this is set to `true`, then the monitor will only check to see if it is running, that is, if the service is set to automatic startup. This means that if the service is disabled or set to start manually, then there would not be an alert if it was not running. Custom application services are often set to manual startup, and so I want an alert whenever the service is not running:

```
<CheckStartupType>false</CheckStartupType>
```

The last section we will be looking at is the **Alert Settings** section. The **Alert Name** field is self-explanatory and the **Alert On State** field is straightforward. The **Alert Description** field, though, is set as follows:

```
The Service $Data/Context/Property[@Name='DisplayName']$ ($Data/
Context/Property[@Name='Name']$) is not running.
```

With the discussion about what surrounding something with $ signs means, this is probably already looking clearer. SCOM should look in the data it has for the `Context` alert for a `Property` called `DisplayName` or `Name`. These properties are returned by the `Monitor Type` property and can be seen in SCOM by looking at the **Alert Context** tab. However, it is helpful to put these into the alert message because many companies use e-mail notifications, and placing this text in the alert message means that this information will be visible in the e-mails.

## There's more...

Because of the flexibility of what is possible in SCOM and the unparalleled capabilities of Visual Studio to support all of this flexibility, we can only scratch the surface of extending basic monitors into more complex monitoring requirements. I hope that you will be able to take the basic skills demonstrated in these recipes and use them to start developing your own custom monitoring.

## See also

Microsoft Virtual Academy course on Management Pack authoring with Visual Studio at `http://www.microsoftvirtualacademy.com/training-courses/system-center-2012-r2-operations-manager-management-pack`

# Monitoring and capturing performance in Visual Studio

As with the recipe for the MP Author editor, the basis for this recipe is the common need to capture performance information as well as monitoring for the value of a counter. We will be using the System Up Time counter as our example, but please be aware that this is already captured in a standard pack.

## Getting ready

To prepare for this recipe, you need to have Visual Studio installed with the Authoring Extensions plugin configured. In order to follow the instructions fully, you should have read and understood the previous recipes, particularly the creation of the Unit Monitors fragment.

## How to do it...

To monitor and capture performance in Visual Studio, follow these steps:

1. Open Visual Studio and the solution containing the management pack from the previous recipe.

2. We need to add the performance library in as a reference. To do this, find the **References** section directly under the project name, right-click on it, and select **Add Reference**. In the dialog box that opens, select the **Browse** tab and then browse through the `Visual Studio Authoring Extensions References` folder. This is normally found in `C:\Program Files (x86)\System Center 2012 Visual Studio Authoring Extensions\References`. Choose the reference folder for the version of the management pack you are creating and then select **System. Performance.Library** and **Microsoft.SystemCenter.DataWarehouse.Library**.

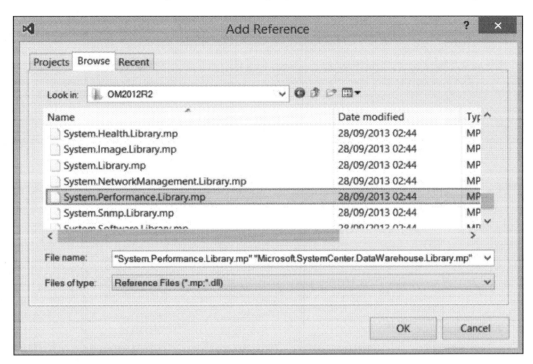

3. Find the **Solution Explorer** and navigate to the **Unit Monitor** fragment. If you have not created this yet, then right-click on the **Monitors and Rules** folder and choose **Add | New Item** to bring up the **Add New Item** dialog. Click on the **Monitor (Unit)** item and enter Unit Monitors in the **Name** field. Click on **Add**.

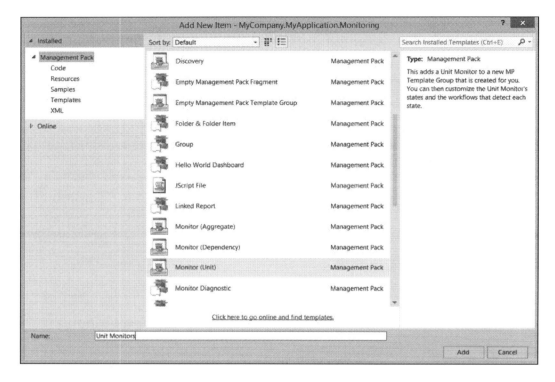

4. If you have already created the unit monitors fragment, then open it and right-click in the window and select **Add Template**. From the dialog box, select **Monitor (Unit)** and then click on **OK**.

5. Whether it is the first or the second, click on the new unit monitor and observe the **Properties** window. By default, this is in the bottom right-hand corner of the screen. We will change multiple properties to get a result that looks like the following screenshot:

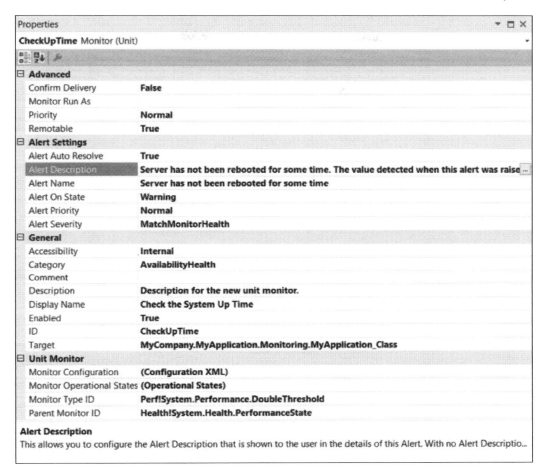

6. Locate the **ID** property in the **General** section. Change the value to CheckUpTime.

7. Locate the **Display Name** property in the **General** section. Change the value to Check the System UpTime.

8. Locate the **Target** property in the **General** section. Click on the ellipsis and select the **MyCompany.MyApplication.Monitoring.MyApplication_Class** class.

9. Locate the **Parent Monitor ID** property in the **Unit Monitor** section. Click on the ellipsis and select the **System.Health.PerformanceState** parent monitor.

10. Locate the **Monitor Type ID** property in the **Unit Monitor** section. Click on the ellipsis and select the **System.Performance.DoubleThreshold** monitor type.

11. Locate the **Monitor Operational States** property in the **Unit Monitor** section. Click on the ellipsis and change the state of **UnderThreshold1** to be **Healthy**. Change the **OverThreshold1UnderThreshold2** state to **Warning** and then click on **OK** to close the window.

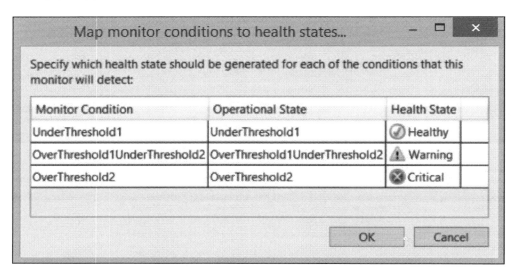

12. Locate the **Monitor Configuration** property in the **Unit Monitor** section. Click on the ellipsis and insert the following XML before the `</Configuration>` tag:

```
<ComputerName>$Target/Host/Property[Type="Windows!Microsoft
.Windows.Computer"]/NetworkName$</ComputerName>
<CounterName>System Up Time</CounterName>
<ObjectName>System</ObjectName>
<InstanceName />
<Frequency>60</Frequency>
<Threshold1>1728000</Threshold1>
<Threshold2>3456000</Threshold2>
```

13. Click on **OK** to close the configuration box.

14. Locate the **Alert On State** property in the **Alert Settings** section. Change the value to **Warning**.

15. Locate the **Alert Name** property in the **Alert Settings** section. Change the value to **Server has not been rebooted for some time**.

16. Locate the **Alert Description** property in the **Alert Settings** section. Change the value to `Server has not been rebooted for some time. The value detected when this alert was raised was an uptime of $Data/Context/Value$ seconds.`

17. Save and close the management pack fragment.

18. Right-click on **Monitors and Rules** and select **Add | New Item** to bring up the **Add New Item** dialog. Click on the **Rule (Performance Collection)** item and enter **Performance Collection Rules** in the **Name** field. Click on **Add**.

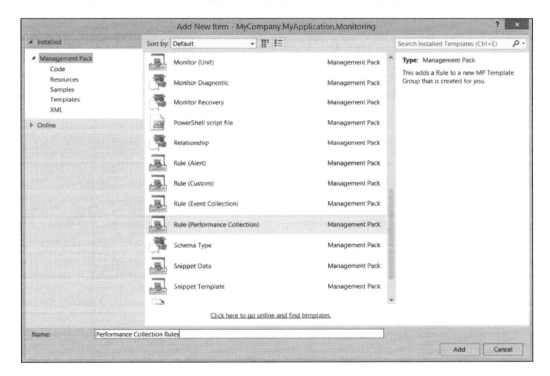

19. Select the **NewPeformanceCollection** rule and locate the **Properties** box. We will change multiple properties to get a result that looks like the following screenshot:

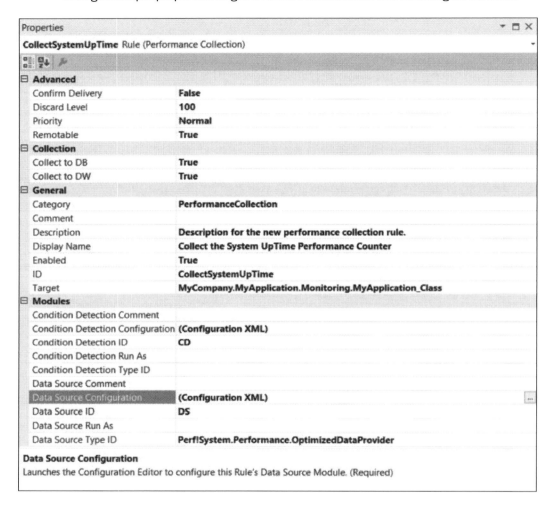

20. Locate the **ID** property in the **General** section. Change the value to `CollectSystemUpTime`.

21. Locate the **Display Name** property in the **General** section. Change the value to `Collect the System UpTime Performance Counter`.

22. Locate the **Target** property in the **General** section. Click on the ellipsis and select the **MyCompany.MyApplication.Monitoring.MyApplication_Class** class.

23. Locate the **Data Source Type ID** property in the **Modules** section. Click on the ellipsis and select the **System.Performance.OptimizedDataProvider** data source.

24. Locate the **Data Source Configuration** property in the **Modules** section. Click on the ellipsis and insert the following XML before the `</Configuration>` tag:

```
<ComputerName>$Target/Host/Property[Type="Windows!Microsoft
.Windows.Computer"]/NetworkName$</ComputerName>
<CounterName>System Up Time</CounterName>
<ObjectName>System</ObjectName>
<InstanceName />
<Frequency>300</Frequency>
<Tolerance>1000</Tolerance>
<ToleranceType>Absolute</ToleranceType>
<MaximumSampleSeparation>6</MaximumSampleSeparation>
```

25. Click on **OK** to close the configuration box.

26. Save and close the management pack fragment.

27. Build and deploy the management pack.

## How it works...

By this time, you should have worked through most of the recipes, and so most of the properties should be self-explanatory. I will just go through the XML configuration we have set up in this recipe.

The first XML configuration is found for the monitor, where we are using a `System.Performance.DoubleThreshold` monitor type. This configuration starts in the same way many monitors do, with detailing the computer that will be monitored:

```
<ComputerName>$Target/Host/Property[Type="Windows!Microsoft.Windows.
Computer"]/NetworkName$</ComputerName>
```

After this is a section to identify the performance counter we will be monitoring. In this case, it is the `System Up Time` counter, which can be found in the `System` object and has no instances:

```
<CounterName>System Up Time</CounterName>
<ObjectName>System</ObjectName>
<InstanceName/>
```

Next, we look at how frequently to check this counter value. Note that this has no link to how frequently we may record the counter as this is configured in another rule. In this example, we check this every `60` seconds:

```
<Frequency>60</Frequency>
```

The final couple of parameters specify the threshold values. These have been chosen to be set at 20 days and 40 days. The monitor type then returns whether it is below `Threshold1`, above `Threshold2`, or between them, and this is translated into a health state by the mapping of the operational states.

```
<Threshold1>1728000</Threshold1>
<Threshold2>3456000</Threshold2>
```

The rule configuration is again very similar. It starts by detailing the computer that will be monitored and then describes the counter that will be recorded:

```
<ComputerName>$Target/Host/Property[Type="Windows!Microsoft
.Windows.Computer"]/NetworkName$</ComputerName>
<CounterName>System Up Time</CounterName>
<ObjectName>System</ObjectName>
<InstanceName/>
```

The next section looks at various parameters that govern the writing of this performance data into the database. Initially, the frequency states the time each sample will be taken, in this case, every five minutes. However, we may not want to record the data into the database for each 5-minute period. While this specific counter will always increase, an error count may sit at zero for months and you may think it is a waste to write a data point of zero every five minutes if the value will not change. To help with this, the tolerance parameters indicate that if the value changes by more than the tolerance (which can be an absolute number or a percentage), then the data will be recorded in the database. The final parameter, `MaximumSampleSeparation`, describes how many samples can be missed before the data will be recorded to the database, even if it has not changed. It is a good practice to ensure that the data is written at least once per hour to make sure that the hourly averages of data used by the data warehouse have some information to process:

```
<Frequency>300</Frequency>
<Tolerance>1000</Tolerance>
<ToleranceType>Absolute</ToleranceType>
<MaximumSampleSeparation>6</MaximumSampleSeparation>
```

These parameters can be used to ensure that the data is stored at an appropriate level of detail in the database without excessive database storage requirements.

## See also

There are several more tips and tricks on using Visual Studio that you can learn from looking at the Microsoft Virtual Academy course, and I would recommend that you look at this to help you make best use of the tool. My favorite feature has to be that you can copy one of these monitors or rules and paste it back in, making it very quick and easy to create multiple copies of similar monitors. The Microsoft Virtual Academy course on management pack authoring with Visual Studio can be found at `http://www.microsoftvirtualacademy.com/training-courses/system-center-2012-r2-operations-manager-management-pack`.

There is also a snippet feature that allows you to create templates similar to the ones used for monitors and rules. This feature is covered very well in Kevin Holmans blog article, *How to use Snippets in VSAE to write LOTS of workflows, quickly!*, at `http://blogs.technet.com/b/kevinholman/archive/2014/01/21/how-to-use-snippets-in-vsae-to-write-lots-of-workflows-quickly.aspx`.

# 9
# Integrating System Center 2012 R2 with Other Components

In this chapter, we will cover the following recipes:

- ▶ Discovering best-practice analysis with System Center Advisor
- ▶ Designing alert and remediation actions with **System Center 2012 R2 Orchestrator (SCORCH)**
- ▶ Enabling Asset Discovery and Incident Management with System Center 2012 R2 Service Manager
- ▶ **Performance and Resource Optimization** (**PRO**) integration with System Center 2012 R2 **Virtual Machine Manager (VMM)**

## Introduction

This chapter will explore how you can utilize other System Center components to provide enhanced monitoring and remediation solutions. We will look at how you can harness the data collected by **System Center 2012 R2 Operations Manager (SCOM)**, feeding this information into other products, and expand your monitoring reach through the use of additional management packs.

The recipes in this chapter will cover the following scenarios:

- ▶ Discovering best-practice analysis with System Center Advisor
    - ❑ Understand what System Center Advisor is and how it can be configured and discuss how it can enhance your monitoring solution

- ▶ Designing alert and remediation actions with SCORCH

  - ❑ Explore how you can take common alerts from within your System Center 2012 R2 Operations Manager environment and autoremediate them using SCORCH

- ▶ Enabling Asset Discovery and Ticketing with System Center 2012 R2 Service Manager

  - ❑ Look at how gathered data can be shared with System Center 2012 R2 Service Manager through the configuration of the CI and Alert connectors

- ▶ **Performance and Resource Optimization** (**PRO**) integration with VMM

  - ❑ Discover how PRO integration can assist with optimization, alert, and remediation actions within VMM

For all these tasks, we will define a process with the required steps in each recipe.

Recipes in this chapter have different requirements and prerequisites, that are detailed within the *Getting ready* section of each recipe. Please ensure you review these requirements before proceeding with each recipe.

# Discovering best-practice analysis with System Center Advisor

This recipe will describe the steps you need to configure System Center Advisor within your SCOM environment. One of the features SCOM brings is out of the box support for System Center Advisor.

What is System Center Advisor? Think of it like having a Microsoft support technician within your team, proactively monitoring and assessing your environment.

System Center Advisor uses operational information gathered through Operations Manager. The data collected from your environment is then compared across a vast array of Microsoft recommended baselines, best practices, and patches. Recommendations are then presented to you on what adjustments to your infrastructure are required or may be beneficial.

Using the power of Microsoft's cloud platform, System Center Advisor is continually updated with the latest information allowing you to stay informed and prevent issues before they occur.

System Center Advisor has been around in various flavors for some time. Deployments in the past required system administrators to deploy gateway servers and certificates, and although this is still available, it can be more complex and time-consuming.

With the integration into SCOM, the gateway role is taken care of by your management servers and we use the Microsoft Monitoring Agent, which is already deployed within your Operations Manager environment to gather the needed information for System Center Advisor.

System Center Advisor not only presents its findings to you through the Operations Console but it also provides you with a graphical dashboard and management interface through `http://www.systemcenteradvisor.com/`.

System Center Advisor analyzes most of Microsoft's top applications including:

- ▶ Microsoft SQL Server 2008 and later
- ▶ Microsoft Windows Server 2008 and later
- ▶ Microsoft SharePoint 2010 and 2013
- ▶ Microsoft Exchange 2010
- ▶ Microsoft Lync 2010 and later
- ▶ Microsoft Virtual Machine Manager 2012 SP1
- ▶ Microsoft Hyper-V 2008 R2 and 2012

## Getting ready

For this recipe, ensure you have appropriate access to your Operations Manager console and that your management servers have Internet access.

You will be required to create or use your existing Microsoft account. This can be either your Live or Office 365 account. If you have neither of these accounts, you will be presented with the option to create a new one.

System Center Advisor supports Windows Server 2008 and higher, and clients are required to have .NET 3.5 SP1 installed.

## How to do it...

To configure System Center Advisor within your environment:

1. Open up your SCOM Console and click on **Administration**.

2. In the **Administration** tree view, select **System Center Advisor | Advisor Connection**:

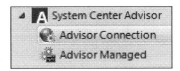

3. On the **System Center Advisor Overview** page, click on the **Register to Advisor Service** link.

4. When presented with the **Sign in to your Microsoft account** page, enter your organization's account details. If you do not have these, you are presented with the option to create one.

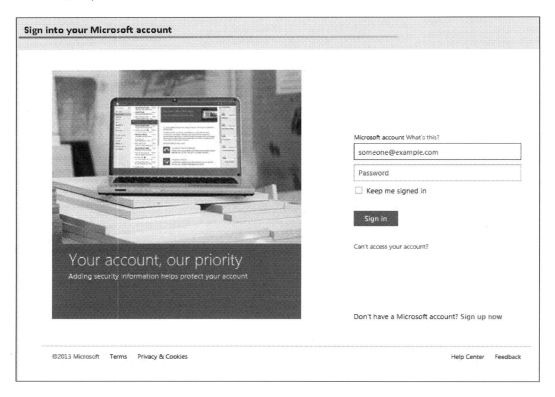

5. Once you have signed in to your Microsoft account, you will be asked to select or enter a new name for your Advisor account. Type a name that is appropriate for your organization such as `OpsMgr Live`:

6. On the **Confirm Settings** page, click on the **Create** button.

7. Click on the close button.

8. In the **Administration** tree view, select **System Center Advisor | Advisor Managed**.

9. On the **Task** pane, click on **Add a Computer/Group**.

10. On the **Computer Search** dialog, click on the **Search** button.

11. From the list of **Available Items**, select a server you wish to add to System Center Advisor and then click on **Add | OK**:

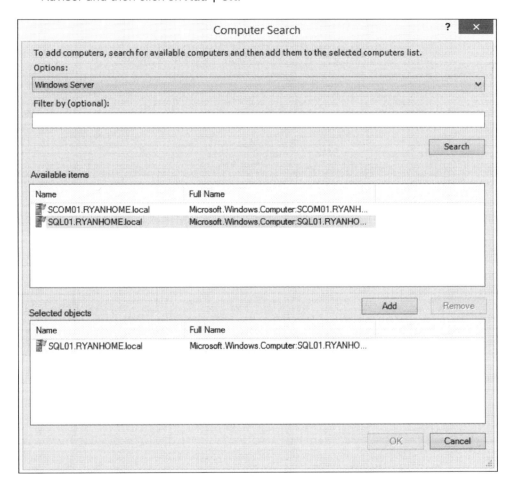

12. Open Internet Explorer and navigate to http://www.systemcenteradvisor.com.

13. Click on **Sign In | Microsoft Account**.

14. Enter the Microsoft credentials you used during the configuration and click on the **Sign In** button.

15. You should now be presented with a dashboard overview detailing advisories regarding your managed agents.

16. Click on the Servers icon on the left-hand side bar. You should see a list of management group along with any agents you have deployed:

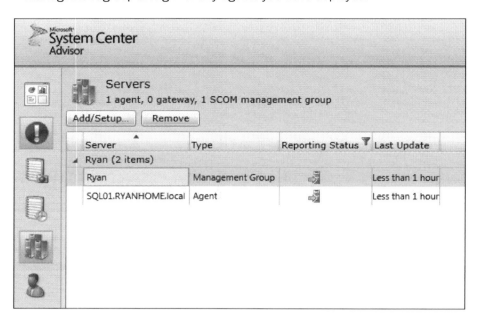

## How it works...

System Center Advisor uses your Operations Manager infrastructure to gather information about your deployed Microsoft software. Then using your Operations Manager management servers, this information is relayed up to the Microsoft System Center Advisor cloud service for analysis.

Communications with the Microsoft System Center Advisor cloud service is done over HTTP (80) and HTTPS (443). For these communications to be successful, you must ensure that your SCOM management servers are able to access services on these ports. More details can be found on Microsoft TechNet using the link provided in the *See also* section.

System Center Advisor then aggregates and analyzes this data and informs you about whether your deployed products deviate from best practices, checks against Microsoft support known issues, and informs you if products require updates to bring them back under mainstream support. If recommendations are found, System Center Advisor notifications can be accessed through the online service and the Operations Manager console.

## There's more...

System Center Advisor will also send out a handy e-mail each week that gives you a summary of the current advisories.

Accessing your dashboard through `http://www.systemcenteradvisor.com` gives you additional options and views:

- ▶ **Overview**: This overview dashboard gives you instant statistics on alerts across your monitored agents and shows you if any agents are not reporting correctly.

- ▶ **Alerts**: The alert view allows you to see detailed information such as the time generated, properties, cause, and possible remediation information. From the alert view, it is also possible to manage the resolution state of the alert and manage alert rules. It is also possible to open a Microsoft service request directly from these alerts.

- ▶ **Configuration current snapshot**: This allows you to view the current configuration of a monitored agent and shows you the properties that have been collected along with the associated values.

- ▶ **Configuration change history**: This allows you to see at a glance any changes made to monitored agents along with detailed information on the properties before and after the change.

- ▶ **Servers**: This option allows you to see which agents are monitored within System Center Advisor and what the current state and last reported time is.

- ▶ **Account**: This allows you to change your account name and user information and manage users who can access your company's System Center Advisor site and also close down your account.

## Azure Operational Insights

System Center Advisor is changing and at the time of writing this Microsoft is currently redesigning the whole Advisor portal to deliver a smarter, faster, and more visual way to investigate your operational data. Giving a more intuitive and consistent feel, Microsoft has reworked the Advisor portal using HTML5, which allows this experience to be viewed across multiple devices with ease while also adopting the familiar tile look and feel found across Microsoft's current product sets.

When first logging in to the Advisor portal, you will notice sets of tiles. These tiles act as entry points in their respective scenario and provide a top-level visual overview of the data gathered by its associated intelligence pack.

Intelligence packs are a collection of data acquisition rules, analytics, and visualizations and act similar to management packs by allowing you to extend your Advisor's capabilities.

These intelligence packs help you target and address key operational issues faster by targeting specific operational scenarios such as updates and malware, auditing, and capacity planning. Intelligence packs can be added to your Advisor experience through the Azure Operational Insights Intelligence Pack Gallery. Currently, the number of intelligence packs is limited; however, this will likely change as time progresses.

Microsoft System Center Advisor LIMITED PREVIEW

 Advisor Gallery

# System Center Advisor - Limited Preview Intelligence Pack Gallery

New intelligence packs for System Center Advisor

## Intelligence Packs for Advisor

Capacity Planning

Calculates current and future utilization of each component of your environment.

FREE | **View** | Remove

Security

Provides the ability to explore security related data and helps to identify security breaches.

FREE | Coming Soon

## About Intelligence Packs

System Center Advisor - Limited Preview Gallery is here. Our gallery contains "intelligence packs" - which contain rich knowledge and visualizations for capacity planning, security, diagnostics, and configuration assessment.

Whether you need to find noisy neighbors, implement thin provisioning or simply ensure configuration compliance, there's an intelligence pack for you. You can choose the intelligence packs that are right for your needs and get rich insights within minutes.

System Center Advisor - Limited Preview gathers data from your on-premise installation and provides rich intelligence. There is no hardware, software, or applications to install, manage or upgrade — everything is cloud-based.

Tiles will lack information initially until enough data has been collected to populate them and is to be expected.

Azure Operational Insights now gives you the ability to collect event logs from across all your managed devices and centrally search upon them with minimal effort, thanks to the new Search Data Explorer feature of Operational Insights. Searching your event logs or other data collected by the various intelligence packs is effortless with the use of predefined search criteria. You can use these as a base for your search and modify the search string to best suit your needs.

Using faceted search, you can quickly compose complex search strings to present the data that matters with the help of facets corresponding to the data each time you drill down:

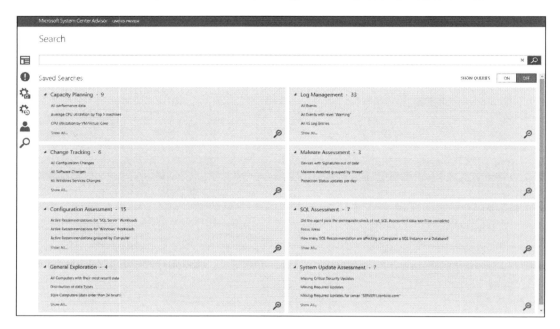

More information on the search syntax and search examples can be found at `http://technet.microsoft.com/library/dn500940.aspx`.

Also new to Operational Insights is the ability to create custom dashboards, allowing you to display operational data relevant to you monitoring requirements. The tile-based dashboard allows you to drag and drop search criteria for display. Options are also given for you to use visual or numerical indicators displayed on the tile.

To use Azure Operational Insights Public Preview, you need to be running System Center Operations Manager SP1 or R2 and the latest update rollup.

Onboarding to Operational Insights is as simple as with the previous version and takes minimal effort to connect your SCOM management group and offer the benefits to you. Existing Advisor users can also upgrade to the public preview version.

Azure Operational Insights is currently free of charge during the public preview. No pricing details are available at this time.

## See also

For more detailed information on methods used in this recipe, refer to the following links of Microsoft System Center Advisor:

- Firewall information: `http://onlinehelp.microsoft.com/en-us/advisor/gg197512.aspx`

- System requirements: `http://onlinehelp.microsoft.com/en-us/advisor/ff962524.aspx`

# Designing alert and remediation actions with System Center 2012 R2 Orchestrator (SCORCH)

Out of the box, SCOM provides many built-in tasks; these allow you to remediate some of the common alerts you may receive. Remediation on Health Service or general Windows Administration can be performed at the click of a button within the Operations Console giving the administrator a feeling of a single pane of glass. In addition to these types of remediation tasks, we also have other types of tasks that perform functions such as diagnostics or data capture, again presenting the results within the Operations Console.

Many management packs come with tasks that are specifically scoped to the products and services they monitor, and in addition to this, we are able to create our own tasks and remediation tasks within SCOM.

Often an administrator wishes to perform alert capture and remediation tasks, which are out of scope of those currently within SCOM. These are often specific to suit your business needs and most often involve several steps with dependencies and often multiple technologies, which makes Orchestrator better suited for these types of remediation tasks.

When creating custom alert and remediation actions, we are able to harness the features and power of other products from within the System Center 2012 R2 suite. SCORCH specifically provides near unlimited possibilities when it comes to automation, allowing you to build complex workflows to achieve your goals.

SCORCH comes with integration packs containing activities for a vast amount of products allowing you to extend your solutions across the whole business and across multiple silos.

In this recipe, you will take a business requirement to run weekly mailbox corruption checks across all of your Exchange 2010 SP3 mailbox servers and take a remediation action if corruption is found. SCOM will be used to track these Exchange events on your mailbox servers not only to notify you once the remediation has completed, but also to ensure that SCORCH is aware when to proceed to the next mailbox server.

## Getting ready

The preparation for this recipe is to ensure you have appropriate access to your Operations Manager console, Orchestrator Runbook Designer, and your Exchange infrastructure. In this recipe, we will be performing tasks against Exchange 2010 SP3; however, this can be adapted for use on Exchange 2013 if required.

Ensure that the System Center 2012 R2 Operations Manager integration pack has been installed and the Microsoft Exchange Admin integration pack for SCORCH has been installed and configured correctly, allowing the execution of remote PowerShell for the user or service account you use to create a connection within SCORCH.

Ensure that the SCOM Exchange management pack has been installed and correctly configured for your environment within SCOM.

## How to do it...

Perform the following steps to create three NT Event Log rules along with three Orchestrator runbooks. At the end of this recipe, you will have an example of how the System Center suite can work for you to discover, automate, and remediate within your infrastructure.

1. Open up your Operations Manager console.
2. Go to the **Authoring** pane.
3. In the tree view, click on **Rules**.
4. On the **Tasks** pane, click on **Create a Rule**.
5. Under **Rule Type**, select **Alert Generating Rules | Event Based | NT Event Log (Alert)**.
6. Select a management pack to save your rule in.
7. Click on the **Next** button.
8. In the **Rule Name** text box, type `Mailbox Repair Request Started`.
9. Select **Maintenance** from the **Rule Category** options.
10. Click on the **Select** button to select a **Rule target**.
11. On the **Select Items to Target** dialog under **Look for**, type `mailbox`.
12. Click the **View all targets** radio button.

13. From the results, select **Mailbox** and click on the **OK** button.

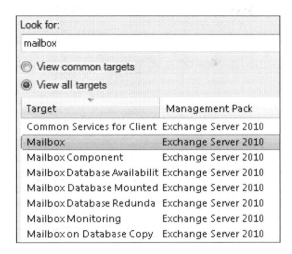

14. Ensure the **Rule is enabled** checkbox is ticked and click on the **Next** button.

15. Ensure the **Log name** field is set to **Application** and click on the **Next** button.

16. On the **Build Event Expressions** page, enter the following:

| Parameter name | Operator | Value |
|---|---|---|
| Event ID | Equals | 10059 |
| Event Source | Contains | MSExchangeIS |

17. Click on the **Next** button.

18. On the **Configure Alerts** page, change the **Priority** field to **Low** and the **Severity** field to **Information**.

19. Click on the **Create** button.

20. On the **Tasks** pane, click on **Create a Rule**.

21. Under **Rule Type**, navigate to **Alert Generating Rules | Event Based | NT Event Log (Alert)**.

22. Select a management pack to save your rule in.

23. Click on the **Next** button.

24. In the **Rule Name** text box, type Mailbox Corruption Detected.

25. Select **Maintenance** from the **Rule Category** options.

26. Click on the **Select** button to select a **Rule target**.

27. In the **Select Items to Target** dialog under **Look for**, type mailbox.

28. Click on the **View all targets** radio button.

29. From the results, select **Mailbox** and click on the **OK** button.

30. Ensure the **Rule is enabled** checkbox is ticked and click on the **Next** button.

31. Ensure the **Log name** field is set to **Application** and click on the **Next** button.

32. On the **Build Event Expressions** page, enter the following:

| Parameter name | Operator | Value |
|---|---|---|
| Event ID | Equals | 10062 |
| Event Source | Contains | MSExchangeIS |

33. Click on the **Next** button.

34. On the **Configure Alerts** page, change the **Priority** field to **Low** and the **Severity** field to **Information**.

35. Click on the **Create** button.

36. On the **Tasks** pane, click on **Create a Rule**.

37. Under **Rule Type**, select **Alert Generating Rules | Event Based | NT Event Log (Alert)**.

38. Select a management pack to save your rule in.

39. Click on the **Next** button.

40. In the **Rule Name** text box, type `Mailbox Repair Request Completed`.

41. Select **Maintenance** from the **Rule Category** options.

42. Click on the **Select** button to select a **Rule target**.

43. On the **Select Items to Target** dialog, under **Look for**, type `mailbox`.

44. Click on the **View all targets** radio button.

45. From the results, select **Mailbox** and click on the **OK** button.

46. Ensure the **Rule is enabled** checkbox is ticked and click on the **Next** button.

47. Ensure the **Log name** is set to **Application** and click on the **Next** button.

48. On the **Build Event Expressions** page, enter the following:

| Parameter name | Operator | Value |
|---|---|---|
| Event ID | Equals | 10048 |
| Event Source | Contains | MSExchangeIS |

49. Click on the **Next** button.

50. On the **Configure Alerts** page, change the **Priority** field to **Low** and the **Severity** field to **Information**.

51. Click on the **Create** button.
52. Open Orchestrator Runbook Designer.
53. From the menu bar, click on **Options | Exchange Admin**.
54. Click on the **Add** button.
55. In the **Name** textbox, type Exchange Connection.
56. Click on the ellipsis next to the **Type** textbox and select **Exchange Configuration** from the list.
57. Enter the following properties:

| Parameter name | Value |
| --- | --- |
| **Exchange Server Host** | Enter the FQDN of the Exchange server you wish to connect to |
| **Exchange Server Port** | 443 |
| **Exchange PowerShell Application** | powershell |
| **Exchange User Name** | Enter the user or account name you wish to use |
| **Exchange Password** | Enter your password |
| **Use SSL** | True |
| **Skip CA Check** | True |
| **Skip CN Check** | True |
| **Skip Revocation Check** | True |
| **Exchange Environment** | On-Premise |

58. Click on the **OK** button.
59. Click on the **Finish** button.
60. On the menu bar, navigate to **Options | SC 2012 Operations Manager**.
61. Click on the **Add** button.
62. Enter the following properties:

| Parameter name | Value |
| --- | --- |
| **Name** | Operations Manager Connection |
| **Server** | Enter your Operations Manager Server |
| **Domain** | Enter your domain |
| **Username** | Enter the user name you wish to use for this connection |
| **Password** | Enter your password |
| **Polling** | 10 seconds |
| **Reconnect** | 10 seconds |

63. Click on the **OK** button.

64. Click the **Finish** button.

65. In the Runbook Designer, expand the connection to the Orchestrator server.

66. Right-click on **Runbooks** and navigate to **New | Runbook**.

67. Right-click on new runbook and rename it `Exchange Corruption Start`. (You may be asked to check out the runbook, and if so, choose **Yes**.)

68. Right-click on **Runbooks** and navigate to **New | Runbook**.

69. Right-click on new runbook and rename it `Exchange Corruption Loop`. (You may be asked to check out the runbook, and if so, choose **Yes**.)

70. Right-click on **Runbooks** and navigate to **New | Runbook**.

71. Right-click on new runbook and rename it `Exchange Corruption Repair Complete`. (You may be asked to check out the runbook, and if so, choose **Yes**.)

72. Expand **Global Settings**.

73. Right-click on **Counters** and navigate to **New | Counter**.

74. In the **Name** textbox, type `ExchangeDB_Counter`.

75. Ensure the **Default Value** is **0** and click on the **Finish** button.

76. Right-click on **Schedules** and navigate to **New | Schedule**.

77. On the **General** page, type `Exchange Mailbox Repair` in the **Name** textbox.

78. On the **Details** page, ensure that **Sun** is the only **Days of week** that is checked and that all **Occurrence** checkboxes are ticked:

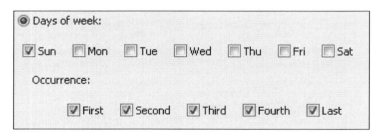

79. Click on the **Hours** button.

80. Adjust **Schedule Hours** so that only **Sunday from 00:00 to 01:00** is permitted:

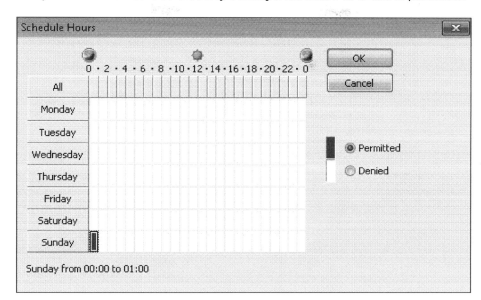

81. Click on **OK | Finish**.

82. Click on **Runbooks** and select the runbook named **Exchange Corruption Start**.

83. Navigate to the **Activities** section in the Runbook Designer, select **Scheduling** and drag a **Monitor Data\Time** activity into the middle pane of the runbook.

84. Right-click on the activity and navigate to **Properties**.

85. On the **Details** page, change the interval to **At: 00:15**.

86. Click on the **Finish** button.

87. Navigate to the **Activities** section in the Runbook Designer, select **Scheduling** and drag a **Check Schedule** activity into the middle pane of the runbook.

88. Right-click on the activity and navigate to **Properties**.

89. On the **Details** page, click the ellipsis next to **Schedule Template** and select **Exchange Mailbox Repair**.

90. Click on **OK | Finish**.

91. Link the **Monitor Data\Time** and the **Check Schedule** activities.

92. Navigate to the **Activities** section in the Runbook Designer, select **Utilities** and drag a **Modify Counter** activity into the middle pane of the runbook.

93. Right-click on the activity and navigate to **Properties**.

94. On the **General** page, type `Initialize Counter` in the **Name** textbox.

95. On the **Details** page, click the ellipsis next to **Counter** and select **ExchangeDB_Counter**.

96. Click on the **OK** button.

97. Under **Action**, select **Reset**.

98. Click on the **Finish** button.

99. Link the **Monitor Data\Time** and **Initialize Counter** activities.

100. Navigate to the **Activities** section in the Runbook Designer, select **Runbook Control** and drag an **Invoke Runbook** activity into the middle pane of the runbook.

101. Right-click on the activity and navigate to **Properties**.

102. On the **Details** page, click the ellipsis next to **Runbook** and select **Exchange Corruption Loop**.

103. Click on the **Finish** button.

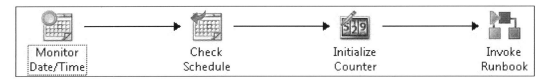

104. On the runbook control bar, click on **Check In | Run**.

105. Click on **Runbooks** and select the runbook named **Exchange Corruption Loop**.

106. Navigate to the **Activities** section in the Runbook Designer, select **Runbook Control** and drag an **Initialize Data** activity into the middle pane of the runbook.

107. Navigate to the **Activities** section in the Runbook Designer, select **Utilities** and drag a **Modify Counter** activity into the middle pane of the runbook.

108. Right-click on the activity and navigate to **Properties**.

109. On the **General** page, type `Increment Counter` in the **Name** textbox.

110. On the **Details** page, click on the ellipsis next to **Counter** and select **ExchangeDB_Counter**.

111. Click on the **OK** button.

112. Under **Action**, select **Increment**.

113. In the **Value** textbox, type `1`.

114. Click on the **Finish** button.

115. Link the **Initialize Data** and **Increment Counter** activities.

116. Navigate to the **Activities** section in the Runbook Designer, select **Utilities** and drag a **Get Counter Value** activity into the middle pane of the runbook.

117. Right-click on the activity and navigate to **Properties**.

118. On the **Details** page, click the ellipsis next to **Counter** and select **ExchangeDB_Counter**.

119. Click on **OK | Finish**.

120. Link the **Increment Counter** and **Get Counter Value** activities.

121. Navigate to the **Activities** section in the Runbook Designer, select **Exchange Admin** and drag a **Run Exchange Management Shell Cmdlet** activity into the middle pane of the runbook.

122. Right-click on the activity and navigate to **Properties**.

123. On the **Properties** page, click on the ellipsis next to **Name** and select **Exchange Connector**.

124. Click on the **OK** button.

125. Enter the following properties:

| Parameter name | Value |
|---|---|
| **Command Text** | ```
if ({Counter Value from "Get Counter Value"}-lt 21)
{
$Count= {Counter Value from "Get Counter Value"}
$DB = "DB" + "{0:D2}" -f $Count
$DBinfo = $DB

New-MailboxRepairRequest -Database "$DB"
-CorruptionType SearchFolder,AggregateCounts,Provisio
nedFolder,FolderView
}
``` |
| | Replace the {Counter Value from "Get Counter Value"} condition by right-clicking on the **PowerShell Script** field and navigating to **Subscribe | Published Data** |
| | Choose **Get Counter Value** in the **Activity** field and select **Counter Value** |
| **Is Exchange Command** | Yes |

126. Click on the **Finish** button.

127. Link the **Get Counter Value** and **Run Exchange Management Shell Cmdlet** activities.

```

128. On the runbook control bar, click on **Check In**.

129. Click on **Runbooks** and select the runbook named **Exchange Corruption Repair Complete**.

130. Navigate to the **Activities** section in the Runbook Designer, select **SC 2012 Operations Manager** and drag a **Monitor Alert** activity into the middle pane of the runbook.

131. Right-click on the activity and navigate to **Properties**.

132. On the **Properties** page, click the ellipsis next to **Connection** and select **Operations Manager Connection**.

133. Click on the **OK** button.

134. Under **Trigger**, ensure only the **New Alerts** checkbox is ticked.

135. Under **Filters**, click on the **Add** button and add the following two filters:

| Name | Relation | Value |
|------|----------|-------|
| Name | Contains | **Mailbox Repair Request Completed** |
| Severity | Equals | **Information** |

136. Click on the **Finish** button.

137. Navigate to the **Activities** section in the Runbook Designer, select **Runbook Control** and drag an **Invoke Runbook** activity into the middle pane of the runbook.

138. Right-click on the activity and navigate to **Properties**.

139. On the **Details** page, click the ellipsis next to **Runbook** and select **Exchange Corruption Loop**.

140. Click on the **Finish** button.

141. Link the **Monitor Alert** and **Invoke Runbook** activities:

142. On the runbook control bar, click on **Check In | Run**.

## How it works...

It is common within your Exchange environment to encounter mailboxes that require some form of maintenance often due to corrupted items. Indications of corruption can appear when performing administrative tasks such as mailbox moves, which may cause errors due to a high bad item count.

Mailboxes can contain different types of corruption such as:

- ▸ Provisioned folders
- ▸ Aggregated counts on folders
- ▸ Search folder corruptions
- ▸ Views on folders

In previous releases of Exchange, repairing this corruption became somewhat of a problem as this often required the database to be dismounted while the maintenance was being performed using Isinteg. One of the changes incorporated with the release of Exchange 2010 SP1 was a new PowerShell cmdlet called `New-MailboxRepairRequest`. This allows corruption detection and repairs to be performed while the database is still mounted with disruption only on a per mailbox basis as the repair is being performed. Mailbox repairs can be performed at either the mailbox or database level.

In this recipe, you were able to use this new feature of Exchange to perform weekly automated maintenance upon your Exchange infrastructure.

First, you created three event log rules within the Operations Manager console that targeted the Mailbox role. These rules specifically look in the application log on your mailbox servers for events raised by the `New-MailboxRepairRequest` cmdlet.

These events serve two purposes: one is to provide informational alerts to Operations Manager to enable you to track when corruption is detected and the task has completed, while the other is to allow Orchestrator to continue to your next mailbox database by monitoring for these alerts.

Owing to the limitations of only one database `MailboxRepairRequest` cmdlet at a time, it becomes vital to ensure these notifications are ready to trigger the next `MailboxRepairRequest` cmdlet within Orchestrator.

Next, you created a series of runbooks. Now, let's break each one down.

## Exchange Corruption Start

The Exchange Corruption Start runbook acts as a trigger for the whole process. Each day at 00:15 hours, this runbook checks against a schedule that you defined to ensure that the Exchange corruption repair process is only performed each Sunday.

Once the schedule criteria are met, you then proceed to initialize the counter that was created and ensure its value is reset to 0. Next, the Exchange Corruption Loop runbook is invoked to carry out the next series of steps.

## Exchange Corruption Loop

The Exchange Corruption Loop runbook begins by incrementing your counter by 1. This counter will be used to define the database number that the `New-MailboxRepairRequest` cmdlet will be performed against. Then, a get counter value is used to return the current database number. This value is later subscribed to within the PowerShell script.

Next, the Run Exchange Management Shell Cmdlet activity from the Exchange Admin integration pack is used. You select a connection that you had created and configured to connect to your Exchange 2010 environment, enabling the remote execution of PowerShell commands within your runbook.

You then initialize the PowerShell script to perform the repair job on your Exchange database within the activity's Command Text property.

The PowerShell script first checks to check whether the counter value is less than 21. This is done to ensure that the runbook will end once the counter value has exceeded this number, which in this example is equal to the number of Exchange databases within your environment.

```
if ({Counter Value from "Get Counter Value"} -lt 21)
```

If the counter value falls within your expected database range, the next section of code is executed and the counter value is formatted to match your database naming convention (in this example, we use the formatting of DB01 through DB20). The `$DB` variable is used to hold your correctly formatted database name that can be then passed as a parameter within your `New-MailboxRepairRequest` command.

```
$Count = {Counter Value from "Get Counter Value"}
$DB = "DB" + "{0:D2}" -f $Count
```

Finally, the `New-MailboxRepairRequest` command is issued to Exchange along with the database parameter and any other options required such as the `CorruptionType` parameter:

```
New-MailboxRepairRequest -Database "$DB" -CorruptionType SearchFolder,
AggregateCounts,ProvisionedFolder,FolderView
```

Once the command has been issued to the Exchange environment, this runbook ends.

## Exchange Corruption Repair Complete

Owing to restrictions, `New-MailboxRepairRequest` only allows one database repair operation to be performed at any one time. When the `New-MailboxRepairRequest` cmdlet finishes, details of the completion are written to the application log.

You created Operations Manager rules to monitor these completion events and create alerts that this runbook monitors. Once the runbook detects that the `New-MailboxRepairRequest` command has completed, it invokes the Exchange Corruption Loop runbook again to begin processing the next database.

## There's more...

In this recipe, we used the database naming convention of DB along with the database as a numerical value of 01 through 20 appended. However, many organizations have different naming conventions, so it is possible that you will need to adjust this runbook to suit your needs.

If a numerical value is used for your naming convention, then it may be possible to adjust the PowerShell section that formats the $DB variable; for example, you could have MailboxDatabase instead of DB or you could adjust the number formatting to use numbers 1–20 as opposed to 01–20.

Another solution could be to utilize the Get-MailboxDatabase command within your runbook, which would return a list of mailbox databases within your environment. These results could then be reused within your runbook allowing you far more scope for database names and ensuring any additional databases are automatically picked up.

Operations Manager gathers a number of alerts in this recipe that are collected from the Event Logs on your Exchange mailbox servers. We log these alerts to allow system administrators or operators to review the progress and status of repairs on a weekly basis. Depending on your requirements, you could reclassify these alerts by modifying the relevant rule, or depending on what you wish, you can have Orchestrator assign these alerts to an Exchange support group or even close them once the runbook has finished with them.

Although we only collect three Event Log IDs, the New-MailboxRepairRequest command logs other events that you may also wish to capture; these events can be captured using the same methods we described in the recipe.

Detailed information on the events logged when using the New-MailboxRepairRequest command can be found by visiting http://technet.microsoft.com/en-us/library/ ff628334(v=exchg.141).aspx.

## See also

For detailed information on methods used in this recipe, refer to the following links:

▶ Information on the events logged when using the New-MailboxRepairRequest command can be found by visiting http://technet.microsoft.com/en-us/ library/ff628334(v=exchg.141).aspx

▶ Overview of Microsoft System Center Orchestrator: http://technet.microsoft. com/en-us/library/hh237242.aspx

▶ Exchange Admin Integration Pack of Microsoft System Center Orchestrator: http://technet.microsoft.com/en-us/library/jj614529.aspx

▶ Events and Rules of Microsoft System Center Operations Manager: http://technet.microsoft.com/en-us/library/hh457603.aspx

> ▶ Create a Mailbox Repair Request of Microsoft Exchange 2010: `http://technet.microsoft.com/en-us/library/ff625221(v=exchg.141).aspx`

> ▶ Get-MailboxDatabase of Microsoft Exchange 2013: `http://technet.microsoft.com/en-us/library/bb124924(v=exchg.150).aspx`

# Enabling Asset Discovery and Incident Management with System Center 2012 R2 Service Manager

In this recipe, we will look at the two types of connectors that are available for Operations Manager with Service Manager; the Operations Manager CI and Alert connectors can be configured to pass objects, attributes, and alerts from SCOM for use within System Center 2012 R2 Service Manager.

We will look at the options that are available when creating these connectors as well as the differences between the two types.

## Getting ready

For this recipe, ensure System Center 2012 Service Manager is running within your environment and that you have the installation folder accessible during the configuration.

You will be required to create two service accounts as described in the following table:

| Connector | Permissions needed |
|---|---|
| Operations Manager CI Connector Account | Operations Manager – Operator Privileges |
| | Service Manager – Advanced Operator |
| Operations Manager Alert Connector Account | Operations Manager – Administrator |
| | Service Manager – Advanced Operator |

## How to do it...

You need to follow a series of steps to configure both the Operations Manager Alert Connector and Configuration Item Connector.

To create the Operations Manager CI Connector:

1. Open the Service Manager 2012 R2 console.

2. Click on **Administration**.

3. Under **Administration**, click on **Connectors**.

4. On the **Tasks** pane under the **Connectors** section, click on **Create Connector** and navigate to **Operations Manager CI Connector**.

5. On the **Before You Begin** page, click on the **Next** button.

6. On the **General** page under **Name**, type Operations Manager CI Connector.

7. Ensure the **Enabled** checkbox is ticked and click on the **Next** button.

8. On the **Server Details** page under **Name**, type the name of your Operations Manager management server.

9. Click on the **New** button to create a new Run As account.

10. On the **Run As Account** screen under **Name**, type OPSMGRCICONN.

11. Type the username and password with appropriate permissions that you created during the prerequisites and then click on the **OK** button.

12. Click on the **Next** button.

13. On the **Management Packs** page, tick the **Select All** and **Do not write null values for properties that are not set within Operations Manager** checkboxes:

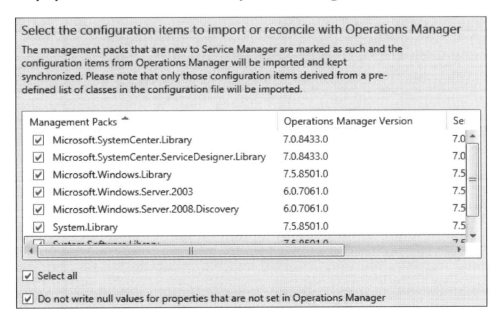

For this example, we select all management packs; however, you can also select only the management packs that contain the Configuration Items you wish to import.

14. Click on the **Next** button.

15. On the **Schedule** page, click on the **Next** button.

16. On the **Summary** page, review the settings and then click on the **Create** button.

17. On the **Completion** page, click on the close button.

18. To force synchronization now, select **Operations Manager CI Connector**, and on the **Tasks** pane, click on **Synchronize Now**.

19. Once the message box confirming the synchronization request has been submitted, click on the **OK** button.

To create the Operations Manager Alert Connector:

1. Open the Service Manager 2012 R2 console and click on **Administration**.

2. Under **Administration**, click on **Connectors**.

3. On the **Tasks** section under the **Connectors** section, click on **Create Connector** and navigate to **Operations Manager Alert Connector**.

4. On the **Before You Begin** page, click on the **Next** button.

5. On the **General** page under **Name**, type Operations Manager Alert Connector.

6. Ensure the **Enabled** checkbox is ticked and click on the **Next** button.

7. On the **Server Details** page under **Name**, type the name of your Operations Manager management server.

8. Click on the **New** button to create a new Run As account.

9. On the **Run As Account** screen under **Name**, type OPSMGRALERTCONN.

10. Type the username and password with appropriate permissions that you created during the prerequisites and then click on the **OK** button.

11. Click on the **Next** button.

12. On the **Alert Routing Rules** page, click on the **Next** Button.

13. On the **Schedule** page, tick the checkboxes next to both **Close alerts in Operations Manager when incidents are resolved and closed** and **Resolve incidents automatically when the alerts in Operations Manager are closed**:

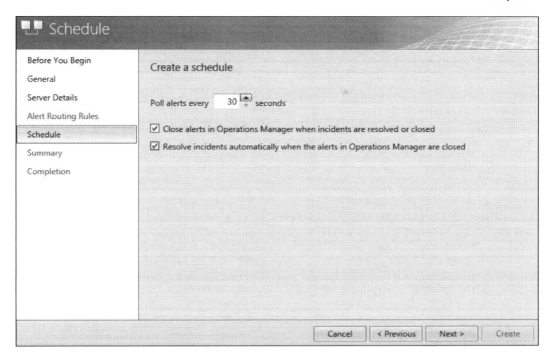

14. Click on the **Next** button.

15. On the **Summary** page, review the settings and then click on the **Create** button.

16. On the **Completion** page, click on the **Close** button.

17. Open the SCOM console and click on **Administration**.

18. Click on **Product Connectors** and navigate to **Internal Connectors**.

19. Select **Alert Sync:Operations Manager Alert Connector** from the list.

20. On the **Tasks** pane, click on **Properties.**

21. On the **Product Connector Properties** dialog, click on the **Add** button.

22. On the **General Properties** page, type All Alerts in the **Subscription Name** textbox.

23. Click on the **Next** button.

24. On the **Groups** page, click on the **Next** button.

25. On the **Targets** page, click on the **Next** button.

26. On the **Criteria** page, click on the **Create** button.

27. Click on the **OK** button.

## How it works...

Service Manager has two types of connectors for Operations Manager, namely the System Center Operations Manager Alert Connector and the System Center Operations Manager Configuration Item Connector also known or referred to as the CI Connector explained as

- **System Center Operations Manager Alert Connector**: The Alert Connector is used to allow the creation of Service Manager Incidents based on Operation Manager Alerts.

  In this recipe, you configured the Alert Connector, which allows for the creation of Service Manager Incidents based upon Operations Manager Alerts. This connector creates a two-way sync between the Operations Manager Alert and the Service Manager Incident that is created allowing the Incident to be resolved if the Operations Manager Alert becomes closed and vice versa.

- **System Center Operations Manager Configuration Item Connector**: The Configuration Item Connector is used to import objects and attributes that have been discovered by Operations Manager and create Configuration Items within the Service Manager **Configuration Management Database** (**CMDB**).

You also configured the Configuration Item Connector. This allows the creation of Service Manager Configuration Items from discovered objects within Operations Manager. The advantage is that once Service Manager is populated with these discovered objects, Configuration Items become available for use within Service Manager, and can be used as affected items for Incidents, Requests, or Change Control.

We have seen that, to import required objects in to Service Manager, you must first have the list of class definitions for these objects. These class definitions are stored within management packs. You import into Service Manager those management packs that contain the object types you wish to bring across while using the Configuration Item Connector.

## There's more...

The example given in this recipe imports some of the more common management packs into Service Manager. Quite often, you have created or imported a wider range of management packs that contain configuration items you may wish bring across to Service Manager. Should this be the case, then the Operations Manager Configuration Item Connector can be edited at any point to change which items you wish to synchronize.

In this recipe, you configured your Operations Manager Alert Connector for the most part using default options. You did not specify any routing rules or scope down the alert sync subscriptions for the connector.

Depending on your environment, using the default options to create the Alert Connector and associated Subscription can lead to a high volume of incidents being created within your Service Manager console or Incidents that are created without using your desired Incident template. To combat this, you can look at customizing the routing rules and/or the alert sync subscriptions to better suit your needs.

Now, we will look at what routing rules and alert sync subscriptions can offer you in the way of customization.

## Routing rules

Adding routing rules allows you to specify the incident template that will be used and what the priority and severity the incident will be based upon given the **Criteria Type** you specify.

You can add any number of routing rules and select their order:

Add Alert Routing Rule

Rule Name

Template

**Select Criteria Type**

○ Operations Manager Management Pack containing the Rule or Monitor raising the alert

Management Pack Name

○ Computer for which the alert was raised

Computer is a member of group

○ Custom Field

○ Operations Manager class for which the alert was raised

Monitoring class name

**Select alert severity and priority**
☐ Priority
☐ Severity

## Alert sync subscriptions

Alert sync subscriptions allow you to have more granular control over the alerts that are passed to Service Manager. By using these subscriptions, you are able to specify the groups, targets, and criteria of the alerts you wish to be forwarded and updated. You can create multiple subscriptions depending on your requirements.

## See also

For more detailed information on methods used in this recipe is available on the following links:

- ► *Using Connectors to Import Data in to System 2012 Center Service Manager*:
  `http://technet.microsoft.com/en-us/library/hh524326.aspx`

- ► *Importing Data and Alerts from System Center Operations Manager*:
  `http://technet.microsoft.com/en-us/library/hh524270.aspx`

# Performance and Resource Optimization (PRO) Integration with System Center 2012 R2 Virtual Machine Manager (VMM)

This recipe will describe the steps you need to configure Operations Manager to monitor your VMM infrastructure and enable PRO features. PRO allows VMM remediation actions to be performed when alerts are raised within SCOM.

We will see how you can provide monitoring of both your VMM hosts and guests by using Operations Manager and VMM integration. In addition, you can monitor the health and availability of components that make up your VMM infrastructure. These include components such as the management server and database server allowing a complete overview through diagram views within the Operations Manager console.

Taking integration a step further, we will see how to enable PRO allowing you to tie remediation actions based on alerts by raising PRO tips. We can either automatically remediate on the basis of these PRO tips or have an administrator manually approve them.

## Getting ready

For this recipe, ensure you have sufficient access to both the SCOM and VMM consoles.

For VMM integration, the following prerequisites should be met before attempting this recipe:

▶ PowerShell Version 3.0 on all Operations Manager Management Servers

▶ Port 5724 needs to be open between VMM and Operations Manager

▶ Operations Manager Console needs to be installed on the VMM Management Server

▶ Microsoft Monitoring Agent needs to be deployed to the VMM Management Server and all VMM managed hosts

▶ The following Operations Manager management packs need to be installed:

    ❑ Windows Server Internet Information Services 2003 6.0.5000.0 or later

    ❑ Windows Server 2008 Operating System (Discovery)

    ❑ Windows Server Operating System Library

    ❑ Windows Server 2008 Internet Information Services 7 6.0.6539.0 or later

    ❑ Windows Server Internet Information Services Library 6.0.5000.0 or later

    ❑ SQL Server Core Library 6.0.5000.0 or later

▶ You will be required to specify two accounts although the same account with the following appropriate permissions will work fine, as often the VMM service account is used:

    ❑ An account that is a member of the Operations Manager Administrators user role

    ❑ An account that is a member of the VMM Administrator user role

## How to do it...

To configure VMM integration with Operations Manager, perform the following steps:

1. Open the Virtual Machine Manager 2012 R2 console.

2. Click on **Settings**.

3. Under **Settings**, click on **System Center Settings**.

4. Right-click on **Operations Manager Server** and navigate to **Properties**.

5. On the **Introduction** screen, click on **Next**.

6. On the **Connection to Operations Manager** page, type the name of a Management Server within your Management Group in the **Server Name** textbox.

7. Select to either use the Service Account or specify an appropriate Run As account depending on how you configured the required accounts in the prerequisites.

8. Ensure the checkboxes for **Enable Performance and Resource Optimization (PRO)** and **Enable maintenance mode integration with Operations Manager** are checked:

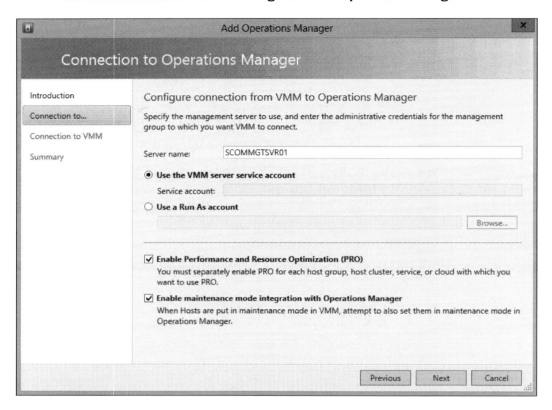

9. Click on **Next**.

10. On the **Connection to VMM** page, enter the user name and password for Operations Manager to connect to VMM. This account should have been configured during the prerequisites.

11. Click on **Next**.

12. On the **Summary** page, review your settings and click on **Finish**.

    The **Jobs** page will now open and you can review the connection creation progress.

| Step | | Name | Status |
|---|---|---|---|
| ✅ | 1 | New Operations Manager connection | Completed |

13. Click on **Settings**.

14. Under **Settings**, click on **System Center Settings**.

15. Right-click on **Operations Manager Server** and navigate to **Properties**.

16. On the **Details** page under **Diagnostics**, click on the **Test Pro** button.

17. Click on **OK | OK**.

18. Click on the **Jobs** section and navigate to **History**.

19. Ensure the **Pro Diagnostics** job completed successfully by selecting the job and viewing the **Details** tab:

| Step | | Name | Status |
|---|---|---|---|
| ✓ | ⊟ 1 | PRO diagnostics | Completed |
| ✓ | 1.1 | Create new PRO tip | Completed |
| ✓ | ⊟ 1.2 | Implement the fix for a PRO tip | Completed |
| ✓ | 1.2.1 | Invoke remediation | Completed |
| ✓ | 1.2.2 | Wait for remediation | Completed |

20. Open the SCOM console.

21. Click on the **Monitoring** section and ensure the Microsoft Virtual Machine Manager monitoring sections are visible:

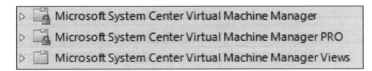

>
> By running the `Test Pro` command, a test alert with the name Pro Diagnostic Alert will be generated within Operations Manager. You can see evidence of this by looking back at closed alerts within the SCOM console.

## How it works...

The configuration of the integration between VMM and SCOM for the most part has been done for you. Having ensured that all prerequisites are met, you are only required to specify account information and the product options you would like to enable.

Behind the scenes, the required Product Connectors, Management Packs, and Run As accounts are all created for you. Configuring the correct permissions for the accounts required is key to ensuring these steps are successful.

If you encounter any issues during the configuration stage, you are advised to check the log file that is generated and review the prerequisites. The log folder and file location can normally be found in `SystemDrive:\ProgramData\VMMLogs\`.

## There's more...

During the configuration of PRO, you enabled maintenance mode integration. This allows SCOM to place the host into maintenance mode (allowing monitoring to be suspended during hardware and software tasks) when maintenance is performed in VMM.

In addition to the Test PRO option within the VMM console, you can also use PowerShell to test the PRO integration between VMM and SCOM using a cmdlet called `Test-SCPROTip`. This cmdlet can be used to ensure PRO integration is functioning correctly.

More information on the `Test-SCPROTip` can be found at `http://technet.microsoft.com/en-us/library/jj613209(v=sc.20).aspx`

## See also

Detailed information on methods used in this recipe is available at:

- *Configuring Operations Manager Integration with VMM*: `http://technet.microsoft.com/en-us/library/hh427287.aspx`

# 10
# Reporting in System Center 2012 R2 Operations Manager

In this chapter, we will cover the recipes that allow you to dig deeper into the data collected within your **System Center 2012 R2 Operations Manager** (**SCOM**) environment:

- ▶ Building SQL queries
- ▶ Creating SQL reports
- ▶ Publishing SQL reports
- ▶ Creating reports within the Operations console
- ▶ Scheduling reports
- ▶ Creating notifications and subscriptions
- ▶ Creating a SharePoint dashboard

## Introduction

This chapter will explore methods for retrieving and manipulating data collected within SCOM and show you how this data can be presented back to your organization in a meaningful way. The methods shown in this chapter can be modified to suit your organizational needs.

The recipes in this chapter will cover the following scenarios:

- Building SQL queries
  - Understand the information you would like to retrieve and how to achieve this by using SQL queries

- Creating SQL reports
  - Understand how to tackle the SQL query you created and explore how you can transform the data returned and present it as a SQL report using SQL Report Builder

- Publishing SQL reports
  - Understand how to publish SQL reports for viewing within the SCOM console

- Creating reports within the Operations console
  - Understand how you can create and save reports within the SCOM console

- Scheduling reports
  - Understand how you can schedule reports within the SCOM console

- Creating notifications and subscriptions
  - Understand how you can subscribe to alert types and how Operations Manager can report these through delivery methods such as e-mail

- Creating a SharePoint dashboard
  - Understand how you can create a simple dashboard within SharePoint to display the reports you have created by using PerformancePoint Services

For all these tasks, we have defined a process with the required steps in each recipe.

For all recipes in this chapter, the requirements are:

- Access to SQL 2012 Management Studio with appropriate permissions to your SCOM databases
- Microsoft Report Builder 3.0
- Appropriate permissions to deploy reports to your SQL Reporting Server

# Building SQL queries

This recipe will describe the steps you need to build a SQL query that will extract application information from your SCOM databases. This method can be used to collect other information from the databases to suit your organizational needs.

In this recipe, we will look at scenarios for which we require data to be extracted from our environment using SQL queries.

This scenario will demonstrate how you can retrieve a list of distributed applications from your environment and identify the health status of each.

## Getting ready

The preparation for this recipe is to ensure you have the appropriate access to read your SCOM databases and access to SQL Server 2012 Management Studio.

## How to do it...

Perform the following steps to build, test, and save your SQL query:

1. Start SQL Server 2012 Management Studio and connect to the SQL server where your Operations Manager database resides.

2. Expand the **Databases** node on the **Object Explorer** pane to see your Operations Manager databases in the tree view.

3. Click on your Operations Manager database (as default named **OperationsManager**) on the **Object Explorer** pane and from the top ribbon select the **New Query** button.

4. Once the **New Query** window opens, we are ready to begin building our SQL query.

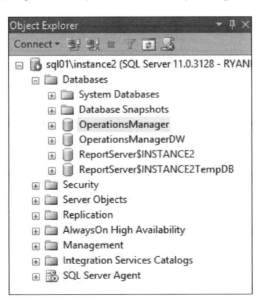

5. Within the **Query** window, type the following SQL statement, and then, in the ribbon, ensure that your **OperationsManager** database is selected and click the **Execute** button.

As a standard, the database name will be **OperationsManager**; however, it is possible that the name specified during installation will differ from this. If this is the case, just replace **OperationsManager** with the name of your database. In addition, you can also add **Use OperationsManager** to the top of your script to automatically select that database when executing your script:

```
SELECT dbo.BaseManagedEntity.DisplayName,
MAX(dbo.State.HealthState) as "Application Health"
FROM dbo.State INNER JOIN

dbo.BaseManagedEntity ON dbo.State.
BaseManagedEntityId =
dbo.BaseManagedEntity.BaseManagedEntityId

where (dbo.BaseManagedEntity.FullName like
'Service_%')

and dbo.state.HealthState between 0 and 3

group by DisplayName
```

6. If we then inspect the **Results** pane in the following screenshot, we can see the SQL query has returned the list of distributed applications that we have created within our environment along with their associated health states as numerical values:

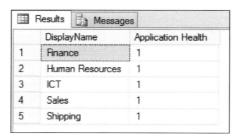

7. Click **File | Save As**, rename the file as `DistrubutedApplications.sql`, and save it to a location of your choice.

## How it works...

This example of a SQL query works in a number of ways. First, you gather all base-managed items by using the following SQL statement:

```
SELECT dbo.BaseManagedEntity.DisplayName,
dbo.State.HealthState as "Application Health"
```

```
FROM dbo.State INNER JOIN
dbo.BaseManagedEntity ON dbo.State.BaseManagedEntityId =
dbo.BaseManagedEntity.BaseManagedEntityId
```

The returned results contain more distributed application items than you may require. The results should only show the distributed applications that you created within your environment and not any that may have automatically been created by the system. You can overcome this by filtering down the results to contain only items matching a specific criteria. In this case, any distributed applications that are created manually will start with the name `Service`, so you can use the following SQL statement to return a filtered set of results:

```
SELECT dbo.BaseManagedEntity.DisplayName,
dbo.State.HealthState as "Application Health"
FROM dbo.State INNER JOIN
dbo.BaseManagedEntity ON dbo.State.BaseManagedEntityId =
dbo.BaseManagedEntity.BaseManagedEntityId
where (dbo.BaseManagedEntity.FullName like 'Service_%')
```

Now, even though your query only returns distributed application items, it still contains more information than you may require. You now need to narrow down the results so that only the health states you are required to report on are returned. In the present example, these results are as follows:

- ▶ **1 – Healthy**: Signifies that the status of the result is healthy
- ▶ **2 – Warning**: Signifies that the status of the result is in a warning state
- ▶ **3 – Critical**: Signifies that the status of the result is critical
- ▶ **0 – Not Monitored**: Signifies that the status of the result is not monitored

You achieve this by only returning items where the health state is between 0 and 3, as follows:

```
    SELECT dbo.BaseManagedEntity.DisplayName,
dbo.State.HealthState as "Application Health"
FROM dbo.State INNER JOIN
dbo.BaseManagedEntity ON dbo.State.BaseManagedEntityId =
dbo.BaseManagedEntity.BaseManagedEntityId
where (dbo.BaseManagedEntity.FullName like 'Service_%')
and dbo.state.HealthState between 0 and 3
```

Finally, you need to filter down your results to contain only one instance of the names of your distributed applications and ensure you select the worst state as your health state. This can be done in SQL by using the `MAX` command along with the `Group By` command.

The MAX command will take the highest numerical value for each health state returned. You then use MAX in conjunction with the Group By command to filter your view:

```
SELECT dbo.BaseManagedEntity.DisplayName,
MAX(dbo.State.HealthState) as "Application Health"
FROM dbo.State INNER JOIN
dbo.BaseManagedEntity ON dbo.State.BaseManagedEntityId =
dbo.BaseManagedEntity.BaseManagedEntityId
where (dbo.BaseManagedEntity.FullName like 'Service_%')
and dbo.state.HealthState between 0 and 3
group by DisplayName
```

## There's more...

Distributed applications that have not been created by the operator will not appear with the execution of this SQL query.

It is possible to add system-created distributed applications into your query using the OR statement.

The following SQL statement uses the OR command to add the Operations Manager Management Group distributed application into your results:

```
 SELECT BaseManagedEntity.DisplayName, Max(State.HealthState) as
"Application Health"
FROM State INNER JOIN
BaseManagedEntity ON State.BaseManagedEntityId =
BaseManagedEntity.BaseManagedEntityId
where (BaseManagedEntity.FullName like 'Service_%'
or BaseManagedEntity.DisplayName = 'Operations Manager Management
Group')
and state.HealthState between 0 and 3
group by DisplayName
```

As you can see on the **Results** pane, the distributed application you added to the query now appears:

| | DisplayName | Application Health |
|---|---|---|
| 1 | Finance | 1 |
| 2 | Human Resources | 1 |
| 3 | ICT | 1 |
| 4 | Operations Manager Management Group | 1 |
| 5 | Sales | 1 |
| 6 | Shipping | 1 |

## See also

Detailed information on the methods used in this recipe is available here:

- ▶ Microsoft Technet—*SELECT Clause*: `http://technet.microsoft.com/en-us/library/ms176104.aspx`

- ▶ Microsoft Technet—*From*: `http://technet.microsoft.com/en-us/library/ms177634.aspx`

- ▶ Microsoft Technet—*WHERE*: `http://technet.microsoft.com/en-us/library/ms188047.aspx`

- ▶ Microsoft Technet—*MAX*: `http://technet.microsoft.com/en-us/library/ms187751.aspx`

- ▶ Microsoft Technet—*GROUP BY*: `http://technet.microsoft.com/en-us/library/ms177673.aspx`

# Creating SQL reports

This recipe will describe the steps you need to build a SQL report using Microsoft Report Builder 3.0.

You will utilize the distributed application SQL query that you created in the previous recipe to act as the foundation of your report.

This method can be used to build other reports from SQL queries to suit your organizational needs. In this recipe, we will look at the returned data from your SQL query and present the information in a way that is easy for business use. This scenario will look at how you can take the results of your SQL query and produce a SQL report that uses visual indicators to show the health status of your distributed applications.

## Getting ready

The preparation for the recipe is to ensure you have access to Microsoft Report Builder 3.0 and appropriate access to read your SCOM databases and the SQL query you saved in the previous recipe.

## How to do it...

To build your SQL report, perform the following steps:

1. Start the Microsoft Report Builder 3.0 application.
2. Click on **File** and navigate to **New**. When the wizard appears, select the **Blank** report.

3. Once your blank report is on the screen, give your new report a title by clicking on **Click to add title** and typing `Distributed Application Status`.

4. Remove the **Execution Time** field by right-clicking on it and navigating to **Delete**.

5. Remove the page footer by right-clicking on it and navigating to **Delete**. You should now be left with a report containing only your title:

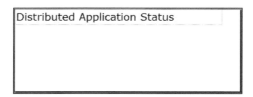

Distributed Application Status

6. Right-click on **Data Sources** from **Report Data | Add Data Source**.

7. In the **Data Source Properties** dialog, type `OperationsManager` in the **Name** field.

8. Click the **Use a connection embedded in my report** radio button.

9. Ensure the connection type is **Microsoft SQL Server** and click the **Build** button.

10. In the **Connection Properties** dialog, type the name of your SQL server on which your Operations Manager database resides.

11. Under **Connect to a database**, select your Operations Manager database.

12. Click the **Test Connection** button to ensure you have the details and permissions correct. Once successful, click the **OK** button:

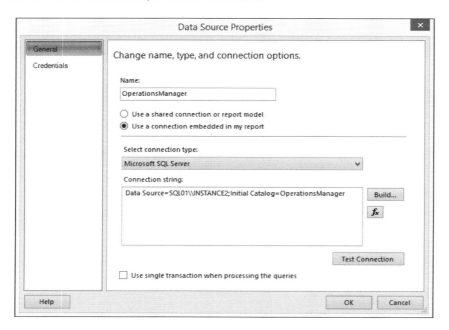

13. Right-click on **Datasets** from the **Report Data** pane and navigate to **Add Dataset**.

14. In the **Dataset Properties** dialog, type `DistributedApplications` in the **Name** field.

15. Click the **Use a dataset embedded in my report** radio button.

16. Under **Data Source**, select the **OperationsManager** data source you created.

17. In the **Query** textbox, paste the SQL query that you created in the previous recipe.

18. Ensure your query is working as expected by clicking **Query Designer...** | **!** buttons. On the **Results** pane, you should see the output from your query. Click **OK** | **OK**:

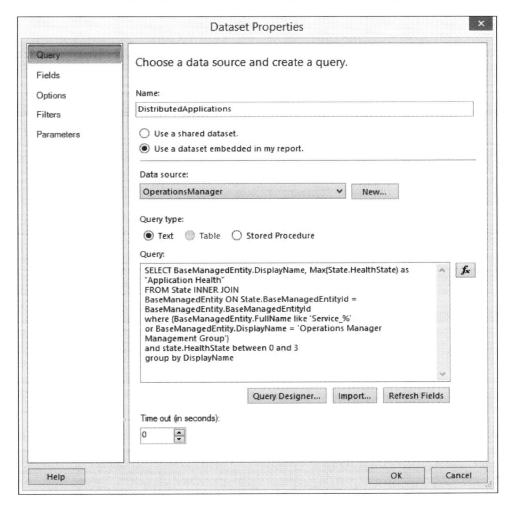

19. From the ribbon, select **Insert** | **Table** | **Insert Table**. Use your cursor to draw the table on your report.

20. From the **Report Data** pane under **Datasets**, drag the **DisplayName** field and drop it in row one, column one of the table.

21. From the **Report Data** pane under **Datasets**, drag the **Application_Health** field and drop it in row two, column two.

22. On row one, column one, click on the field and rename it to `Application Name`.

23. On row one, column three, click on the field and type `Application Status`.

24. Highlight each column and, on the ribbon, click **Paragraph** and navigate to **Middle | Centered**.

25. Highlight the top row. On the ribbon, click **Font**, select the font size as **14**, and click the **bold** button.

26. From the ribbon, select the **Insert** tab and click on the **indicator** button.

27. On row two, column three, click on the cell.

28. When the **Indicators** dialog box appears, click **Symbols | Circled | OK**.

29. Right-click on the **Indicator** icon that has appeared and click on **Indicator Properties**.

30. In the **Indicator Properties** dialog, type `Status` in the **Name** field and then click on **Values and States**.

31. Under **Value**, select **[Sum(Application_Health)]**.

32. Under **States Measurement Unit**, select **Numeric**.

33. Click the **Add** button under **Indicator States**.

34. Under **Indicator States**, adjust the indicator **Start** and **End** values to match the color state: **3** for red, **2** for yellow, **1** for green, and **0** for no color:

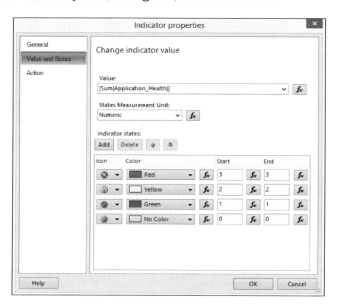

35. Click **OK** to return to the report.

36. Right-click on column two and click **Visibility**.

37. In the **Column Visibility** dialog, select the **Hide** radio button then click **OK**.

38. From the ribbon, click the **Run** button to preview your report:

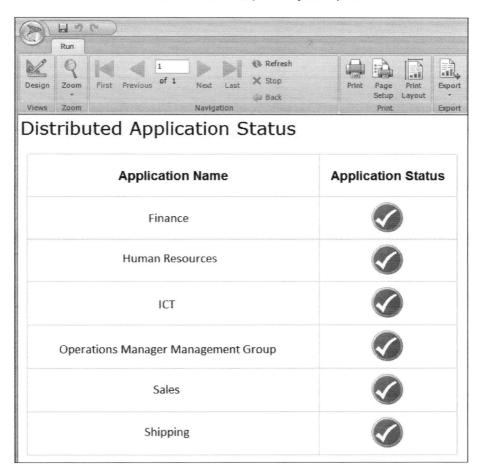

39. You may wish to adjust the column widths as required to ensure all data is visible.

40. Click **File | Save As**, name the file as `DistributedApplicationReport.rdl`, and save it to a location of your choice.

## How it works...

In this recipe, you have completed a number of tasks to produce your required SQL report.

First, you took a blank report and customized it by removing the **Execution Time** field and **Page Footer** and adding your own title for the report.

You can modify the layout and content of your report to suit your organizational needs. Now try adding images or additional text.

After that, you established your data source. This is the connection you would use to access your Operations Manager databases and perform queries against.

Having created your data source, you proceeded to create a dataset. Your dataset will use the SQL query that was created in the previous recipe and return to you a collection of data that you can present within your report:

Next, the data returned from your dataset was added by creating a new table within your report and placing the required fields into the columns.

You then modified the font styles and sizes to make your report stand out to its viewer, as default font sizes can be small and formatting can look out of place.

If you were to run the report at this stage, you would see numerical values for the health states; however, for this report, you require a visual indication so that the health states of your distributed applications can be seen at a glance.

You achieved this by using indicators. Indicators allow you to adjust the indication images shown on the basis of the values that are passed to it. In this case, you used the numerical values returned for the health state of your distributed applications.

You inserted an additional column on which you placed the circled indicator image set. Then, you set the indicator properties to take the numerical value of your **Application_Health** and set your indicators to match the health state value relevant to the indicator icon you wished to be displayed:

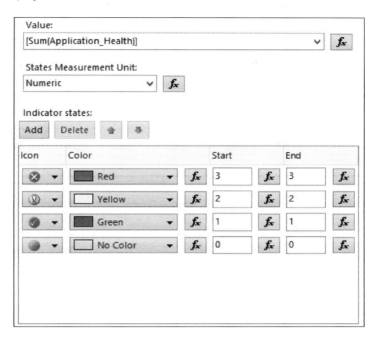

Now when you run your report, you can see that the numerical values have been replaced with indicator icons that represent your distributed application health states.

## There's more...

Indicators and tables are just some of the components that SQL reports can contain. Other items such as lists, gauges, maps, and even subreports can be added to create a rich report to suit your organization's needs.

The following screenshot shows the type of components that can be added to SQL reports through Report Builder:

## See also

Detailed information on the methods and tools used in this recipe is available here:

▶ Microsoft Technet—*Report Builder 3.0*: `http://technet.microsoft.com/en-us/library/dd207008(v=sql.105).aspx`

# Publishing SQL reports

This recipe will describe the steps you need to publish reports to your SQL reporting server.

In this recipe, we will look at scenarios for which we require access to your newly created SQL reports from within the SCOM console.

## Getting ready

The preparation for this recipe is to ensure you have the appropriate access to your SCOM reporting server.

## How to do it...

Perform the following steps to publish your SQL report to your SCOM reporting server:

1. Start the Microsoft Report Builder 3.0 application.
2. Click **File | Open**.
3. Navigate to the location of the `DistributedApplicationReport.rdl` file you saved in the previous recipe, select the file, and click **Open**.
4. Click **File | Save As**.
5. In the **Name** textbox, type the web address of your Operations Manager reporting server and click **Save**.
6. Once you are connected to your SQL report server, double-click on the folder named `My Reports`. Now, in the **Name** textbox, type `Distributed Applications` and click **Save**:

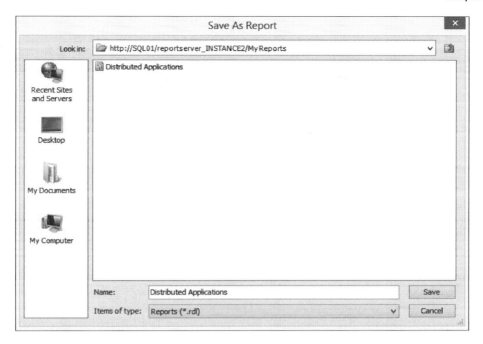

7.  Close the Microsoft Report Builder 3.0 application.

8.  Open the Microsoft Operations Manager console.

9.  Navigate to **Reports**.

10. Select the **Authored Reports** folder.

11. Select the report named **Distributed Applications**.

12. Click **Tasks | Report | Open**.

## How it works...

In this recipe, you have published a SQL report to your reporting server and verified it is accessible through the SCOM console.

First, you opened the distributed application report that you created in the previous recipe within Microsoft SQL Report Builder 3.0.

You then connected to your Operations Manager reporting server through the **Save** dialog box and saved the report to the My Reports folder located on the report's server.

 If you are unsure of your reporting web service URL, this can be found by using the **Reporting Services Configuration Manager** application on your reporting server.

Once your report had been saved, you verified access to the report using the SCOM console.

## There's more...

Using the Report Builder application is not the only way you can manage reports within your environment. Reports on your reporting server can be administered using the Report Manager URL, which can be found within the Reporting Services Configuration Manager application on your reporting server.

When accessing your report server through the Report Manager URL, you can perform a number of more advanced administrative tasks such as creating folders, uploading reports, and managing security. The various SQL Server reporting services are shown in the following screenshot:

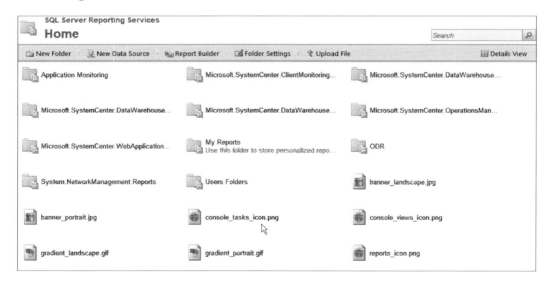

## See also

Detailed information on the methods and tools used in this recipe is available here:

- ▶ Microsoft Technet—*Report Builder 3.0*: `http://technet.microsoft.com/en-us/library/dd207008(v=sql.105).aspx`

- ▶ Microsoft Technet—*Reporting Services (SSRS)*: `http://technet.microsoft.com/en-us/library/ms159106.aspx`

# Creating reports within the Operations console

This recipe will describe the steps you need to create reports within the System Center 2012 R2 Operations Manager console.

This method shows how you can set parameters within your reports to customize their output to suit your business needs.

In this recipe, we will look at a scenario for creating reports that enable you to identify underutilized resources on servers over the previous month. This scenario will look at how we can produce easy-to-use reports that can later be used to inform other business units on the performance of servers they may be responsible for, and where possible, resources and costs may be recovered.

## Getting ready

The preparation for this recipe is to ensure you have the appropriate administrative access to your Operations Manager console and **Windows Server Operating Management Packs** deployed within your environment. This recipe assumes you have sufficient data within your environment on which to report on.

## How to do it...

1. Open your Operations Manager console.
2. Select **Reporting**.
3. On the **Reporting** pane, select the folder named **Windows Server Operating System Reports**.
4. On the **Reports** pane, double-click on the report named **Performance by Utilization**.
5. On the **Performance by Utilization** report options page under **Aggregation**, select **Daily**.
6. Under **From**, select **Previous Month | First Day | 08:00 AM**.

7. Under **To**, select **Previous Month | Last Day | 05:00 PM**.

8. Tick the **Use business hours** checkbox.

9. From the **Group** drop-down menu, select **Windows Server Computer Group**.

10. From the **Utilization** drop-down menu, select **Least**.

 Changing parameters on this report will also allow you to report on the most utilized servers. You can also change which server group you report on and how many results you would like to be displayed within your report.

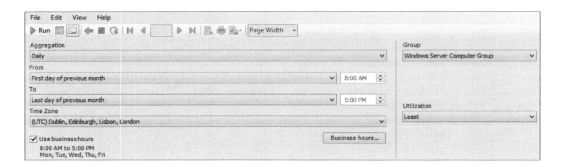

11. Click the **Run** icon to preview the report.

12. Click **File | Publish**.

13. In the **Name** textbox, type `Top 10 Least Utilized Server Resources`.

14. In the **Description** textbox, type `Shows the top 10 least utilized server resources for the last whole month`.

15. Click **OK**.

## How it works...

Taking the requirement to find the least utilized servers within your environment, you were able to make use of one of the standard reports that are available within the Operations console.

The Windows Server Operating System Management Pack contains a report called **Performance by Utilization**, which allows you to pass a number of parameters to achieve your report. The report includes the following information:

▶ Aggregation type

▶ Time period required

- ▸ Business hours only requirement
- ▸ Group on which to report on
- ▸ Utilization type, **Least** or **Most**
- ▸ Number of systems to return

You then set the parameters of your report to return daily aggregated data that covered the whole of the previous month during business hours and returned the least utilized resources from 10 systems from the group of Windows Server Computers.

Then, you ran the report to ensure your data was returned as expected before publishing the report for future use.

The results of this report can be helpful in identifying systems that may be underutilized or over-resourced and could form part of a monthly review.

## There's more...

Out of the box, Operations Manager provides you with a vast amount of reports that you can use to obtain insights into your infrastructure. Additional management packs that you may install within your environment often come with reports that focus upon the product they monitor.

Most reports within Operations Manager can be passed parameters, allowing you to tailor them to the specific needs of your business.

Reports can also be sent to different business units using subscriptions and notification channels, which will be covered in the next recipes. The reporting options are as follows:

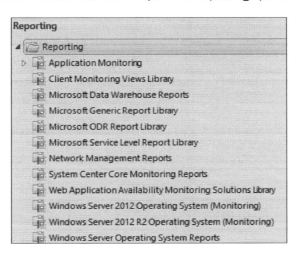

## See also

Detailed information on the methods and tools used in this recipe is available here:

▸ Microsoft Technet—*Using Reports in Operations Manager*: `http://technet.microsoft.com/en-us/library/hh212786.aspx`

# Scheduling reports

This recipe will describe the steps you need to schedule reports within the System Center 2012 R2 Operations Manager console.

## Getting ready

The preparation for this recipe is to ensure you have the appropriate administrative access to your Operations Manager console and to Reporting Services Configuration Manager on your Operations Manager SQL reporting server.

## How to do it...

1. On your Operations Manager SQL reporting server, open the Reporting Services Configuration Manager application through the Windows Start menu.

2. When prompted to connect to your reporting server instance, select the appropriate server for your environment and click the **OK** button.

3. From the tree view on the left-hand side, select **E-Mail Settings**.

4. Check whether e-mail settings are already configured. If they are, you can close down the **Reporting Services Configuration** tool and continue from step 9 of this recipe.

5. Under **E-Mails Settings | SMTP Settings | Sender Address**, type the e-mail address you wish your Operations Manager reports to be sent from.

6. Under **E-Mails Settings | SMTP Settings | SMTP Server**, type the SMTP address of your mail server.

7. Click the **Apply** button.

8. Verify the settings have applied correctly and then click **Exit**:

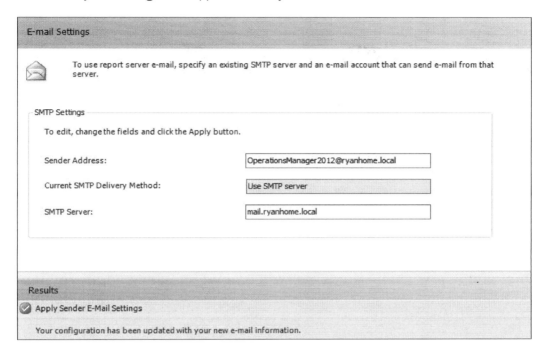

9. Open up your System Center 2012 R2 Operations Manager console.

10. Select **Reporting**.

11. Under **Reporting**, click **Authored Reports** in the tree view.

12. On the **Reports** pane, right-click on the report titled **Top 10 Least Utilized Server Resources** and click **Schedule**.

13. In the **Subscribe to a Report** dialog, type Top 10 Least Utilized Server Resources - Monthly Report in the **Description** textbox.

14. Under **Delivery Method**, select **E-Mail**.

15. In the **Settings** section, enter the following properties:

| Name of parameter | Value |
| --- | --- |
| To (required) | Enter your recipient e-mail address |
| CC | Leave blank |
| BCC | Leave blank |
| Reply-To | Enter the address which any replies will be sent to |
| Include Report | Checked |

| Name of parameter | Value |
|---|---|
| Render Format | **MHTML (web archive)** |
| Priority | **Normal** |
| Subject (required) | `@ReportName` |
| Comment | Leave blank |
| Include Link | Unchecked |

The final screen after all the fields are filled will look like the following:

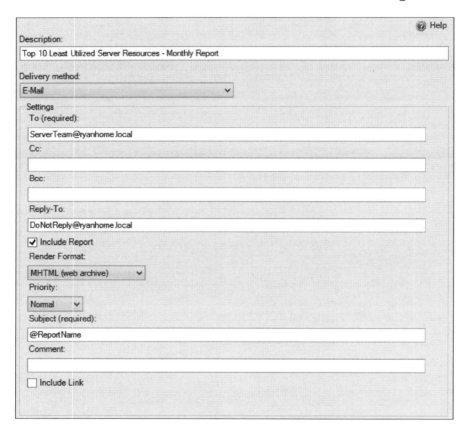

16. Click **Next**.

17. On the **Schedule** page under **Generate the Report**, select the **Monthly** radio button.

18. Ensure boxes for months **January** through **December** are ticked.

19. Check the **Every** radio button and set the drop-down list to **1st**.

20. Uncheck days Tuesday through Sunday and ensure only **Mon** is ticked:

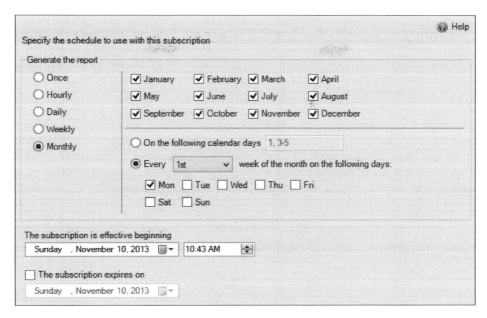

21. Click **Next**.

22. On the **Parameters** page, click **Finish**.

23. In the SCOM console, select **Scheduled Reports** from the **Reporting** tree view. Your scheduled report should now be listed.

## How it works...

Unlike subscribers and subscriptions, **Scheduled Reports** do not use the e-mail (SMTP) notification channel within Operations Manager to send reports through. Scheduling a report relies upon SQL Reporting Services to be correctly configured to allow the use of SMTP e-mail.

In this recipe, you checked your SQL Reporting Services configuration to ensure that the settings had been configured to suit your environment. An indication that this configuration has not been complete is the lack of the **E-Mail** option when scheduling a report through the SCOM console.

Once SQL Reporting Services were confirmed as configured, you began to schedule your report that was created in the previous recipe.

Scheduling the report allowed you to specify options such as who the recipient will be, what format the report should be rendered in, and the priority and subject of the e-mail.

 Operations Manager allows your report to be rendered in a variety of different formats to suit your business requirements. Depending on the reporting methods, type of report, or recipient, you may wish to adjust this to find a render format most suited to your needs.

Next, you specified a schedule on which you would like your report to be executed. This **Schedule** page allowed you to set granular options for the day, date, time, and frequency of when your report would run. The parameters of your report were set to gather data over the previous month. A schedule of the first Monday of each month was set, allowing for this data to be delivered promptly.

 Scheduling options are unique to you and your business and may require adjustment. You can also give the start and expiration times for scheduled reports if you wish reports to be sent at or for a specific period of time.

You left the options on the **Parameter** page alone as these had already been configured within your report. However, if needed, these can be adjusted.

Your report schedule was then saved and you verified this by checking **Scheduled Reports** within the SCOM console.

## There's more...

In addition to the e-mail delivery method, reports can also be scheduled for delivery to a Windows File Share.

The following screenshot shows options that are available when saving reports to a Windows File Share:

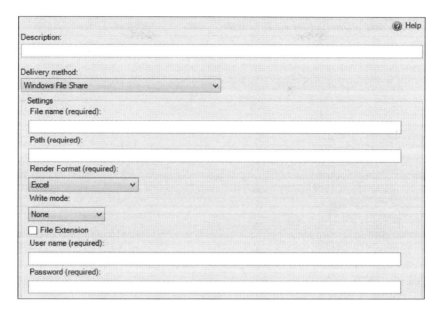

Using the delivery to a **Windows File Share** method may be handy for a number of uses, which include:

▸ Saving to a central reporting repository

▸ Saving to different areas of the business

▸ Delivery where **E-Mail** is not an option

▸ Saving to a file share for manipulation using System Center 2012 R2 Orchestrator or other such tools

The file share method also allows for saved reports to be either overwritten or auto incremented if required.

## See also

Detailed information on the methods and tools used in this recipe is available here:

▸ Microsoft Technet—*E-Mail Delivery in Reporting Services*: `http://technet.microsoft.com/en-us/library/ms160334.aspx`

# Creating notifications and subscriptions

This recipe will describe the steps you need to create and subscribe to alerts and reports for business units from within the Operations console.

In this recipe, we will take a scenario where you may require your server team to be notified through e-mail of any monitored servers that experience a heartbeat failure. This can be useful if operators are not always within the Operations console or have limited access such as field engineers.

This scenario will look at how you can create an e-mail notification channel as well as create a subscriber and then a subscription to the heartbeat alert in order to ensure your server administrators are notified.

## Getting ready

The preparation for this recipe is to ensure you have the appropriate administrative access to your Operations Manager console, details of your SMTP server, and e-mail addresses of your intended recipients.

## How to do it...

1. Open your Operations Manager console.
2. Select **Administration**.
3. On the **Administration** pane, select **Notification | Channels**.
4. On the **Task** pane, select **New | E-Mail (SMTP)**.
5. In the **E-mail Notification Channel** dialog, click **Next**.
6. Click the **Add** button.
7. Under **SMTP Server (FQDN)**, type the name of your SMTP server in the textbox.
8. Under **Port Number**, type the port number on which your SMTP server accepts traffic.
9. Click **OK**.

You can add multiple SMTP servers to provide failover, ensuring e-mail notifications are not missed due to outage.

10. In the **Return Address** textbox, type the e-mail address to which you wish replies to be sent.

11. Click **Next | Finish**:

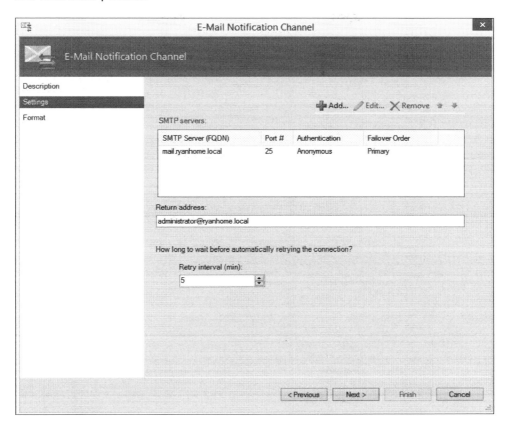

12. On the **Administration** pane, select **Notification | Subscribers**.

13. On the **Task** pane, select **New**.

14. In the **Notification Subscriber Wizard** dialog, type `Server Team` in the **Subscriber Name** textbox.

15. Click **Next | Next**.

The **Schedule options** pages allow you to specify when notifications are sent. These can be restricted by day and time and can apply to both the subscription and subscribers. These options are useful if you have teams working within shift patterns or alerts that are only relevant at certain times.

16. On the **Address** page, click the **Add** button.

17. On the **General** page, type `Server Team` within the **Address Name** textbox and click **Next**.

18. On the **Channel** page, select **E-Mail (SMTP)** as **Channel Type**.

19. In the **Delivery Address for the Selected Channel** textbox, type the e-mail address of your server team.

20. Click **Finish**.

21. On the **Administration** pane, select **Notification | Subscriptions**.

22. On the **Task** pane, select **New**.

23. On the **Description** page, type `Server Heartbeat Failures` in the **Subscription Name** textbox.

24. In the **Description** textbox, type `Subscription to notify upon server heartbeat failures`.

25. Click **Next**.

26. On the **Criteria** page under **Conditions**, tick the checkboxes next to **created by specific rules or monitors (e.g., sources)** and **with a specific resolution state**.

27. In the **Criteria Description** box, click the first instance of the **specific** link.

28. In the **Filter by** textbox, type `Health Service Heartbeat Failure` and click the **Search** button.

29. Under **Available rules and monitors**, select **Health Service Heartbeat Failure** and click the **Add** button.

30. Click **OK**.

31. In the **Criteria Description** box, click on the second instance of the **specific** link.

32. Tick the checkbox next to the **New** resolution state then click **OK**:

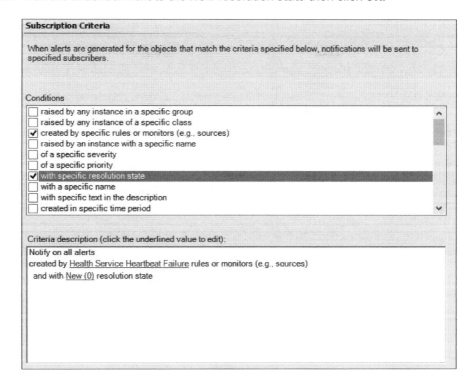

33. Click **Next**.

34. On the **Subscribers** page, click the **Add** button.

35. Click the **Search** button.

36. Under **Available Subscribers**, select **Server Team** and click **Add | OK**.

37. Click **Next**.

38. On the **Channels** page, click the **Add** button.

39. Click the **Search** button.

40. Under **Available Channels**, select **SMTP Channel** and click **Add | OK**.

41. Click **Next**.

42. On the **Summary** page, ensure that the **Enable this notification subscription** checkbox is checked and click **Finish**.

43. Once the subscription is saved, click **Close**.

## How it works...

First, you created your notification channel, which allows you to configure the delivery mechanism through which Operations Manager sends notifications. In this example, you configured the **E-Mail (SMTP)** mechanism. To achieve this, you entered details such as:

- ▸ Mail server address
- ▸ Port number
- ▸ Return e-mail address

 The formatting of your notification can be customized to include additional parameters or wording. You can also modify the importance level at which your alert reports are sent.

Next, you created your subscriber. In this example, we created one for your server teams. Subscribers are people or groups to whom you wish notifications or reports to be sent.

You created a subscriber for your server team, which was set to allow notifications at any time of the day using the **E-Mail (SMTP)** notification channel you configured. Notifications can be set to be sent between scheduled hours or by certain notification channels, all of which can be tailored to suit your business needs.

Once your notification channel and subscriber were created, you identified the type of alerts for which you wished to be notified. For this example, you used server heartbeat failures and a subscription was created that allowed you to specify the criterion for notifications to be sent.

The criterion was set to trigger notifications on any server heartbeat failures that had a resolution state of new.

 The alert criterion can be adjusted to cover most required scenarios.

For example, you may wish to create similar subscriptions to notify teams when servers are experiencing low disk space. In this example, you could specify a source condition to ensure your Windows and Linux server teams are notified only when it affects a certain platform.

You then added the subscriber and notification channel you created before ensuring your subscription was enabled.

## There's more...

One notification channel that is available is called **Command Notification Channel**. This notification channel differs from the other methods as it is used to run command-line executables and scripts in response to alerts.

You could use **Command Notification Channel** for a number of reasons, such as:

- ► PowerShell and VBS scripts
- ► Logging in
- ► Auto remediation
- ► Updating alerts

You can also pass parameters of the Operations Manager alert across to your command line to perform actions targeted at the properties of your alerts:

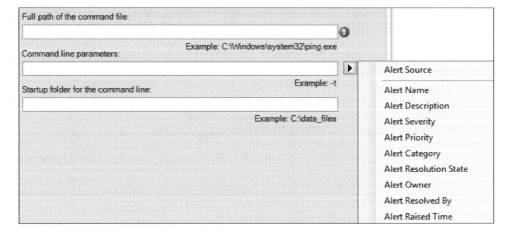

As you can see, using this method enables you to open up endless possibilities and extend Operations Manager's reach by truly customizing it to meet your operational needs.

 Command notifications will be executed under the local system account.

## See also

Detailed information on the methods and tools used in this recipe is available here:

- ▶ Microsoft Technet—*Subscribing to Alert Notifications*:
  `http://technet.microsoft.com/en-us/library/hh212725.aspx`

- ▶ Microsoft Technet—*How to Enable an Email Notification Channel*:
  `http://technet.microsoft.com/en-us/library/hh212914.aspx`

- ▶ Microsoft Technet—*How to Enable a Command Notification Channel*:
  `http://technet.microsoft.com/en-us/library/hh212711.aspx`

- ▶ Microsoft Technet—*How to Create Notification Subscribers*:
  `http://technet.microsoft.com/en-us/library/hh212812.aspx`

- ▶ Microsoft Technet—*How to Create Notification Subscriptions*:
  `http://technet.microsoft.com/en-us/library/hh212789.aspx`

# Creating a SharePoint dashboard

This recipe will describe the steps you need to create a SharePoint dashboard to display information gathered from within your SCOM environment.

In this recipe, we will look at how you can leverage Microsoft SharePoint 2013 PerformancePoint Services to present Operations Manager data in a meaningful way to your business.

 PerformancePoint Services requires SharePoint Enterprise Edition.

This recipe will look at how you can take your SQL reports and quickly present them through dashboards using PerformancePoint Designer.

We will then look at how these dashboards can then be presented to your business by publishing them to your company's SharePoint 2013 site.

Dashboards can comprise of a number of components, such as score cards, SQL reports, and KPIs, which connect to one or more data sources, allowing you to collate and present your information more easily.

## Getting ready

As the preparation for this recipe, it is assumed you have a SharePoint 2013 infrastructure already deployed and have your PerformancePoint site running.

You also need to ensure you have the appropriate access to your SharePoint 2013 PerformancePoint site.

## How to do it...

Perform the following steps to create a SharePoint dashboard containing your **Distributed Application Status** report:

1. Using your web browser, connect to your SharePoint 2013 PerformancePoint site.

2. From the ribbon, select the **PERFORMANCEPOINT** tab and click the **Dashboard Designer** button:

3. Once the **PerformancePoint Designer** application has loaded, under **Workspace Browser**, right-click on **PerformancePoint Content** and navigate to **New | Report**.

4. Select the **Reporting Services** template and click the **OK** button.

5. On the **Editor** tab, enter the following properties:

| Name of parameter | Value |
|---|---|
| **Server Mode** | **Server Center** |
| **Server Name** | Type the address of your Operations Manager 2012 R2 Reporting Server: `http://<<server name>>/reportserver` |
| **Report** | Click the **Browse** button and select your **Distributed Application** report located in the `My Reports` folder |
| **Show Toolbar** | Unchecked |
| **Show Parameters** | Unchecked |
| **Show Docmap** | Unchecked |
| **Zoom** | **100** |
| **Format** | **HTML4.0** |
| **Section** | Leave blank |
| **Docmap ID** | Leave blank |
| **Report Parameters** | Leave blank |

6. On the **Properties** tab, type `Distributed Application Report` in the **Name** textbox.

7. Click **File | Save Item**.

8. Under **Workspace Browser**, right-click on **PerformancePoint Content** and navigate to **New | Dashboard**.

9. Select the **1 Zone** template and click the **OK** button.

10. On the **Editor** tab, change the **Page Name** value from **page 1** to **Distributed Applications**.

11. On the **Details** pane, expand **Reports | PerformancePoint Content**.

12. Drag **Distributed Application Status Report** on to the **Dashboard Content** zone.

13. On the **Properties** tab, type `Distributed Application Dashboard` in the **Name** textbox.

14. Click **File | Save Item**.

15. On the **Workspace Browser** pane under **PerformancePoint Content**, right-click on **Distributed Application Dashboard** and select **Deploy to SharePoint**.

16. In the **Deploy To** dialog, select the appropriate folder in which to deploy your dashboard and click **OK**:

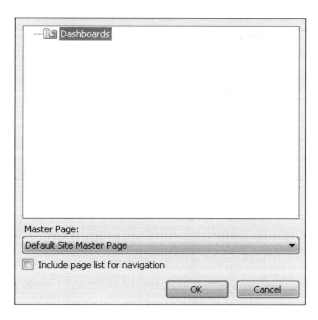

17. Once the dashboard has been deployed, your web browser should open and display the content.

## How it works...

This recipe has shown how Operations Manager information can be embedded within SharePoint dashboards quickly and easily for presentation to the business.

SharePoint is in use in many organizations as a collaboration tool, whether that be document management, team portals, business intelligence, or social collaboration. The list is endless, and as such, SharePoint is an ideal tool to present operational data.

In this recipe, you utilized your SharePoint PerformancePoint Services site and, using the Dashboard Designer tool, created the **Distributed Application** dashboard.

Within the Dashboard Designer tool, you created a `Reporting` object. Using this SQL `Reporting` object, you were able to connect to your Operations Manager SQL reporting server from which you browsed and selected the distributed application report that you published in the previous recipe. Other reporting types can be used depending on your requirements:

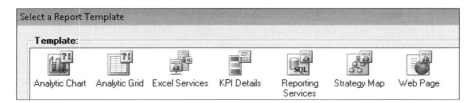

You then configured the `Reporting` object properties, which ensured that the report was displayed on your dashboard as required, removing items such as the toolbar and parameter options. Depending on your report requirements, you may wish to modify these report options.

Next, you created a new dashboard object. Dashboards can be configured for a number of layout styles allowing for multiple horizontal or vertical content zones depending on your requirements. For this recipe, you selected the **1 zone** template.

Be careful when adding additional content to your dashboards. The more content added, the more difficult it can become to layout the page correctly:

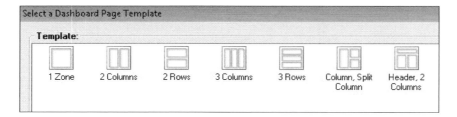

Once the dashboard object was created, the dashboard page was given a name. This example uses only one dashboard page, but dashboards support the addition of multiple pages if required. Your dashboards can contain other SharePoint items if required, allowing you to group your information in a central place.

You were then able to browse any content you had previously created via SharePoint Dashboard Designer by browsing through the content types in the **Details** pane. Dragging the `SQL Reporting` object you created, you enabled it to be placed on your dashboard's content zone.

Once your dashboard was complete, you saved the item and used the **Deploy** option to place the dashboard on to your PerformancePoint site.

Once deployed, the dashboard page was opened within your browser. At this point, your report can be reviewed, and if any changes are needed, you can modify the report and redeploy it from within the designer:

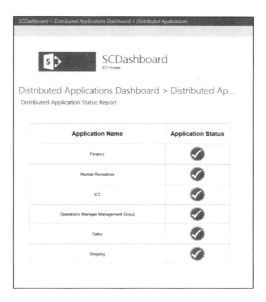

 There's more...

Once you have deployed your dashboards, business units can access them as required. However, another way to present this information could be using a projector or large display to create a team operational dashboard. Using popular web browsers that support tab rotation plugins, you can quickly create operational dashboards that can rotate between different business sites, allowing information to be continually refreshed and on hand.

Another feature of Operations Manager available in SharePoint is the Operations Manager web part. This web part allows you to display dashboards from within the web console. This can be useful in providing performance and availability metrics to the business.

> If the SharePoint farm is running SharePoint Foundation 2010, you can only deploy the web part in the same domain as the web console, and you cannot use shared credentials.

At the time of writing, the Operations Manager SharePoint web part is available and supported only to users of SharePoint 2010.

You may also wish to take a look at the Visio and SharePoint extensions for System Center 2012. With the Visio extension, you can create live dashboard views that connect to your Operations Manager data to ensure your dashboards display the most up-to-date status of your managed objects.

Taking this a step further, you can display these Visio dashboards in your SharePoint environment using the SharePoint extension.

## See also

Detailed information on the methods and tools used in this recipe is available here:

- Microsoft download—*Microsoft Visio 2010 and SharePoint 2010 Extensions for System Center 2012*: `http://www.microsoft.com/en-us/download/details.aspx?displaylang=en&id=29268`

- Microsoft Technet—*SharePoint 2013*: `http://technet.microsoft.com/en-us/library/cc303422.aspx`

- Microsoft Technet—*PerformancePoint Services in SharePoint Server 2013 overview*: `http://technet.microsoft.com/en-us/library/ee424392.aspx`

- Microsoft Technet—*Create reports by using Dashboard Designer (SharePoint Server 2013*: `http://technet.microsoft.com/en-us/library/ff806339.aspx`

- Microsoft Technet—*Using SharePoint to View Operations Manager Data*: `http://technet.microsoft.com/en-us/library/hh212924.aspx`

# Resourceful Links

In this appendix, you will find useful links to community content and third-party System Center 2012 R2 Operations Manager extensions.

## Notable community blogs

- Kevin Greene: `http://kevingreeneitblog.blogspot.co.uk/`
- Tao Yang: `http://blog.tyang.org/`
- Marnix Wolf: `http://thoughtsonopsmgr.blogspot.co.uk/`
- Cameron Fuller: `http://blogs.catapultsystems.com/cfuller/default.aspx`
- Dieter Wijckmans: `http://scug.be/dieter/`
- Bob Cornelissen: `http://www.bictt.com/blogs/bictt.php`
- Steve Buchanan: `http://www.buchatech.com/`
- Stanislav Zhelyazkov: `https://cloudadministrator.wordpress.com/`
- Patrick Seidl: `http://www.systemcenterrocks.com/`
- The Official Operations Manager Engineering blog: `http://blogs.technet.com/b/momteam/`

## Notable community sites

System Center Central: `http://www.systemcentercentral.com/`

SCOM Management Pack wiki: `http://social.technet.microsoft.com/wiki/contents/articles/16174.microsoft-management-packs.aspx`

# Third-party SCOM extensions

- ▸ Squared Up (http://squaredup.com/): Squared Up HTML5 dashboards provide rich data visualizations and fast, modern, and intuitive web access to the entire wealth of your SCOM data

- ▸ BlueStripe Software (http://bluestripe.com/): Extending distributed applications via dynamic discoveries and presentation of information within SCOM and Windows Azure Pack

- ▸ Savision (http://www.savision.com/): These are business service management dashboards for SCOM, helping you understand the dependencies between your company's business services and the underlying IT infrastructure and applications

- ▸ Derdack (http://derdack.com/): Derdack's Enterprise Alert® automates critical incident communication and transforms it into an intelligent, real-time, reliable, and mobile experience

- ▸ Bridgeways (http://bridgeways.com/): Turnkey management pack solutions and cloud-based systems monitoring

- ▸ OpsLogix (http://www.opslogix.com/): Oracle, Blackberry, VMware, and Swift management and capacity reports

- ▸ Veeam (http://www.veeam.com/): Veeam Replication & Backup, Hyper-V, and VMware management packs

# Index

# About Packt Publishing

Packt, pronounced 'packed', published its first book, *Mastering phpMyAdmin for Effective MySQL Management*, in April 2004, and subsequently continued to specialize in publishing highly focused books on specific technologies and solutions.

Our books and publications share the experiences of your fellow IT professionals in adapting and customizing today's systems, applications, and frameworks. Our solution-based books give you the knowledge and power to customize the software and technologies you're using to get the job done. Packt books are more specific and less general than the IT books you have seen in the past. Our unique business model allows us to bring you more focused information, giving you more of what you need to know, and less of what you don't.

Packt is a modern yet unique publishing company that focuses on producing quality, cutting-edge books for communities of developers, administrators, and newbies alike. For more information, please visit our website at www.PacktPub.com.

# About Packt Enterprise

In 2010, Packt launched two new brands, Packt Enterprise and Packt Open Source, in order to continue its focus on specialization. This book is part of the Packt Enterprise brand, home to books published on enterprise software – software created by major vendors, including (but not limited to) IBM, Microsoft, and Oracle, often for use in other corporations. Its titles will offer information relevant to a range of users of this software, including administrators, developers, architects, and end users.

# Writing for Packt

We welcome all inquiries from people who are interested in authoring. Book proposals should be sent to author@packtpub.com. If your book idea is still at an early stage and you would like to discuss it first before writing a formal book proposal, then please contact us; one of our commissioning editors will get in touch with you.

We're not just looking for published authors; if you have strong technical skills but no writing experience, our experienced editors can help you develop a writing career, or simply get some additional reward for your expertise.

**System Center 2012 R2 Virtual Machine Manager Cookbook**
**Second Edition**

Over 70 recipes to help you design, configure, and manage a reliable and efficient virtual infrastructure with VMM 2012 R2

Edvaldo Alessandro Cardoso

# System Center 2012 R2 Virtual Machine Manager Cookbook

*Second Edition*

ISBN: 978-1-78217-684-8          Paperback: 428 pages

Over 70 recipes to help you design, configure, and manage a reliable and efficient virtual infrastructure with VMM 2012 R2

1. Create, deploy, and manage datacenters and private and hybrid clouds with hybrid hypervisors using VMM 2012 R2.

2. Integrate and manage fabric (compute, storages, gateways, and networking), services and resources, and deploy clusters from bare metal servers.

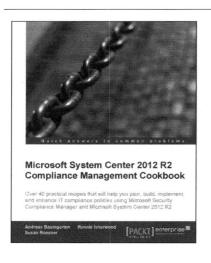

**Microsoft System Center 2012 R2 Compliance Management Cookbook**

Over 40 practical recipes that will help you plan, build, implement, and enhance IT compliance policies using Microsoft Security Compliance Manager and Microsoft System Center 2012 R2

Andreas Baumgarten    Ronnie Isherwood
Susan Roesner

# Microsoft System Center 2012 R2 Compliance Management Cookbook

ISBN: 978-1-78217-170-6          Paperback: 284 pages

Over 40 practical recipes that will help you plan, build, implement, and enhance IT compliance policies using Microsoft Security Compliance Manager and Microsoft System Center 2012 R2

1. A step-by-step guide filled with practical recipes that will show you how to start your compliance project using Microsoft System Center and other supporting technologies.

2. Demystify the compliance deployment myth; bridge the gap between IT, audit, and compliance programs.

3. Maximize your return on investment using the System Center product components.

Please check **www.PacktPub.com** for information on our titles

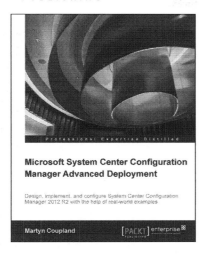

**Microsoft System Center Configuration Manager Advanced Deployment**

Design, implement, and configure System Center Configuration Manager 2012 R2 with the help of real-world examples

Martyn Coupland

[PACKT] enterprise 88

# Microsoft System Center Configuration Manager Advanced Deployment

ISBN: 978-1-78217-208-6          Paperback: 290 pages

Design, implement, and configure System Center Configuration Manager 2012 R2 with the help of real-world examples

1. Learn how to design and operate Configuration Manager 2012 R2 sites.

2. Explore the power of Configuration Manager 2012 R2 for managing your client and server estate.

3. Discover up-to-date solutions to real-world problems in System Center Configuration Manager administration.

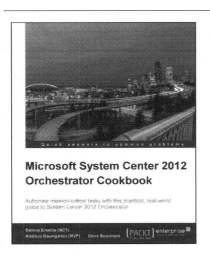

**Microsoft System Center 2012 Orchestrator Cookbook**

Automate mission-critical tasks with this practical, real-world guide to System Center 2012 Orchestrator

Samuel Erskine (MCT)
Andreas Baumgarten (MVP)   Steve Beaumont

[PACKT] enterprise 88

# Microsoft System Center 2012 Orchestrator Cookbook

ISBN: 978-1-84968-850-5          Paperback: 318 pages

Automate mission-critical tasks with this practical, real-world guide to System Center 2012 Orchestrator

1. Create powerful runbooks for the System Center 2012 product line.

2. Master System Center 2012 Orchestrator by creating looping, child and branching runbooks.

3. Learn how to install System Center Orchestrator and make it secure and fault tolerant.

Please check **www.PacktPub.com** for information on our titles

Made in the USA
Lexington, KY
22 April 2015